The Rebirth of Hasidism

The Rebirth of Hasidism

1945 to the Present Day

Jacques Gutwirth

Translated by Sophie Leighton

FREE ASSOCIATION BOOKS

First published in 2005 by
FREE ASSOCIATION BOOKS
57 Warren Street
London W1T 5NR

www.fabooks.com

Copyright © Jacques Gutwirth 2005
English-language translation © Sophie Leighton 2005

The right of Jacques Gutwirth to be identified as the author
of this work has been asserted by him in accordance
with the Copyright, Designs and Patents Act 1988.

All rights reserved. No part of this publication may be reproduced, stored in a retrieval system, or
transmitted, in any form or by any means, without the prior permission in writing of the publisher.
The book is sold subject to the condition that it shall not, by way of trade or otherwise, be lent,
resold, hired out or otherwise circulated without the publisher's prior consent in any form other than
that supplied by the publisher.

A CIP catalogue record for this book is available
from the British Library.

ISBN 1 85343 774 3 pbk

BM
198
.G825
2005

Designed and produced for the publisher by
Chase Publishing Services Ltd, Sidmouth, EX10 9QG
Printed and bound in the European Union by
Antony Rowe Ltd, Chippenham and Eastbourne, England

Contents

Introduction	1
1. From the Birth to the Rebirth	4
The environment	4
Baal Shem Tov; main characteristics of Hasidism	5
Expansion and decline	8
Five stages in two and a half centuries	12
1945: a new departure	12
2. A European Staging-post: Antwerp	15
Staging-post and place of settlement	15
The role of the diamond industry	16
Diverse communities	17
A new dynasty	19
Complex interactions	22
3. Williamsburg, a Satmar Bastion	27
The United States, a 'non-kasher' destination	27
The district	28
Professions	29
Poverty, state assistance, solidarity	31
A meticulous kashrut	32
Satmar, principal community of the district	34
Satmar: Zionism and American politics	37
The Satmar economy	39
Satmar beyond the walls: Kiryas Joel	41
Political, juridical and legislative wrangles	43
A dynasty in transition	44
Williamsburg: an ultra-orthodox assembly	47
4. Borough Park: a 'Bourgeois' District	49
The district	49
Composite regrouping	52
Bobov: the principal community	54
Bobov: a model	59
5. Crown Heights, Seat of the Lubavitch Movement	60
A highly turbulent district	60
Lubavitch, a specific form of Hasidism	63
An original rebbe	64
The Lubavitch zeal	66

	A specific social structure	69
	Kashrut: observance and inculcation	71
	Local – and Israeli – politics	72
	Personality cult	75
	Is the rebbe the Messiah?	76
	The movement without the rebbe	79
6.	Jerusalem	81
	Hasidism in the Holy Land	81
	Mea Shearim and its ultra-orthodox	82
	Bratzlav: the 'dead Hasidim'	84
	Toldot Ahronot, a dynasty of the district	85
	Many communities: Belz, one of the largest	89
	Belzer rebbe at the age of seventeen	91
	Community expansion and mutual assistance	92
	Belz and politics	93
	Belz, a successful movement	94
	Ger, a major Hasidic movement	95
	A resolute dynasty	96
	Traditionalism without confinement	98
	Missionary work	99
	Ger and politics	100
7.	Bene Beraq and Other Locations	102
	Bene Beraq, ultra-orthodox citadel	102
	Expansion and poverty, but also solidarity	105
	Principal religious constituents	107
	Numerous rebbes	108
	Vishnitz, a major dynasty	109
	The Vishnitz way of life	111
	The Vishnitzer rebbe today	112
	Conflicts and rivalries	113
	Various Hasidic centres: Tel-Aviv, a special case	114
	Lubavitch settlements	115
	Natanya: a community and a hospital	116
	Occupied territories	117
8.	Lubavitch in France	120
	A highly distinct form of Hasidism	120
	Historical outline	120
	A specific form of expansion	123
	Lubavitch in France and Sephardic culture	125
	Lubavitch institutions: the educational system	126
	Financial difficulties: professions	129
	National and 'community' politics	130
	Conclusion	132

9. Overview 134
   An unexpected rebirth 134
   Origin of the survivors: identifications past and present 135
   The community cocoon: a source of psychological support 137
   Marriage and demography 138
   Traditionalism and modernity 141
   The position of women: some minor advances 142
   A spiritual or intellectual revival? 145
   A favourable context 147
   A genetic nucleus? 150

Appendix 153
Notes 155
Bibliography 178
Glossary 187
Index 192

Introduction

In the early 1960s, as an ethnologist practising 'participant observation',[1] I conducted a study that involved an extensive period of immersion in a Hasidic* community. This was a group of ultra-orthodox Jews who belong to a major Jewish movement that had been adopted in the course of a few decades by a substantial proportion of the Jewish population in Eastern Europe since its emergence in the 18th century. My research led to a doctoral thesis and then to a book.[2] The community of Belz Hasidim* that I studied had been founded in Antwerp, Belgium, after the Second World War by survivors of the Nazi genocide. On 1 January 1963, it consisted of 418 people in total, two thirds of whom were under the age of 20 years, and were for the most part born in Antwerp after the Second World War, which already testified eighteen years after the Shoah* to a strong demographic dynamism. At present, notwithstanding a schism and the departure of around thirty families, the community consists of 250 households, which with three children on average (at a very modest estimate) represents at least 1,250 people. This demographic growth is almost universal among the Hasidim, whether this is in Antwerp, New York, Jerusalem or elsewhere. Whereas in 1945 there were around 20,000 Hasidim worldwide – survivors of the Shoah living in small communities in Palestine and in London and New York – today there are probably between 350,000 and 400,000,[3] around half of whom live in Israel, with many large families, in which early marriages and births provide the movement with continuing growth. This phenomenal expansion stands in contrast to the limited demographic dynamism of the Jewish people worldwide: in 1945 there were eleven million Jews. Fifty-two years later, in 1997, this figure had only risen to just over thirteen million.[4]

In this book, which is a distant continuation of the one devoted to the Belz Hasidim, I shall present the main centres of Hasidism today, which are essentially in Antwerp, New York, Jerusalem, Bene Beraq and Paris. For the reader who may be more or less familiar with Hasidism, I shall begin with a concise account of its main characteristics, including its contribution to Jewish spirituality and religiosity. One of the matters that I shall be addressing in the final chapter is the ambiguous question of the spiritual and intellectual contribution of contemporary Hasidism. In Chapter 1, I shall also give a brief historical account of the movement from its beginnings in the mid-18th century to the end of the Second World War. I shall then demonstrate in the course of several chapters the vigour of the rebirth of the Hasidic world today in its principal strongholds. I shall discuss the movement in France, which evidences some highly specific characteristics. Finally, in a general overview, I shall seek to analyse the astounding dynamism and vitality of this ultra-orthodox movement and to explain its intricacies.

Notwithstanding the traditionalism of the Hasidim, the reconstitution of the movement has not led to any replication of the extremely difficult conditions that usually prevailed before 1945 in Eastern Europe, where the majority of the followers had previously lived. In fact, this revival has to be understood both in a more international Jewish context and in terms of the rather favourable environment of the countries in which the Hasidim settled after 1945. Hasidism is something more than a religious doctrine, a form of religiosity and a specific way of life; its development, most clearly evidenced in its demographic expansion, is also connected with global political and economic conditions, to which the Hasidim bring their own influence to bear in turn. This can range from a relatively strong impact, such as in the *kasher** food industry in the United States and political life in Israel, to a more limited influence, for example in their contribution to the diamond industry, particularly in Antwerp and New York, and their political activity in the non-Jewish world, especially in the United States.

Despite their desire to protect their way of life with social and even spatial barriers, which extends to creating their own towns and villages, the Hasidim lead a life that is deeply rooted in both the Jewish and the non-Jewish world, from which they are in no way separated, especially in the urban areas in which the vast majority of them live. Furthermore, despite the hostility or at best the mistrust across much of the Jewish world towards the Hasidim, leaders of powerful institutions in the American Jewish establishment, such as the American Jewish Committee and the American Jewish Congress, or, in France, the leaders of the CRIF and the FSJU,[i] have been more or less quick to grasp that in the context of demographic decline in the Jewish world, especially outside Israel, mainly as a result of intermarriage and an assimilation that is insidious rather than overt (the phenomenon gets a bad press today), Hasidism, with its intense religious and community life, its assiduous practice of a Talmudic culture and its maximal endogamy represents a particularly strong model of Jewish identity, which is precisely what these institutions wish to foster. Therefore, certain branches of Hasidism, principally its 'missionary' wing, the movement known as Lubavitch or *Habad*,* obtain various forms of financial and other assistance from organizations that belong to this establishment and also from certain Jewish communities with a limited religious potential, which they help to increase,[5] as well as from sponsors and other Jewish donors who often have very few religious ties themselves but are aware of their role at this level.

Moreover, in Israel Hasidism, particularly through the ultra-orthodox political parties such as *Agudath Israel** and more recently *Degel Hatorah*,* has been participating in the nation's political life since it gained independence in 1948, including with shorter or longer periods of participation in government. They have thereby made their mark on national life, securing the domination of the *haredim*,* literally the 'God-fearing' – the ultra-orthodox, including the Hasidim – over every Jew in Israel, for example as concerns marriage, as a fundamental civil act of state, which has to be sanctioned by the orthodox rabbinate[6] and is only permitted between men and women who are Jewish

---

i   CRIF: 'Conseil représentatif des institutions juives en France' – the representative council of Jewish institutions in France; FSJU: 'Fonds social juif unifié' – the united Jewish social fund (*Translator's note*).

according to its very strict conception of the Jewish Law. There are many other acute conflicts in Israel between more or less secular Jews and the *haredim*, including the Hasidim, especially surrounding the vexed question of military service, from which ultra-orthodox men and women are exempted. In any case, the Hasidim are major players and therefore a force to be reckoned with in political discussions, implementation of laws and so on, while various questions such as housing subsidies for large families are of specific concern to them.

Finally, in this book I am seeking to provide an introduction that is as objective as possible to this highly complex movement.

1
From the Birth to the Rebirth

THE ENVIRONMENT

In 1648, led by the hetman Bogdan Khmelnitsky (1595–1657), the Cossacks launched a war to liberate Ukraine from several centuries of oppression by the kingdom of Poland. These battles, which continued till 1654, took place in Poland, Ukraine, Belarus and Lithuania.

Most historians of Judaism take the view that this war produced a turning-point in the Jewish condition in these regions. During the persecutions of the feudal age, particularly from the 11th century to the 14th century, especially in Germany but also in France and England, the Ashkenazi* (literally 'German' but more generally Northern European) Jews found refuge and a favourable welcome in Poland and the neighbouring states from the second half of the 13th century. The Polish kings and other princes wanted to introduce the benefits of a market economy into their lands, which were still essentially feudal. The Jews then began to work there as merchants, intendants for the extensive lands of the aristocracy, tax-collectors and landlords of drinking establishments, but also as artisans and small shopkeepers. The Jewish communities, the *kahalim** (H, singular *kahal**) to which the Jews were required to belong had a great deal of religious, cultural and juridical autonomy; they also raised taxes, generally on behalf of the Polish authorities.

However, feudal society was breaking down. The above-mentioned war was a consequence of the intolerable conditions from which the Ukrainian peasants in particular were suffering. These peasants often found themselves in a much more directly subordinate relationship to Jewish tax-collectors and intendants acting on behalf of the Polish feudal landowners than to the landowners themselves. The Jews therefore turned themselves into 'scapegoats' and became particularly vulnerable targets of the insurgents. Many Jews were slaughtered in terrible ways in the course of the hostilities. There were further insurrections in the 18th century and there was great insecurity within the Jewish communities. In Poland, the Catholic clergy promulgated a virulent anti-Semitism; the Church and the civil authorities were constantly demanding taxes and bribes from the Jewish communities. Living conditions were particularly hard for the poorest classes.

It was in fact precisely at this period that messianic expectations, which had certainly always existed in latent form at the heart of the Jewish faith and imagination – albeit principally in terms of the distant future, found concrete expression in the emergence of the false messiah Shabbetai Tzevi (1626–1678). Born in Smyrna, present-day Izmir, in Turkey, Shabbetai Tzevi managed to gain recognition as a Messiah by many Jews in the East; the influence of the

'Sabbatean' movement also spread to Poland and the neighbouring regions, which had been the site of tragedies that made the Jews particularly receptive to a message of imminent salvation and redemption.[1] Shabbetai Tzevi, who specifically advocated sexual licence and the abrogation of the Jewish commandments, finally converted to Islam in 1666. However, this apostasy did not put an end to the phenomenon: many followers secretly continued to believe in Tzevi's ideas. The latter also had a follower in Poland, another false messiah, Jacob Frank (1726–1791), born in Podolia, Ukraine. A charismatic figure who presented himself as the reincarnation of Tzevi, he had a substantial following in Ukraine, Galicia and Hungary, all regions in which Hasidism later developed. Frank rejected the authority of the Talmud* – a collection of Biblical commentaries that has been an authoritative source within Judaism for two millennia; he also advocated sexual licence, practised magic and claimed to have prophetic gifts. In 1759, Frank and 600 of his followers converted to Catholicism, with the approval of the Polish clergy. He nevertheless spent thirteen years in prison, which only seems to have increased his prestige among his followers. The movement finally disappeared at the beginning of the 19th century, by which time Hasidism was already flourishing.[2]

Sabbateanism and Frankism may have provided a fertile ground for Hasidism but, unlike the latter two movements, Hasidism remained faithful to the foundations of Judaism, its commandments and its moral rigour. In fact, if these two forms of messianism were in some sense 'rebellions against the ghetto',[3] Hasidism represented a rebellion within the 'ghetto', that is against the prevailing conditions within the official Jewish communities, the *kahalim*, recognized by the non-Jewish authorities. To meet the Polish financial demands, those who were oppressed by the tax-collectors, intendants and merchants imposed heavy taxes on the poorest and most disadvantaged Jews: peddlers, artisans and beggars.[4] In these modest conditions, many believed in the power of the amulets, miracles and conjuration of demons that were offered to them by itinerant preachers, the *maggidim*.* Many of these miracle-workers and healers were called *baalei shem*,* 'masters of the (divine) name', because the efficacy of their gifts was thought to derive from their knowledge of the ineffable name of God.

BAAL SHEM TOV; MAIN CHARACTERISTICS OF HASIDISM

One of these preachers and healers, Israel ben Eliezer (1700–1760), born to a humble and devout family in Okopy in Galicia,[5] became famous under the name Baal Shem Tov (the good master of the name), and was also known by the acronym Besht,* based on the initials of his pseudonym. He was not only an exorcist, a healer of melancholia and sterility and a miracle-worker like his fellow prophets, but he also proved to be a charismatic guide and master of some small groups of disciples, of *Hasidim*,* that is, of 'pious ones', forming a movement that showed a propensity for gradual expansion. Having lived for a while in Slusk in Lithuania, between 1740 and 1745[6] he settled in Miedzyboz in Ukraine, a small town in the count Czartoryski's lands, where he lived until his death.[7] The tensions between the Jewish social classes were acute there, particularly between the *arendators* (a Polish term), tax-collectors, millers and so on – who were generally Jewish servants of the Czartoryskis – and the poorer people, the Jewish artisans and small shopkeepers. However, throughout his long stay in this town, Baal Shem Tov managed to stay on the right side of the various Jewish groups there. The instigator of a major religious reform was therefore not perceived in any sense by his contemporaries as a dissident or a charlatan, nor in fact as the founder of a new movement. However, Hasidism – *hassidut** in Hebrew, *hessides** in Yiddish, literally meaning piety – went on to become a powerful force that soon encountered opposition from many authorities in the Jewish communities of the region.

Baal Shem left no writings but his disciples undertook to transcribe his sayings, while accounts of his life, some more accurate than others, spread by word of mouth.[8] Furthermore, his main disciple, the *maggid** Dov Baer of Mezhirech (1710–1772) became the organizer and theoretician of the emerging Hasidic movement, disseminating its main ideas.[9]

The foundations of Hasidism lie in the Kabbala,* a set of texts that have been collected together from the early centuries of the common era, along with the Talmud. The Kabbala, the principal work of which is the Zohar or Book of Splendour, is a highly complex and esoteric body of work and the overwhelming majority of Hasidim, both at the beginning of the movement and today, have no knowledge of these texts, which are read by certain scholars of mysticism. Certain Kabbalistic concepts, especially those developed by Isaac Luria (1534–1572), have had a particularly strong influence on the thought of the founders of Hasidism. One of these is *devekuss*,* mystical and affective communion with God. For Hasidim, this state can be attained at will in the most commonplace activities such as eating, drinking, working and also in sexual relations, for the 'divine sparks' permeate everything and every action. Accordingly, and this was a specific innovation, the founders of Hasidism emphasized the possibility for every believer, however illiterate, of attaining this *devekuss* in any situation. Moreover, happiness was supposed to be conducive to this affective state, a view that contrasted with the austere attitude that generally prevailed in the synagogues.

Liturgical prayer certainly remained an essential means of attaining a mystical communion for the Hasidim. Fervent swaying during prayer was not unknown in the synagogue but the Hasidim began to make more systematic recourse to this way of praying and they added to it ecstatic roars and postures. Moreover, dancing in the oratory, only practised by men, quickly assumed a feverish quality; for Baal Shem Tov and his disciples it was certainly a valuable way of attaining religious enthusiasm and *devekuss*. These forms of dancing and prayer are also much practised by Hasidim today.

In Hasidic oratories, the pre-eminence given to fervour in prayer and also to dancing gave rise to a new scale of values in religious activity. The importance attributed to these modes of expression conferred on the illiterate and uncultured person, usually from the lowest social categories, a respectability that was denied him in the synagogue because Talmudic knowledge and study, hitherto the prerogative of rich people and scholars, were the principal criteria of merit there. While the founders of Hasidism certainly did not reject the study of Talmudic texts, which was to become an essential component of the religious modes that they would establish, it was the regular practice of study, of *lernen** (Y-G), rather than erudition as such that mattered.

Baal Shem Tov and his disciples had forcefully rejected the moral permissiveness and dispensations from the Jewish laws instituted by Shabbetai Tzevi and Jacob Frank. The Hasidim remained faithful, moreover with an extraordinary vigilance, to the 613 commandments – 248 prescriptions and 365 prohibitions – that originate from the Torah* and are codified in the *Shulhan Aruh** (H), the code of Jewish laws that was compiled in the 16th century.[10] The messianic expectations exacerbated by Tzevi and Frank were also swept aside. Although the belief in the advent of the Messiah and messianic times persisted, these were relegated to an indeterminate point in the future. Hasidism was in no sense a messianic movement; as we will observe, however, messianic predilections have surfaced there at times, including in our own day.

As we know, the *maggidim*, including Baal Shem Tov himself, performed miracles and cures and these thaumaturgic functions have persisted to this day in Hasidism. Moreover, it went on to develop, according to Kabbalistic theories, a cult of the *tzadik*,* the holy, the righteous one, who has received from God a superior soul and extraordinary powers, including clairvoyance, and who is therefore a powerful intermediary between ordinary Jews and God. Accordingly, the followers of a *tzadik* – for which *rebbe** (Y) and more recently, mainly in Israel, *admor*,* became the more general term – confer an intense veneration on 'their' spiritual leader in the Hasidic oratories. They pay him frequent visits to ask him to perform miracles, for advice, including on business matters, to listen to his addresses, to ask him to resolve disagreements with other followers and so on. In return for rebbe's care, the followers offer him gifts, sometimes considerable sums of money, to finance the various projects that he sponsors, but also for his living costs and those of his immediate family. Furthermore, this cult of the rebbe, which was theorized by one of the movement's early leaders, Elimelech of Lyzhansk (1717–1787), continues today with the same intensity as during the first generations of Hasidim.

As Gershom Scholem expresses it: 'The whole development [of the movement] centers round the personality of the Hasidic saint; this is something entirely new. *Personality* takes the place of *doctrine*; what is lost in rationality by this change is gained in efficacy'.[11] In fact, on the social level, this cult helped to consolidate and unite the emerging movement around the *tzadik*, for the followers came from various places and a range of different social groups. Furthermore, today the distinctly charismatic authority of the rebbe has fostered the regrouping of the Hasidim who survived the Nazi genocide, for the latter came from diverse regions and countries and often had very different mentalities.

However, this cult of the rebbe was severely criticized by the adversaries of Hasidism and it remains a source of contention between Hasidim and non-Hasidic orthodox Jews to this day.

EXPANSION AND DECLINE

Baal Shem Tov's first successor was therefore Dov Baer of Mezhirech (1710–1772), also known as 'the great maggid' (preacher). He is said to have visited the Besht in Miedzyboz to obtain a miracle cure and he became his disciple. After the death of Baal Shem Tov in 1760, he was recognized as one of his principal successors. Dov Baer settled in Mezhirech, a town in Podolia, Ukraine, where he instigated the spread of Hasidism to the neighbouring regions, particularly Poland. By contrast, it encountered strong resistance in Lithuania and White Russia (Belarus). There was not even an attempt to introduce it into France, Germany or the Netherlands. Western Jewish circles, which were impervious to mysticism, belief in miracles and the cult of the rebbe were resistant to Hasidism because in these countries rationalism and science, or Talmudism, prevailed; it later met with similar resistance in Eastern Europe. In fact, Hasidism appealed to people who were immersed in a traditional faith, remote from modern society and culture.[12]

Dov Baer instituted a liturgical innovation that was certainly minor in itself but which contributed to the creation of separate Hasidic oratories. The Hasidim were no longer required to use the *sidder*,* the customary prayer-book in the Ashkenazi synagogues, but the book created by the great Kabbalistic scholar Isaac Luria (1534–1572) which included prayers from the Sephardic* liturgy, in particular *piyyutim*,* liturgical poems and blessings that contained Kabbalistic references. Another distinctive characteristic of the emerging Hasidic communities was the development of a specific method of *kasher** ritual slaughter, using highly sharpened knives, which implied that the meat slaughtered under the supervision of the official community was not in fact proper. This attitude had some major economic effects because the imposition of a tax on the slaughter of each head of cattle or piece of poultry was a major source of revenue for the *kahalim*; the establishment of a dissident slaughter method therefore reduced their income.[13] This special slaughter method probably constituted a greater challenge to the authority of the official communities than the institution of a slightly different *sidder*. As we will see, the Hasidim use ritual slaughter and the *kashrut** in many components of their diet to assert their distinct identities to this day.

Confronted with these dissident attitudes, the rabbinical authorities of the *kahalim* often reacted harshly. In 1772, Elijah ben Solomon Zalman, the 'Gaon of Vilna' (1720–1797), the highest religious authority in Lithuania, who was particularly outraged at the decline of Talmudic ideals among the Hasidim and suspected them of being influenced by Sabbateanism,* issued them with a vigorous excommunication, a *herem.** Nevertheless, not all the official authorities behaved in this extreme manner.[14] The new movement, which was certainly reformist in religious matters, certainly demonstrated no form of social rebellion. Neither Baal Shem Tov nor his disciples, who included some dignitaries in their ranks,[15] proposed to reform the *kahal* and although they criticized the prosperous Jews for their lack of charity and their irreligiosity, they certainly did not suggest any end to their preponderance within it. The rebbes were undoubtedly concerned with the followers' everyday difficulties, particularly with their charitable initiatives, but their teaching accorded little importance to social matters; and concerning each person's means of subsistence, they believed that men depended on the will of God, although this could be influenced by religious acts.[16]

After Dov Baer's death, other Hasidic leaders took over and Hasidism spread and grew across Eastern Europe. It developed as a set of distinct communities that were certainly connected by the shared legacy of the Besht and Dov Baer but in which each autonomous group was governed by its own *tzadik* or leader.[17] These gradually gave rise to Hasidic 'dynasties'; at the death of a famous rebbe, one of his close relatives – son, grandson or son-in-law – would succeed him. Thus, the Lubavitch dynasty dates from the end of the 18th century and continues to this day (see Chapter 5); other contemporary dynasties date back to the 19th century. This persistence of dynasties is due to the prestige of the *tzadik* and to his aspiration, shared by his followers, to provide continuity to the life of their communities and their specific traditions and customs.[18] It is the rebbe himself who names his successor, usually one of his sons – not necessarily the eldest – or one of his sons-in-law; on other occasions, when the rebbe had not expressed his choice, a council of 'greats', prominent figures in the movement, would nominate a new leader after his death.

The rebbe, his family members and his close colleagues, usually live in what has come to be known as their 'court', *hoif*, generally a vast house with a large adjoining oratory and sometimes with lodgings for followers who visit their *tzadik* for longer or shorter periods, although many visitors stay with the local residents. Some of the 'courts' remained modest; others were luxurious, particularly in the 19th century.[19] In any case, the rebbe's residence is the rallying point for the followers, especially the men who, often leaving their wives and children for several weeks, stay there sometimes for long periods. This takes place especially in the autumn, during the cycle of festivals for the New Year, *Roshe Shoune*,* which lasts three weeks,[20] or in spring during *Paiseh*,* the eight-day festival of the Passover.

The rebbes govern their movements autocratically. The *shtiebleh* (Y sing. *shtiebl**), the Hasidic oratories in which the followers of a particular dynasty gather together in the various regions of Eastern Europe, are run by rabbis or other prominent figures who are favoured by the rebbe.

The various dynasties establish at the 'court' and in the communities *minugem** (singular *minek**), particular customs, for example introducing particular melodies and chants into the liturgy. By adopting specific sartorial practices, many rebbes engender particular customs concerning the appearance of the followers. According to the prescriptions in Leviticus (XVIII, 3) and restated in the code of Jewish laws, the *Shulhan Aruh*, the rabbinical authorities in Eastern Europe had often prohibited Jews from wearing Christian garments even as late as 1809.[21] The Hasidim rigorously applied these prescriptions but the rebbes also established a physical appearance that was almost compulsory for the followers. Accordingly, the Hasidim do not cut their beards and sidelocks, *peyes** in Yiddish, either with scissors or a razor. These practices originate from the Bible (particularly Leviticus XIX, 27) and from reflections in the Kabbala.

Nevertheless, attitudes towards the beard and sidelocks vary because each Hasidic dynasty institutes a slightly different model among its followers, which may not amount here to a *minek*, or custom, but rather expresses a more or less strong desire to distinguish themselves from non-Jews, or even from Jews who are either non-religious or not highly religious. Certain rebbes and their followers more or less remove their sidelocks or hide them from view (see Chapter 5). Moreover, some *minugem* serve the function of distinguishing the various movements through their clothing. The Belz Hasidim, followers of a major Galician dynasty, wear the *shtreimel*,* a wide fur cap, from the time of their marriage on festival days and the Sabbath, in common with the followers of other dynasties, but according to their own custom established by one of their rebbes, they wear it askew, tilted towards the right ear. Also, the Ger Hasidim, also followers of a prestigious line of descent, wear another kind of tall fur cap, the *spodek** (a Polish term). The various dynasties have also adopted further characteristics of dress – such as frock coats of a particular length or hats of a particular size – that distinguish them from each other.[22] Although a non-believer cannot tell them apart, the Hasidim themselves can fairly easily recognize the dynasty from which a particular unknown *Hasid** encountered in the street originates. Furthermore, each dynasty of rebbes and sometimes even a particular local community, also has a set of customs that relate to many other spheres.

Under the auspices of Baal Shem Tov's disciples and their various successors, Hasidism therefore gained in influence, especially at the end of the 18th century and the beginning of the 19th century, in Ukraine, Poland and even to some extent in Lithuania, a country in which the *misnaggedim*,* literally the 'adversaries', the orthodox who were opposed to Hasidism, still exerted a strong influence.[23] However, in the same period, the established Jewish communities were confronted not only with Hasidism, but also in the larger towns, with another formidable adversary, the *Haskule** in Yiddish or *Haskalah** in Hebrew, the Jewish Enlightenment movement. The Haskule had first developed at the end of the 18th century in Germany but its influence spread towards Eastern Europe, particularly in Galicia, in the towns of Brody, Tarnopol and Lemberg (today Lvov in Ukraine).[24] The *maskilim** ('enlightened ones'), followers of the Haskule, who were found mainly among the shopkeepers and artisans of the major cities, wanted to extend to all Jews a secular academic education that included learning the languages – particularly German, Polish and Russian – of their countries of residence. Moreover, they condemned the 'obscurantism' of the Hasidim.[25] The latter in turn nursed an intense hatred for the *maskilim*.[26]

The ideology of the Haskule certainly resonated with the spirit of the age. The Enlightenment had particularly influenced the Edict of Tolerance issued by Joseph II, implemented in 1781–1782 in the Austro-Hungarian Empire, which included the regions in which many Jews were living: Hungary, Bohemia, Slovakia and later Galicia (where the edict was not in force until 1789). The Edict made the study of the national languages compulsory in Jewish schools and abolished the juridical prerogatives of the rabbis in the *kahal* (from 1784), liberating the *maskilim* but also the Hasidim from the control of the 'official' community. The 'tolerance' was only relative because many forms of discrimination persisted. In a much more radical sense, the Revolution brought the emancipation of Jews in France in 1789, and this was granted to Jews in Eastern Europe in the wake first of the revolutionary armies and then of the Emperor's troops, but the gradual departure of the French meant that the measures adopted were later abrogated on many occasions. Moreover, a dispute arose between two rebbes concerning Napoleon's advances in Poland and Russia. One of these, the *tzadik* of Rymanow, argued that the Emperor's victories would be beneficial for the Jews, whereas the Ropshitzer rebbe asserted that these would contribute to the spread of unbelief and would force young Jews to attend Christian schools and carry out military service, which would seal the fate of Hasidism and destroy faith in the *tzadikim*.*[27]

However, over the second half of the 19th century, some other ideological and political trends were to jeopardize the influence of the Hasidim. Rural poverty drove many Jews into an exodus towards the cities, in which they generally became workers or artisans. Many of them were then drawn to the ideas and the ranks of secular socialist political movements, particularly the associations of Jewish workers who formed the trade union 'Bund'[28] in 1897, but also to universal socialist parties supported by both Jews and non-Jews. Moreover, the Jews from the 'bourgeois' social classes – shopkeepers, small manufacturers and so on – were increasingly wanting to adopt the lifestyle of their non-Jewish peers, leading to an acculturation that often came to distance them from the Jewish community and that fostered assimilation through intermarriage and conversion. From the end of the 19th century, particularly following the disappointments in these assimilation processes (in particular with the sensational Dreyfus affair), a proportion of these same social classes and a (smaller) minority of the artisans and workers were attracted to the Zionism that was then emerging.

Furthermore, the extremely strong demographic growth among the Jews of Eastern Europe – they exceeded six million in 1880 – the Russian pogroms from 1881 to 1884 and from 1903 to 1906, as well as the poverty, discrimination and economic difficulties, drove four million Jews to leave these regions between 1881 and 1932, the majority – 70% – for the United States. These mass emigrations brought major upheavals for those concerned; emigration to the United States in particular produced a strong disaffection with religious observance.

The influence of Hasidism remained relatively strong in Eastern Europe, especially in independent Poland where three million Jews were still living between 1918 and 1939 – accordingly, the *Agudath Israel** (union of Israel) party, founded in 1912 and strongly influenced by the Hasidim, had six of a total of thirty-five Jewish representatives elected to the Polish Diet in 1922.[29] However, Hasidism proved unable to respond to the dangers that would destroy Polish Judaism: it dissuaded its followers from going to the United States and, because it rejected political Zionism, it also discouraged them from settling in Palestine, although the position on this matter modified slightly after 1930.

Hasidism therefore appeared to be in great difficulty just before the outbreak of the Second World War. The Shoah was almost to deal it the final death blow.

FIVE STAGES IN TWO AND A HALF CENTURIES

Using the model of the stages in the history of Hasidism established by Simon Dubnow, the great historian of Hasidism, its history can be classified into five phases – Dubnow identifies four,[30] but I am adding the present period with which I am dealing in detail in this book.

1. *1740–1782*. A dynamic period in the establishment of Hasidism, with Besht and his immediate disciples. It is also the period of the first struggles with the authorities of the *kahalim*, the official communities recognized by the non-Jewish authorities.
2. *1782–1815*. The Hasidim cease to be a dissident 'sect'; Hasidism becomes a majority movement within the Jewish population of Eastern Europe. At the same time, it branches out with various dynasties of *tzadikim* and a consequent increase in Hasidic centres with fairly diverse orientations. There is intense conflict with the *misnaggedim*, the Rabbinical 'adversaries'.
3. *1815–1870*. The cult of the rebbe intensifies but an alliance simultaneously develops with rabbis from non-Hasidic communities to oppose the 'enlightened ones' and their movement, the Haskalah.
4. *1870–1945*. The period of decline, followed by destruction. Hasidism remains influential but the above-mentioned secularizing forces dominate the scene in Eastern Europe. The emigration of millions of Jews from Eastern Europe to the United States leads to the secularization of emigrants; there are very few Hasidic communities in this country. Moreover, in the Soviet Union, the new regime persecutes Hasidism, which only survives clandestinely. The invasion of Poland in 1939 and the Second World War that it triggers inflict hell on the Jews and particularly to the Hasidim. At the end of the war, very few Hasidim have survived 'the final solution'.
5. *1945 to the present day*. The period of the dynamic rebirth of Hasidism. The survivors recreate communities not in Eastern Europe but in Belgium, England and Canada and particularly in the United States and Israel. As we will see, the energy and vitality demonstrated by the surviving Hasidim are not the only factors in this revival. The Hasidim also find political and economic contexts that are favourable to their demographic expansion. Furthermore, they become models of a *yiddishkait*, 'Jewishness',[31] a way of being Jewish that is particularly distinctive and intense.

1945: A NEW DEPARTURE

The fate of the Hasidim at the end of the Second World War had been especially tragic because their distinctive appearance, their way of life and their strong presence in certain areas made them particularly vulnerable victims of the German forces.

There were, however, some survivors. Among the surviving Hasidim in Poland, very few had survived the Nazi massacres in Poland itself and the periods spent in the death camps. Some nevertheless owed their survival ... to their obliviousness. Having taken refuge in the area of Poland occupied by the Soviet Union shortly after the German invasion of the country in 1939, they were required either to return to the Nazi-occupied zone or to become Soviet citizens and live more than 100 kilometres away from the border. Some Hasidim chose to return to the places (under German occupation!) from which they had come, which paradoxically saved their lives because the Soviet authorities deported everyone who made this choice to Siberia. The former group thereby escaped the German invasion of the Soviet Union in 1941 and despite many hardships the majority of them managed to survive.[32]

However, there were also some Hasidim in Hungary and Rumania before the war. In Hungary, a country allied with Germany, there were certainly anti-Semitic persecutions and bloody pogroms, but systematic deportations to the Nazi death camps did not begin until March 1944, when German troops occupied the country. More than 550,000 Jews, two thirds of the 825,000 Hungarian Jews, were deported and assassinated. The fact that the German crimes could not take place until the end of the war allowed the survival – in slightly greater numbers proportionally than in Poland – of Hungarian Hasidim, including in the Nazi camps, particularly some of the youngest.[33] In Rumania, despite the persecutions and massacres that issued from the country's fascist regime, which was also allied with the Germans, Rumanian Jews were also able to survive in greater numbers, at least in certain regions of the country. Moreover, the Rumanian surrender to the USSR in August 1944 blocked the deportation plans prepared by the Nazis.

Whereas before 1939 the Hasidim in Poland were broadly predominant, the surviving Hasidim in Hungary and Rumania, henceforth as numerous as if not more so than those in Poland, went on to play an important role in the rebirth and development of the contemporary Hasidic movement, particularly in their stronghold of Williamsburg in Brooklyn, but also in other places.

There had also been small Hasidic communities in Palestine, England and the United States that had been fortunate enough to escape the clutches of the Nazis. However, although these groups were not impervious to the post-war rebirth of Hasidism – and their solidarity and their presence in these two countries facilitated the settlement of survivors there – the actual dynamic of the revival came from the survivors of Eastern Europe.

The first site of the regeneration was within the displaced persons camps in occupied Germany. Some survivors of the death camps quickly regrouped there and were joined in 1946 by Polish Jews returning from the Soviet Union.[34] Surviving rebbes helped the Hasidic survivors to assemble in communities and prayer groups in these camps. Yekutiel Judah Halberstam (1904–1994), the Klausenburger rebbe who had survived the Nazi camps, was particularly active in this way. Despite his own tragedy – he had lost his wife and eleven children – he listened to and comforted the orphaned children, the parents who had lost their children, the widows and the widowers in various displaced persons camps in Germany. He later founded Hasidic communities in New York, Montreal and Natanya in Israel.[35] Furthermore, the Lubavitcher rebbe Joseph Isaac Schneerson, who had managed to flee Europe and had settled in New York in 1940, established a *yeshive*,* a Talmudic academy, at a camp in Bavaria, which had 300 pupils in 1947.[36]

For the surviving Hasidim, these 'displaced persons' camps constituted an almost compulsory prelude to emigration to the United States, which was henceforth being unreservedly urged by the surviving rebbes; this country had become a favoured destination in the immediate post-war period. However, not everyone left for the United States: Belgium, with the city of Antwerp; Canada, mainly in Montreal; London in Great Britain and Israel were also places where surviving Hasidim went to rebuild their lives. It is through a consideration of the particularly important centres of Hasidism today that I shall be examining the evolution and state of the movement and its main characteristics in the chapters that follow. In the final chapter, I shall present an overview of the 'fifth stage' of Hasidism.

2
A European Staging-post: Antwerp

Antwerp, the major Belgian port, is certainly not one of the places in the world with the most Hasidim, but it is one of the cities with the highest proportion within the Jewish population. For more than fifty years, it has also been a vibrant centre of Hasidism, in which its post-war regeneration was very rapid. I shall therefore take Antwerp as the starting-point for this journey through the Hasidic world; furthermore, it was an important staging-post for Hasidim who travelled through Antwerp and stayed after 1945 until around 1960 and went on to form communities elsewhere, such as in Canada, the United States and Israel.

STAGING-POST AND PLACE OF SETTLEMENT

Although Antwerp, a major port on the River Schelde near the North Sea, had a Jewish population of no more than 8,000 in 1900, this figure rose to 35,000 by 1927 and to 55,000 in 1939, following the arrival of thousands of refugees from Germany under the Nazi regime, mainly after 1933.[1]

Since the 15th century, the city had been a centre for the diamond industry and trade, and *Marranos** from Spain and Portugal had been working in this sector at least since the 17th century. Although Amsterdam remained the main international diamond centre until after the First World War, from the 1880s this industry also expanded in Antwerp.[2] In the same period, the mass Jewish emigration from Poland and Russia to the United States had begun and Antwerp had already become a crossing-point and a port of embarkation for many emigrants. Some migrants chose to stay there because they were able to earn a living in the rapidly expanding diamond industry and trade. Many of these Jews, particularly workers who were Bund members or socialists and others who later became communists, were highly secularized; nevertheless, a religious way of life had also developed well, with synagogues, schools, *kasher** shops and so on. Between 1928 and 1939, eight Hasidic communities were established in Antwerp, formed by emigrants from Eastern Europe.[3]

In May 1940, after the German lightning offensives in the Netherlands, Belgium and France, Antwerp experienced the horrors of occupation. Although just over half of the Jews in Belgium managed to escape the clutches of the Germans, 25,631[4] were deported, almost all of whom perished in the Nazi camps.

However, after the Liberation in September 1944, Jewish life, with around 800 people who had managed to survive in hiding, quickly resuscitated in this city, which had survived the bombardments relatively unscathed. With the support of the Belgian government, the diamond trade and industry also underwent a rapid recovery. The city councillors in Antwerp also sought to persuade Jewish diamond-workers from Antwerp who had managed to find refuge abroad to return. Furthermore, both for humanitarian reasons and from enlightened self-interest, the local administration allowed Antwerp to become a crossing-point for Jewish refugees again. Thus, during the first few years after the Second World War, some thousands of Jewish survivors of the death camps and survivors from Poland, Hungary, Rumania and other parts of Eastern Europe found at least a temporary refuge in Antwerp.[5] Moreover, some international and local Jewish philanthropic institutions organized the reception of emigrants[6] and various religious institutions were quickly established: the damaged synagogues were rebuilt and Jewish schools, a *mikve** ritual bath, a kasher food industry and so on were established.

The newcomers included some orthodox Jews, who found the necessary infrastructures in Antwerp for a way of life that accorded with Jewish laws. Finally, while waiting to emigrate to the United States or to Israel, it was possible to earn a living in this city, particularly within the reviving diamond industry.

THE ROLE OF THE DIAMOND INDUSTRY

Through this integration into the diamond sector, many Hasidim and other Jewish emigrants finally settled permanently in Antwerp.[7] Although almost no Hasid* from Eastern Europe had ever worked in this sector before, many of them had been small shopkeepers or artisans. The diamond industry and trade were still dominated at this period by relatively primitive techniques for transforming the rough diamond into precious stones – this has been less the case in the last twenty years – and by a traditional form of trade, with long discussions and haggling. Unlike gold or silver, raw diamonds are not uniform precious materials: in a raw state and even when cut, the stones have highly diverse qualities, colours and purity and their value is assessed in a subjective and intuitive way. This fosters haggling in commercial transactions, in which each party, buyer and seller, has his own idea of the approximate value of the batches of stones under negotiation.

Moreover, the diamond business in Antwerp but also in New York and even in Israel, is often conducted in Yiddish, a true *lingua franca* that is reputed to be discreet within this economic sector. In these conditions many immigrant Hasidim, often former small shopkeepers who were used to haggling and for whom Yiddish was already the habitual language – in daily life and also in the practice of Talmudic commentary – found favourable openings in the diamond trade, particularly as brokers, an intermediary activity that required little or no capital, of which they had none available then. Furthermore, one of the main techniques in the transformation of diamonds in Antwerp was the stone cleaving, which was an entirely artisan and manual practice.[8] It was a craft that could be practised in small workshops or even at home. The youngest Hasidim found in it a trade that was well suited to their religious way of life because most of them were able to adapt their working hours to the religious services and Jewish festival days.[9]

DIVERSE COMMUNITIES

In the immediate post-war period, the first Hasidim to arrive in Antwerp, as followers of various rebbes, joined their meagre forces to establish a shared oratory in a makeshift building. However, in subsequent years several Hasidic groups, as followers of different dynasties, created their own *shtiebleh,** oratories. In around 1960 there were six of these, five of which belonged to more or less long-established Hasidic movements and dynasties – Belz, Ger, Satmar, Chortkov, Vishnitz – and finally a sixth around a new rebbe, reb* (master) Ytsekl Gewuerzman (see below p. [31]). The community of the 'Belzer', followers of the Belz dynasty, was the largest, with seventy-four families. There were sixty Ger families, while Vishnitz and reb Ytsekl's community each had fifty-five, Satmar had forty-five and Chortkov had thirty-five families, making a total of around 334 families, which is of course an approximate figure.[10] By the beginning of the 1960s, just fifteen years after the war, the Hasidim in Antwerp were in strong demographic expansion. The seventy-four Belz families included 276 children, giving a total of 418 people. It can be estimated that the Hasidic communities as a whole represented at least 1,500 people, admittedly with a large proportion of children, but this nevertheless represented around 12% of the total Jewish population, around 10,500 people, even at that period.

I shall return to discuss the Belz dynasty at greater length in my chapter on the Hasidim in Jerusalem, where it has now settled, but the composition of the Belz community in Antwerp already provides some interesting information concerning this important component of contemporary Hasidism.[11]

The Belz Hasidim in Antwerp, with financial assistance from followers in England and elsewhere, were certainly among the very first to create their own community, acquiring a house in 1946 in which to establish their own oratory, *shtiebl.** The community had been formed at the outset by two groups of different origin, the first originating from Poland, the others from Hungary, in approximately equal numbers. This is a rather exceptional phenomenon that can be explained by the history of this movement.

The Belz dynasty, dating from the beginning of the 19th century, was founded in Belz, a small town that held regional trade fairs in Eastern Galicia, a region that belonged to the Austro-Hungarian Empire from 1815 to 1918, became Polish in 1918 and since 1945 has been situated in Ukraine, not far from the Polish border. Belz had a substantial Jewish population, comprising up to 50% of its 5,000 inhabitants before 1940. The first rebbe, Shalom Rokeah (1779–1855) was originally the rabbi there. After the death of Jacob Hachoze, the 'seer' of Lublin (1745–1815), one of the founders of Hasidism in Galicia, of whom he was a disciple, Rokeah was considered as a *tzadik,** a holy rebbe, by the Hasidim of the region.

Until 1914, the influence of the dynasty was restricted to Galicia, but during the First World War, the third rebbe, Issachar Dov, who had left Belz, which was situated in a combat zone, settled in Hungary, in particular in Ujfeherto and Mukacevo (Munkacs), and he attracted a number of followers. This is how the post-war Antwerp community, which did not in fact include any followers from the pre-war community in that city, came to be constituted of approximately equal numbers of Polish and Hungarian survivors.[12] The local customs or traditions brought from the countries of origin were not exactly the same, particularly in relation to clothing. Whereas in Antwerp the Poles[13] wear long frock coats in everyday life, the Hungarians wear double-breasted jackets that are midway between the frock coat and the suit jacket in length. Also, the Polish wear large soft black hats with a longitudinal vent in daily life, whereas the Hungarians wear hats that are certainly the same colour but have wide brims, shaped with a rounded hollow or sometimes a bump. Many Magyar Hasidim from other Antwerp communities also observe the Hungarian sartorial habits or customs, and they still predominate in the Hasidic districts inhabited mainly by Hasidim of this origin, particularly in Williamsburg, New York (Chapter 3).[14]

Furthermore, the Polish Belzer, the majority of whom had lived through the war in the Soviet Union without being able to express their religious faith, were less traditionalist in the post-war period than their Hungarian counterparts. However, it was Polish Hasidim who officiated at principal festival days for they were more familiar then with the style and certain customs, *minugem*,* liturgical practices from the 'court' in Belz, and fidelity to traditions of the past remains an important concern for the Belzer as for other Hasidic communities. Over time and with new generations, born and brought up together in Antwerp, these differences of origin have undoubtedly attenuated.

In Eastern Galicia, the very poor region in which the Belz dynasty had developed, the rebbe maintained a rather austere 'court' and a lack of ceremony and ostentation continues to characterize Belz Hasidism today, particularly in Antwerp, where the *shtiebl*, the community oratory, is extremely sober, although following reconstruction in recent years it appears luxurious in comparison with its original form. The community house was in fact established in a disused factory, premises with limited comfort and aesthetic qualities.

In the post-war years, despite the predominance of Polish Hasidim in various communities, particularly Ger, Bobov and Chortkov, Hasidism in Antwerp was influenced by the arrival of Hungarian Hasidim, who were in a large majority for example in the Satmar and Vishnitz communities, which as we will see have a particularly strong presence in Brooklyn, New York and Bene Beraq in Israel, respectively.

The various dynasties have their own customs and style, and the ambiance in the various Hasidic oratories in Antwerp also varies. The Belz Hasidim are well-known for their austerity but the Satmarer and the Vishnitzer also have very sober oratories, whereas the Gerer, based in a beautiful manor-house, have a distinctly more comfortable *shtiebl*. The Gerer are also known for their tendency to pray very quickly, which reduces the duration of the services, whereas the Belzer tend to prolong their liturgical procedure.

One of the major concerns of the Hasidim in Antwerp but also elsewhere is the separation of the sexes, particularly in places of prayer. Because the oratories in Antwerp were established in pre-existing buildings, each community deployed some ingenuity in order to ensure that when they arrived at the oratory[15] the men and the women did not mingle as they went to their places of prayer, which were adjacent but separate. To this day, despite the construction of a modern oratory on the site of the old one, the Belzer use the same passageway, some ten metres away from the main entrance, which enables the women to access the *waber shil*,* the 'women's synagogue', adjacent to the men's shtiebl, through a garden at the back. In the 1960s, the Vishnitzer, for the same purpose, had constructed a long and high wooden partition in the corridor leading to their oratory so that there were two entrances there as well.

In the last fifty years, the Hasidic communities have increased in Antwerp; today there are eighteen on record, three times as many as in the 1960s![16] Most of them are experiencing a major demographic dynamism. The Belz dynasty, with 250 families (see above), is by far the largest and this expansion has occurred despite the departure of around thirty families who have formed a group that does not recognize the authority of the current Belzer rebbe. Their official name, 'Chassidei Belz-Haichal Aharon', proclaims their affiliation both with the Belz dynasty and with the previous rebbe, Aaron Rokeah, but they have placed themselves under the authority of another spiritual leader, the Machnovker rebbe, Joshua Rokeah, who is also associated with the Belz dynasty. They also have less traditionalist ideas than their rivals, particularly concerning secular education (see below p. [36]).[17] The next largest groups are the Satmarer and the Gerer, each with one hundred families, then the Bobover with fifty families. All these communities belong to dynasties that were also influential in other countries.

Furthermore, some decades ago the Vishnitzer split into two groups, one reputed to be relatively 'modern' – including a large number of 'beardless' followers who wear modern clothing – and the other more 'traditional'. Like the Belzer, the two groups ultimately adopted different and rivalrous leaders; one, particularly influential in Israel, settled in Bene Beraq (see Chapter 6) and the other, in Monsey near New York. Finally, there are various other small groups in a range of different areas. The Lubavitch Hasidim, a particularly important and original movement today, who have institutions in many cities worldwide that urge Jews to 'return' to religious orthodoxy, also have a strong presence in Antwerp, with two groups who are divided as to belief in the future messianic 'resurrection' of the last rebbe, Menahem Mendel Schneerson, who died in 1994 (see Chapter 5). I estimate that there are at least 950 Hasidic families in Antwerp today, which with three or four children per household – a modest estimate – represents between 4,750 and 5,700 Hasidim. The Jewish population in Antwerp is estimated at around 18,000 people and the Hasidim therefore represent at least one quarter of this figure and possibly more.[18]

A NEW DYNASTY[19]

One example of the rebirth, the dynamism and even the innovative capacity of Hasidism in Antwerp is the creation in 1954 of a 'court', *hoif*,* around reb Ytsekl, considered as a rebbe by his followers since the post-war period. Since his death in 1977, he has already had two consecutive successors, and a community of followers grew around them from around sixty families in the 1960s to around one hundred today. The 'court' – the rebbe's residence adjoining the oratory – is in an old house in Mercatorstraat, about one kilometre away from the centre of the diamond trade and the city's main station.

Ytsekl is the informal and affectionate name given by the followers to the founder of this group, taken from his real name, Isaac Gewuerzmann. A short and fragile-looking man (I knew him in the early 1960s), he nevertheless died a nonagenarian in 1977. He was deeply revered by his disciples and even by Hasidim who were followers of other rebbes in Antwerp. His followers, very much according to Hasidic tradition, came to ask him for advice and especially for miraculous intercessions. According to a custom that dates from the development of the cult of the miracle-working rebbe (see Chapter 1), and still practised by most rebbes, wishes expressed by visitors were noted down on a *kvitel*,* literally 'receipt', by an assistant and follower of the rebbe. Reb Ytsekl's assistant was known for his complete discretion concerning the content of the petitions.[20] In exchange, the petitioner, who might be a man or a woman, would put a small sum of money towards the charitable works sponsored by the rebbe. One visitor might want his daughter to find a suitable match; another might wish for the cure of an illness afflicting himself or a loved one; a third might hope that the infertility in his couple would be overcome; yet others simply aspired for prosperity in their business. After a longer or shorter waiting period, the petitioner would be introduced to the rebbe, who would talk with him about the subject of his request, then answer by expressing the wish for God to provide him with help. Among the rebbe's followers, there would be boasts about this or that example of a wish that had been fulfilled.

Hasidim with other affiliations (generally in total discretion!) and people from further afield would also come to ask for his intervention. Through a third party and by post, he also received letters and messages, with requests usually accompanied by gifts. On many occasions, these letters would come from people living abroad but reb Ytsekl also received travellers for whom this meeting was one of the fundamental reasons for the journey if not the sole purpose. These visitors could be sure of finding a sympathetic hearing for their worries and problems and they could hope for miracles following his intervention; they also imbibed the fraternal and traditional atmosphere of a *shtiebl*, which was often lacking in their existing place of residence.

Like other rebbes, on Friday evening after the Sabbatical service, reb Ytsekl would preside over a meal in which his family and various guests participated: he 'held table' – in Yiddish, *tish halten.** Having started on a traditional dish from the Sabbatical meals of Eastern Europe, consisting of stuffed carp, boiled chicken and broth, reb Ytsekl would distribute *shrayim*,* the remains of the meal, to his guests. The guests thereby partook of the rebbe's holiness in the hope of obtaining 'good things'. As for the audience with *kvitel*, it therefore consisted in a form of thaumaturgic intervention, but with a collective dimension. The *kvitel* and *tish halten* rituals, with a few exceptional differences, are practised by most rebbes today.

To his disciples reb Ytsekl was certainly a *tzadik*, a holy man, a rebbe. But how did reb Ytsekl become the founder of a Hasidic dynasty? He was born in Sieniawa, a small town in Eastern Galicia where he was a follower of the Sieniawer rebbe, the leader of a local dynasty. Before the Second World War, he was an itinerant preacher, or *maggid*,* known particularly for his collections on behalf of those in need. He already had a great reputation for piety, spirituality and benevolence. When the Second World War came, reb Ytsekl survived in the Soviet Union (see Chapter 1). After the Nazi genocide, on his return to Poland, he assumed the role and functions of a rebbe, thus effectively replacing the *tzadikim** who had disappeared in the turmoil with the surviving Hasidim who, in the tragic circumstances of the time, had more need than ever of consolation and miraculous interventions. In 1948, reb Ytsekl left Poland and spent several years in Paris, in the district of the Rue des Rosiers. However, Hasidism was not highly esteemed in the capital at that time and in 1954 he accepted the invitation from a group of followers settled in Antwerp to establish himself among them. They bought the house that became his residence and from then on the community took care of his needs.

Reb Ytsekl was accompanied by his family, including his son-in-law, reb Yankele Leizer (1907–1998). The use of the forename Yankele, a Yiddish diminutive of Jacob, expresses as with reb Ytsekl an affectionate and direct relationship that often existed among the Hasidim from Poland.[21] Reb Yankele was in any case highly regarded by the regular visitors to the *shtiebl*, for which he provided the administration. He was also appreciated as an illuminating commentator on the Talmud, who interspersed what he said with long digressions illustrated with anecdotes. Furthermore, long before the reb Ytsekl died, he appeared to be his likely successor. Thus already in the 1960s, when Ytsekl was indisposed, it was reb Yankele who presided at a *tish halten* and distributed the *shrayim*, thus carrying out a rebbe's functions. Moreover, the followers did not hesitate to seize the 'leftovers', with their mystical significance, thereby attesting that Yankele was considered to have a rebbe's thaumaturgic powers.

After reb Ytsekl's death in 1977, reb Yankele in effect became the leader of the community. He fulfilled his office to general satisfaction and he died in November 1998, at a similarly advanced age of 91 years old. Around 1,500 people, including Hasidim from other communities, attended the funeral ceremony in front of the house in Mercatorstraat, which has since been known as Beth Jitschok, 'house of Isaac', after the forename of the first rebbe of this new Hasidic dynasty. The reb Yankele's only son, Leibish Leizer, then took over the succession and he has since been known as the Przeworsker rebbe, after the small town of Przeworsk, around 15 kilometres from Sieniawa, where reb Ytsekl was born. This reference to a more or less mythical origin in the Eastern European past – reb Ytsekl was never a rebbe in Przeworsk – has since been current in Hasidic circles, especially for new dynasties or rebbes with a limited or localized influence.[22]

Reb Ytsekl, but also reb Yankele, were renowned for their charitable activities. Both managed to obtain gifts from rich followers or sympathizers for good works, *tzedoke*,* which they distributed to the needy, particularly for time-specific needs such as the traditional constitution of a trousseau and a dowry for a fiancée from a poor family, *hahnosses kale.** The rabbi's residence also provided shelter to impecunious visitors (often in fact having travelled to Antwerp to earn some money), who obtained food and lodging there. It thus functions both as a *shtiebl* and as a 'court' that provides accommodation for the rebbe and his family.

The community that has grown up around reb Ytsekl shows how Hasidim 'orphaned' of their former *tzadikim* produced a new Hasidic structure in 1954, a new dynasty that has now lasted nearly fifty years and is on its third rebbe. The 'creation' of a rebbe is certainly the result of an interaction between the 'holy one' and his followers. Reb Ytsekl and his successors have also gathered around them people from a very wide range of social and geographical backgrounds over more than fifty years. This dynasty is a good example of the current dynamism of the movement. The conditions in Antwerp were certainly favourable: the valuable presence of many other Hasidic groups – the 'Przeworsker' sent their children to Satmar Hasidic schools – the economic prosperity from the diamond industry in the post-war years and the benevolence of the city and the State authorities all contributed, as for other Hasidic communities in Antwerp, to the efflorescence – albeit limited – of this dynasty and the community that formed around it.

COMPLEX INTERACTIONS

Many Jews in Antwerp send their children to three Jewish schools that are recognized and subsidized by the State, which provide a high standard of secular education along with Jewish instruction. In accordance with a model that most Hasidim strive to put in place everywhere, four Hasidic communities in Antwerp have established their own schools specifically in order to be able to limit the proportion of secular education. This is the case with the Belz, Satmar, Vishnitz and Bobov Hasidim – the first three communities have schools both for boys and for girls. These schools also accept pupils from other Hasidic communities: children from the Przeworsk community attend the Satmar school.

For the girls, the secular education, with a substantial amount of practical knowledge for domestic life, but also languages, conducted entirely in Flemish, is relatively advanced and these schools are therefore state-subsidized. Moreover, the girls only receive a limited religious education; in the Hasidic orthodox tradition religious learning is the prerogative of men. For boys, the traditional education begins as early as three years of age in the *haider,** literally the 'chamber', with the Hebrew alphabet and the teaching of prayer, extending gradually to the *Humesh,** the Pentateuch and then to the Talmud and to the study of the code of Jewish laws, the *Shulhan Aruh**. At the age of twelve, the boys enter the *Talmud Torah,** the school for the study of the Talmud and the Torah, then at around the age of sixteen the *yeshive,** the Talmudic academy itself. All this teaching is conducted in Hebrew and Yiddish and the boys in these schools receive only a limited education (just a few hours) in secular subjects: Dutch and French, arithmetic and some basic geography. Talmudic questioning and debate (fairly limited in this type of school) certainly constitute a beneficial form of mental 'gymnastics' but these boys' ignorance of secular knowledge – science, history, chemistry, physics and so on – hinders their access to many professions. As we will see, this disadvantage also applies to the Hasidim in New York and elsewhere. Certainly in Antwerp, from 1950 until 1980, a period in which the Hasidim found work fairly easily in the diamond industry, these deficiencies did not have too much impact. For being a broker, usually speaking Yiddish, or for cleaving diamonds these kinds of knowledge were not indispensable, but today there are fewer professional openings in the diamond sector and the lack of secular knowledge is having an impact. Moreover, the group of Belz Hasidim that has formed a dissident community is specifically rejecting the narrowness of the curriculum in the ultra-traditional school. In common with the Gerer, the Lubavitcher and many other Hasidim of diverse affiliations, they are sending their boys to the Jesode Hatorah school belonging to the Antwerp orthodox community, *Mahzikei Hadas* (the defenders of the faith), where the secular teaching, recognized and subsidized by the State, is much more substantial than in the Belzer, Satmarer or Vishnitzer schools.

There is therefore, at least at the scholastic level, some continuity and interaction between the orthodox and the Hasidic communities. It is true that the orthodox community is being 'infiltrated' by the Hasidim; there is even one major oratory that uses the Hasidic prayer-book (see the previous chapter). Many of the followers are also former Hasidim who settled in Antwerp before the war, or their descendants. Furthermore, many Hasidim, particularly within the most traditionalist groups such as the Satmarer and the Belzer, are ritual slaughterers, *kashrut** supervisors in butchers' and kasher restaurants and so on, on behalf of this community. The Hasidim also run many of the shops and outlets selling religious articles, bakeries, butchers', fishmongers' and so on that supply Hasidic but also orthodox and even 'conservative' Jews (less strict than the orthodox) who belong to a second official Antwerp community, *Shomer Hadas*, 'Guardians of the faith'. There is therefore continuity between Hasidim and other more or less religious sectors in Antwerp at various levels. Many Hasidic diamond-traders work alongside non-religious manufacturers and shopkeepers who often originate, either directly or through their parents or grandparents, from the same towns in Hungary or Poland as themselves – and are frequently also of Hasidic origin. This leads to forms of contact and informality that make light of differences in lifestyle.

Moreover, friendly social relations between Hasidim of various affiliations, including orthodox and conservative Jews, also develop at many 'rites of passage' ceremonies. For instance, at around midday on Saturdays at the end of the Sabbatical service, there is a great to-ing and fro-ing between the various oratories and synagogues. Many Hasidim hurry to another *shtiebl* to take part in a *kiddish*,* a light meal intended to celebrate an attainment of male religious majority (at the age of thirteen years), a *bar mitsve*,* or a forthcoming marriage and so on. This involves congratulating the families concerned, who are often business associates in the diamond sector, and chatting with acquaintances. It is also one of the occasions on which Hasidim can be seen wearing their *shtreimel** or *spodek,** fur caps, in the majestic 'conservative' synagogue in the city.

Since 1980, the economic situation of the Hasidim has been transformed. Antwerp remains a major trading centre for both rough and finished diamonds, but it is no longer the main centre for polishing the stones; this has relocated to other countries – Russia, Vietnam, India and Israel. The craft of cleaving, a Hasidic speciality in Antwerp, has largely given way to fragmentation by laser equipment. Moreover, the Hasidic brokers are now confronted with the presence of competing commercial diamond networks, particularly Indians from Gujarat,[23] and they have fewer opportunities today for exercising their intermediary role. Many Hasidim have therefore entered other sectors of activity: kasher pizzerias (sic!), mobile phone shops, religious bookshops and other retail businesses. A few black sheep became involved in heroin trafficking, and in 1997 a rich follower of the Vishnitzer rebbe and a sponsor of his movement, was implicated in a financial and property scandal that caused a great sensation.

However, the vast majority of Hasidim are decent people and the difficulties in the diamond industry, as well as the need to provide for large numbers of children, sometimes six or more, have produced many situations of hardship; some Hasidim receive financial assistance from their local Jewish charitable institution. However, as we will see in later chapters, the economic situation of the Hasidim is often much more difficult in other places, particularly in Israel.

In any case, confronted with economic difficulties, the expansion of Hasidism in Antwerp seems to have slowed today. However, it remains a major component of Jewish life in Antwerp; the eighteen Hasidic communities of varying sizes constitute the hard core of religious practice, for the observance in the classical orthodox and conservative communities is considerably less rigorous. The rhythm of celebrations among the various Hasidic groups, particularly from sunset on Friday until Saturday evening or during the festivals, with the street processions of Hasidim in their ceremonial dress, accompanied by their many children, going to the oratory or returning from it, lends a particular atmosphere to several streets in the city, mainly south of the central station.

Over the years, the intense Hasidic religiosity has had an influence on the more or less religious or traditionalist Jews of the city and even beyond. In the immediate post-war period, a Jewish butcher (of Dutch origin) who had settled in the heart of the Jewish quarter was selling non-kasher meat![24] Today that seems inconceivable; kashrut observance has generally become stricter and more widespread. Even fish, which does not require any particular religious preparation (although certain shellfish and crustaceans are forbidden), which in the immediate post-war period many Jews would obtain from a Flemish fishmonger, also settled in the Jewish quarter, is now bought almost exclusively in fishmongers' run by Hasidim.

Today, many Hasidim but also some orthodox work very little if at all during the half-holiday period, *Hol-hamoed,** during certain religious festivals (festival of the Tabernacle, Sukkot* and during the Passover), whereas previously they attended to their businesses. Like the Hasidim, the orthodox no longer go to the cinema and men and women are separated at weddings and *bar mitsve* celebrations. Increasingly, the men wear beards and the untrimmed and extremely thick 'Hasidic' beards have proliferated. Among the non-Hasidim, more and more women are wearing wigs. Among the Hasidim themselves, a certain emulation is also in play. Thirty years ago in the streets of the city, sidelocks around the face remained discreet; today many Hasidim sport long sidelocks that unroll in curls around the face. Hasidic hyper-religiosity and ritualism now imbue the life of wide sectors of Jewish life in Antwerp.[25]

For its part, the intense Hasidic way of life is highly dependent on the presence of the non-Hasidic Jewish majority in Antwerp. Major institutions such as the orthodox school, which takes a significant number of pupils from Hasidic families, and an efficient charitable institution that helps Hasidic families in need, as well as the funeral organizations run by the orthodox community, and finally the diamond sector with many Jewish employers, have provided the Hasidim with many economic opportunities. This remains the situation today, albeit to a lesser degree. Also, in various Jewish districts of the city, Yiddish is the language in current use. This is the language of daily use for the Hasidim, but also for many other Polish, Hungarian or Rumanian Jews for whom it was already the mother-tongue or language of everyday use before the war. Together they use it in abundance in their daily interaction, particularly in the diamond trade. As a result of this, Yiddish continues to thrive in Antwerp.

As I have said, many Antwerp Jews originate from the same towns or villages as the Hasidim, leading to affinities and some benevolence among the former towards the latter. These affinities are important for the Hasidim because these *landsman** or compatriots, whom they do not fail to solicit, provide financial support for many enterprises and projects in the Hasidic communities – schools, construction and reconstruction of oratories and so on – and very often, at the request of their Hasidic relatives, they help families or individuals in difficulty. The interdependence and interaction between the Hasidic world and much of the Jewish community in Antwerp are therefore very real.

Furthermore, Belgium is clearly benevolent towards the Hasidim. The religious freedom that prevails there and the democratic nature of the country allow their various religious institutions to be created and governed without difficulty. Moreover, Belgian social legislation, with a family policy strongly influenced by the Flemish and francophone Christian social-democratic parties, provides financial support and tax concessions to many Hasidic families. Furthermore, the high standard of living, clean conditions and medical care in this country help to reduce infant mortality, which has of course favoured the demographic expansion of Hasidism.

The strong correlation in Antwerp between the diamond industry, Jewish life and Hasidism is a striking fact; in Brussels, where as many if not more Jews live as in Antwerp, but where there is less religiosity and no diamond industry, there is almost no Hasidic presence.[26] This strong correlation also exists elsewhere, particularly in New York, without the major role that it continues to play in the Flemish city. In any case, the growth and contemporary dynamism of

Hasidism, which contrasts with the pre-war situation, is dependent everywhere, as we will see, on the existence of an encompassing Jewish and non-Jewish environment that is somewhat favourable. Beyond the 'Diaspora', the State of Israel clearly constitutes a rather different case but, as we will see, Hasidism also has a presence there, with important interactions in both directions, playing an active part in Israeli society as a whole.

3
Williamsburg, a Satmar Bastion

THE UNITED STATES, A 'NON-*KASHER*'* DESTINATION

Although Hasidism has a very strong presence in New York today, this was far from the case before the Second World War. Certainly, among the millions of Jewish emigrants from Eastern Europe who had settled in the United States between 1880 and 1940, there were some highly religious Jews, including a minority of Hasidim. However, during that period economic necessities often prevented Jews from observing the Sabbatical day of rest, as well as other Jewish prescriptions. Furthermore, the attendance of state schools –there were just five full-time Jewish schools in the country in 1917[1] – meant that the orthodox faith that might have been introduced from Eastern Europe rapidly lost ground to less rigorous forms of religious practice, particularly to 'conservative' and 'reform' Judaism,[2] or simply led to the abandonment of religious practices. The attraction of the prevailing American way of life also had an impact, particularly among the younger members of the second generation who were born in the country. In 1937 to 1938, just one quarter to one third of Jews were members of a synagogue and the majority of these were somewhat elderly people.[3] Religious orthodoxy seemed to be on the brink of disappearing.

The *rebbes** in Eastern Europe were aware of this situation and they discouraged and sometimes even prohibited their followers from emigrating to the United States, that *trefe medine** or non-kasher country.[4] There were in fact some exceptions to this, but these were Hasidic figures without great influence and only a small number of followers.[5] The true beginnings of the Hasidic expansion in the United States date back to the beginnings of the Second World War, with the arrival in 1940 of the sixth Lubavitch rebbe, Joseph Isaac Schneerson (1880–1950), who came from an ancient and renowned dynasty (see Chapter 5). Having managed to flee occupied Poland, he settled in Crown Heights, Brooklyn. With just a few followers from the Lubavitch dynasty and some other orthodox Jews, almost all of whom had recently emigrated from Eastern Europe, he formed a small but vigorous Hasidic community with just a few dozen people.

Crown Heights is one of the three districts, along with Williamsburg and Borough Park, that became prime settlement areas for Hasidic immigrants after the Nazi genocide. All three are situated in Brooklyn, one of the five vast boroughs of New York City. However, after the Second World War it was in Williamsburg, one of the oldest districts of Brooklyn, that Hasidism underwent its major boom.[6] This area is near the Williamsburg Bridge over the East River, which connects Brooklyn to Lower East Side in Manhattan, a densely populated area in which many Jews had lived just after immigrating from Eastern Europe and where some still live today. In fact, the strong Hasidic presence in Williamsburg, where many non-Jews – mainly Puerto Ricans – also live, came to be located in one part of the district only. This consisted of around 120 blocks of houses or other buildings; it was a triangular area with boundaries correspondingly approximately to Broadway, Kent and Flushing Avenues; the centre of the Hasidic district is situated around Bedford, Lee, Marcy and Division Avenues and some lateral roads.[7] The Hasidic population consists of around 40,000 people belonging to various Hasidic movements, the main one of which is called Yetev Lev D'Satmar, 'the charitable heart'[8] of Satmar. The other communities present include the followers of the rebbes of Klausenburg (Kolozvar in Hungary), Munkacz, Papa, Tzelem, Vishnitz, Spinka and Krasna. These dynasties and their followers mainly originate from regions of Transylvania, Slovakia, Lower Carpathian Ruthenia and some that are strictly speaking in Hungary; in every case, they are regions that belonged for a very long period, from the 18th century to the breakdown of the Austro-Hungarian Empire in 1918, within the sphere of Hungarian influence.[9] The Hasidism in Williamsburg is therefore essentially 'Hungarian',[10] in clear contrast both to Antwerp Hasidism (see previous chapter) and to the other major Hasidic centres that I shall next be examining.

THE DISTRICT

Towards the end of the 1920s and during the subsequent decades, there were some orthodox Jews of Russian and Polish origin living in Williamsburg, who were relatively moderate in their religious practice. There were nonetheless a few Hasidic oratories in the district, established in shops or basements. It was in the immediate post-war period, with the arrival of the first survivors of the Nazi genocide, mainly from Hungary and Rumania (particularly Transylvania, a region that had belonged to this country from 1918), that the district developed a Hasidic character. In 1948, there were already around 1,500 Hasidim in the district. This presence of a first core attracted other Hasidim survivors of the Nazi genocide, including various rebbes. As in Antwerp, families were rebuilt and they rapidly brought large numbers of children into the world. In 1959, the Hasidic population already numbered between 10,000 and 12,000 people. By 1972, there were some 35,000 Hasidim in the area and towards the end of the 20th century there were 40,000,[11] although some of them had left for new Hasidic settlements (see below p. 41). Meanwhile, the overwhelming majority of 'moderate' orthodox Jews left the district. There are still a few small communities of this kind, but the Jews in Williamsburg have essentially been Hasidic for a number of decades.

The Jewish quarter has some highly contrasting characteristics. From their arrival, the Hassidim created oratories, schools and ritual baths, often investing in buildings – sometimes with neo-Gothic architecture – abandoned by the moderate orthodox Jews who had left for other places. Although there are also tall apartment blocks with comfortable rental accommodation, much of the Hasidic housing is located in dilapidated houses that pre-date the Second World War. The heart of the quarter, with its shops, residential buildings, synagogues and schools, mainly consists of old houses. On the main streets, particularly Lee and Bedford Avenues, there are many shops, some of which are set up in cramped basements. Signboards in English and Yiddish advertise the specialities: butchers', dairies, bakeries, groceries, snack bars and small restaurants, of course all strictly kasher. There are also many traders in religious items, who display prayer-shawls, phylacteries and suchlike in their windows, bookshops selling large numbers of religious books – editions of the Talmud, writings of more or less renowned rebbes – and gentlemen's tailors, who chiefly supply traditional Hasidic garments.[12] There are also, in increasing numbers in the last twenty years, car-hire firms, estate agents and financial advisers, and even legal practices and medical and dental surgeries, usually belonging to more or less religious non-Hasidim who nevertheless speak Yiddish. The new shops also include many selling children's items – often run by women – in response to the demographic expansion of the district.

The shopping streets are often extremely busy, especially between midday and two o'clock and at the end of the afternoon: there are many regular customers and passers-by, and the trucks and other vehicles that pass and stop to make deliveries often create traffic congestion. The drivers, who are often young, frequently wear overcoats that in no way conceal the *tzitses*,* the fringes of the ritual shawls, *talles koten*,* that they sport over their shirts;[13] also their caps – the traditional hats would be cumbersome – tend to emphasize their long sidelocks falling down in curls. The married women, wearing the traditional Hasidic wigs and scarves or hats, take their children with them when they go shopping; they take advantage of chance meetings to stop and chat with other women, as the men do with their male acquaintances.

Neither Borough Park nor Crown Heights have such a large number of people of both sexes in their streets with such a distinctive ultra-orthodox appearance. This creates a very specific atmosphere in the roads lined with specialized shops, oratories, traditional schools for younger and older children, both boys and girls, and many other Hasidic institutions, particularly in the centre of the district.

Since settling in Williamsburg, the Hasidim have scrupulously observed the Biblical prescription to 'be fruitful, and multiply'. Today, many of the Hasidim in the district already belong to a third generation of adults; also, many passers-by in the streets of the district are noticeably young, whereas the many children of school age, now of the fourth generation, are less in evidence, since they are shut away all day in their schools from the age of three years. According to a recent survey of a sample of women, all the married women over 25 years of age had on average four to eight children![14]

Despite all this, the Hasidic population of the district has not grown very much – since the 1970s, some of the followers have settled outside New York (see below).

PROFESSIONS

According to George Kranzler,[15] nearly half the male Hasidim of the district are workers and employees. The more or less skilled Hasidim work as mechanics, locksmiths, electricians, diamond-polishers and so on. The employees are generally secretaries, bookkeepers, salespeople or lower-ranking executives. Around 10% work in the public sector, for example as postal workers. Twenty-five percent of Hasidim are self-employed, particularly in the diamond industry and trade, and in jewellery and silverware, but also in the sector of cameras, video cameras and other electronic goods. Others work as insurance brokers, estate agents or securities brokers. A significant number of the Hasidim have posts as *kashrut** supervisors and ritual slaughterers and, finally, some are teachers and administrators in Hasidic scholastic institutions, which are expanding rapidly in Williamsburg and in the other Hasidic districts in Brooklyn and elsewhere.

Particularly in the immediate post-war period, some of the newly arrived followers worked, often in difficult conditions, in the textile industry, as cutters, sewing-machine operators or tailors, or in shops connected with this industry. Many newcomers also went into the diamond industry and trade, which remains a sector in which the Hasidim work, mainly as brokers, polishers or diamond-sawyers. They can be observed in large numbers – naturally all bearded and dressed in black – in 47th Street, between 5th and 6th Avenue in Manhattan, which is the heart of the diamond trade and industry in New York.[16]

However, the Williamsburg Hasidim, men and women alike, do not exercise professions that require university qualifications. They do not become doctors, lawyers, or high-ranking executives in industry or finance. In fact, the overwhelming majority of the Hasidic movements reject any form of university education for their children, which is in any case almost impossible for them to access given the meagre secular education acquired in their schools. University is considered to pose a threat to young people, with the exposure they would receive both to teachings on evolution, philosophy and suchlike and to the deleterious environment of the campuses with their non-religious students and lecturers. The advent of the counter-culture and the hippy movement towards the end of the 1960s has only reinforced this rejection of the academic world.

By contrast, computer training, particularly in offices where many Hasidim are employed, can now be obtained in schools where the instructors are orthodox Jews; furthermore, the teaching of these essentially technological skills is not thought to present a challenge to Jewish values. In fact, the Hasidim do not feel threatened by the use of new technology for practical purposes such as telephones, fax machines and cars. By contrast, most Hasidic movements are fiercely opposed to use of the internet, as well as television and to a lesser extent the radio. However, the reality experienced by followers working in offices and even in shops is often more sophisticated and electronic mail and information obtained from the Web then become extremely valuable, which means that the computers have internet access, leading to many dangers and temptations ...

During the early post-war decades, when the demands of caring for their (many) children permitted, or when the children were old enough, the women had worked in the textile industry or as teachers in religious schools for girls – more often the case for young women who were not yet married – while others helped their husbands to run shops in Williamsburg. Today they have an increasingly strong presence in the businesses of the district but also in the shops selling photographic, electronic or other manufactured goods, often situated in Manhattan or Borough Park; they also do office jobs that require them to use computers. Moreover, some women in Williamsburg run shops selling wigs (an important accessory for married women),[17] lingerie, women's clothes that accord with the Hasidic code of decency (loose dresses that conceal the figure, dark tights, 'decent' underwear etc.). Orthodox women come from all over New York and even further afield to do their shopping there. Some Hasidic women are employed in the jewellery and diamond sector in Manhattan but for many years now they have also been opening shops selling silverware, jewellery and bric-a-brac in Williamsburg itself.

POVERTY, STATE ASSISTANCE, SOLIDARITY

Although more and more women are working, many are unable to do so because of their large numbers of children. Also, one third of the Hasidim of the district are elderly people with very modest pensions. Finally, many young people pursue extensive Talmudic studies, at the *kolel*,* a Talmudic academy for married men, for a year or two after their marriage. It is therefore not entirely surprising that in Williamsburg in 1985 one third of the population had incomes of less than $10,000 a year for a family of four, a figure then considered as the official poverty line.[18]

In 1984, after ten years of intense juridical and political struggle, in which the Satmar community played a particularly active part, the Williamsburg Hasidim obtained 'disadvantaged minority' status, which is generally accorded to Native Americans, Hispanics or blacks. This status gave the Hasidim who wanted for instance to set up their own businesses or to renovate or construct buildings in the district access to financial assistance from a federal agency, the Opportunity Development Association (ODA). This also subsidized the establishment of a mental health centre called Pesach Tikvah, 'door of hope', the first institution of its kind in Hasidic circles. Moreover, various sources of state aid also provide Hasidim in difficult financial circumstances with coupons for buying food, housing subsidies and assistance with medical care (Medicaid). Sixty-two percent of the customers in the pharmacies, shoe-shops and children's clothing shops depend on these various subsidies.[19]

However, the Hasidim themselves, who have a very strong sense of the tradition of *tzedoke*,* good works or charity, practised among the Jews for so many centuries,[20] operate a great many forms of mutual aid, which are also organized at present in a highly systematic way. For instance, there is the tradition of visiting the sick, *bikur holim*;* today there is an entire network of organizations, projects and programmes, which begin with initiatives on the part of individuals or small groups, designed to provide assistance to the latter. Some organizations use a fleet of vehicles and have teams of volunteers, men and women, who provide the sick with daily material assistance and kasher meals as well as moral support.[21] Furthermore, according to a strong ancient tradition, called *hahnosses kale*,* literally, 'leading the bride' (under the wedding canopy), individuals and small organizations collect 'dowries' for young women from poor families or who are orphans so that they can marry in suitable conditions and with minimal basic equipment for their future accommodation. This assistance is particularly welcome for impecunious parents who have several daughters to marry.

Moreover, in around 1967 a non-profit-making paramedical organization developed in Williamsburg for the first time in the Hasidic world; known as *Hatzoloh** (rescue), it is run by a group of young Hasidic volunteers who are well-versed in the Jewish rules and laws concerning medical practice. Hatzoloh has a fleet of ambulances and other vehicles, authorized by the health departments and by the police, which constantly travel the district, including – for emergencies – on the Sabbath and festival days; the circulation of these vehicles in the streets of the district has come to form an integral part of its life. As well as first aid, this organization provides Hasidim with the guarantee that everything will be carried out in accordance with the Jewish prescriptions, for example in how the dead are treated, or how female modesty is respected. Shortly after its creation in Williamsburg, branches of Hatzoloh were created in other districts of New York and beyond. Since then, similar institutions have been set up in other American towns and in other countries, such as Israel.

Moreover, in the context of the urban violence, theft and other delinquent phenomena that characterize many districts of New York, the Williamsburg Hasidim have created a security organization known as *Shomrim*,* 'supervisors', who patrol the streets and have helped to make them safer. Hatzoloh and Shomrim are therefore modern contributors to Hasidic mutual social assistance in the Diaspora.

In any case, the *tzedoke* plays an essential part in Hasidic Williamsburg, with its large contingent of economically disadvantaged families and individuals. In fact, with a few rare variations, an equally strong organized solidarity exists in other places where Hasidism is strong, particularly in Israel.

A METICULOUS KASHRUT

As soon as they arrived, the Hasidim began to institute a kashrut[22] with very strict rules, thereby creating a specific economic kasher system applying to many products. Even food such as preserved fruit that in theory is not affected by these rules[23] has gradually become part of this system. In fact, if the preparation of such food is not supervised by *mashgihim** (singular *mashgiah*), appropriate religious supervisors, fears can arise concerning the possible introduction of unauthorized substances during their preparation. Doubt, mistrust and anxiety even on this score often know no bounds.

At the heart of this system are the meat-based foods, mainly beef, veal, chicken, duck and goose, which are subject to particularly strict rules concerning slaughter and preparation.[24] In the small semi-rural Jewish communities of the past in Eastern Europe and elsewhere, the weekly slaughter of one or two animals by a ritual slaughterer, *shoihet*,* under the local rabbi's supervision, was enough to supply their needs. However, with increasing urbanization, and also because of the increasingly strict statutory obligations in matters of hygiene, and consequently also in the use of preserved food, slaughter could no longer be practised in such traditional conditions. Thus, at the beginning of the 19th century in France the consistories in Paris and the provinces became the guarantors of the operation of the kashrut with the agreement of the authorities.[25] At the end of the 19th century in the United States, some orthodox rabbis assembled to establish a systematic organization for kasher slaughter.[26] Since then these religious authorities have had their own slaughterers, who work in the major slaughterhouses, and supervisors, *mashgihim*, who monitor both the work in the slaughterhouse and the butchers who sell the products to which the rabbis grant their seal of approval. The Jewish communities to which these rabbis belong receive a levy for their intervention and this represents an important source of revenue.

The religious authorities that issue their seal of approval also have an evident economic power over those who work in the kasher sector, especially the butchers and poultry merchants, because their guarantee is critical to consumer confidence; its repeal can bring financial ruin to the trader disowned in this way.[27] The existence of this economic sector also gives rise to 'religious' occupations, such as slaughterers, supervisors and kasher butchers and poulterers. Until the 1950s most American Jews, even the orthodox, were satisfied with the system that had existed until then but the newly arrived Hasidim had only limited confidence in the kashrut that was not under their supervision. Gradually butchers', groceries and restaurants transformed Williamsburg into the bastion of a kashrut that was supervised by the rebbes and rabbis originating from Europe. This development was instigated by the Tzelemer rebbe,[28] Levi Y. Grunwald, who had been one of the first leaders to create in the district a small Hasidic community of a hard-line 'Hungarian' style,[29] which still generally characterizes the Hasidism of the district.[30] These Hasidim who were very strict in matters of kasher food included the Satmar rebbe and his followers; within a few years of their arrival, they succeeded in creating their own kasher products, particularly milk products, bread and cakes, and finally and importantly, meat and poultry.[31]

In 1952, a central organization of Hasidic rebbes and rabbis was created, the Central Rabbinical Congress of the United States and Canada, under the presidency and direction of the Satmarer rebbe.[32] This Congress set up its own production and marketing networks, particularly for a new 'type' of kasher meat, the *glatt kasher** meat, from cattle and poultry in perfect health that have been impeccably slaughtered using ultra-smooth knives.[33] The businesses that produce and sell the food under the supervision of this institution clearly owe it levies on their turnover. Soon *glatt kasher* meat also found sales outlets in other ultra-orthodox districts of New York and some traders organized the distribution of their merchandise in various towns in the United States and in Canada. From the 1960s, the purchase and consumption of *glatt kasher* food spread to a wide non-Hasidic orthodox public in the United States because these products are reputed to provide excellent guarantees of adherence to the Jewish prescriptions. The existence of the *glatt kasher* sector has contributed to a general reform of the American kasher industry and trade, in which dubious practices were prevalent.

SATMAR, PRINCIPAL COMMUNITY OF THE DISTRICT

The principal community of the district, which is also the most dynamic, having played a major role since 1945 in creating the Williamsburg of today, belongs to the Satmar Hasidic movement. This has developed under the leadership of its rebbe, Joel Teitelbaum (1887–1979). Born in Sighet (today Sighetul in Rumania), he was the second son of Chanania Teitelbaum, the rabbi in that town, and at the same time the rebbe of the local Hasidic community. When Chanania Teitelbaum died in 1904, his elder son, Hersch Teitelbaum, took over the succession, while Joel Teitelbaum, aged seventeen years, settled in Satu Mare (also in Rumania today), where a small community of Hasidim who were attracted by his learning, his piety and his personality gathered around him. Joel Teitelbaum was also a rabbi in some other towns of the region and he gained a strong influence there among many orthodox Jews. In 1934 he returned to Satu Mare, where he had been made a rabbi by the orthodox community. He was known as a staunch champion of both Jewish laws and Hasidic traditions. Under his spiritual leadership, the most traditionalist form of Hasidism gained influence among a population that was certainly religious but had previously been relatively impervious to Hasidism.

From 1940 to 1944, the Satu Mare region was annexed by Hungary and the authorities introduced a large number of discriminatory measures towards the Jews; then in March 1944 Hitler's Germany occupied this country, which had previously been its ally, and undertook the assassination of its approximately 825,000 Jews, more than 550,000 of whom were murdered.[34] On 3 May 1944, Joel Teitelbaum was arrested in Satu Mare and deported first to Cluj in Hungary (now in Rumania) and then to Bergen-Belsen. In December 1944, during some negotiations between Rudolf Kasztner, Vice-President of the Zionist organization in Budapest and the SS leader Adolf Eichmann, who stated that he wanted to ensure the safety of one million Jews' lives in exchange for some goods that were useful to the Germans, 1,684 Jews, including Joel Teitelbaum, were released as a 'good-will gesture' from the camp at Bergen-Belsen and transported after some dramatic incidents to Switzerland.[35] After spending a few months in Geneva, Teitelbaum settled in Palestine in 1945; in 1947, he left for the United States and he settled at 554 Bedford Avenue in Williamsburg; he was then 61 years old. In 1948, he founded the Satmar community with no more than a few dozen followers. Thirteen years later, in 1961, the community already comprised 860 families.[36] This growth was only partly due to the presence of the rebbe's former disciples in Europe; 40% of the followers, albeit already ultra-orthodox and generally originating from the same parts of Transylvania as the older followers, were newcomers to the movement. As with the community surrounding reb Ytsekl in Antwerp, here too a Hasidic figure gathered around him people who had lost their spiritual leaders of the pre-war period. This phenomenon also occurred in many other Hasidic communities created after 1945.

In any case, Satmar Hasidism expanded considerably. Today there are 5,000 to 6,000 families in the United States,[37] half of whom live in Williamsburg. The others live mainly in Borough Park, another Hasidic district in Brooklyn, or in Kiryas Joel, a new town populated exclusively by followers, or in Monsey, a small ultra-orthodox town, both of which are situated in the New York region (see p. 41 below). If we calculate that there are on average six people per household (two adults and four children), there would be between 30,000 and 36,000 Satmar in New York as a whole, including 15,000 to 18,000 in Williamsburg, representing 37.5% to 45% of the Hasidic population in the district. This illustrates the importance of Satmar in Williamsburg.

As the movement developed, oratories, ritual baths and schools were created. Immersed in study and prayer, and also heavily occupied with the numerous religious aspects of community life, the rebbe entrusted the practical problems that arose from this expansion to some people with experience of business and dealings with the 'secular' world. It was they who raised funds, obtained loans for the community's various housing projects, negotiated with the local administrations and police and so on.[38] Success in this field was essential for ensuring the continuation of a viable community and Satmar, notwithstanding its traditionalism, proved to be highly adept in managing its relationships with society at large.

One of the community's major achievements was the development, commensurate with the community's demographic dynamism, of its own scholastic system, providing education to girls and boys from the age of three years until adulthood. This was vital to the continuance of the Hasidic faith in the new generations born after the war within an open society dominated by secular and materialistic concerns. At the beginning of the 1960s, there were 3,000 pupils in the entire Satmar school community, as against 10,000 today, albeit across the movement's four geographical settlements.[39] As I showed in the previous chapter, in their educational system the Hasidim reduce secular teaching to the minimum in favour of an emphasis on religious education conducted in Yiddish and Biblical Hebrew. The Satmar scholastic system extends from the *haider** to the *yeshive gdole*,* the Talmudic academy for advanced students, not forgetting the *kolel* for married men. The forms of teaching are derived from the ultra-orthodox Satmar principles that were established before the war.

The rebbe and his followers originate from north-eastern Transylvania, a region in which a strict orthodoxy predominated, which the Hasidim further reinforced. To maintain a complete fidelity to the values, the model of social and familial organization and the Jewish prescriptions, it was necessary to maintain as much distance as possible from the non-Jewish world, all the more so from some of the Jews of the region, who led a way of life that bore little relation to such a strict system.[40] In the United States, where the temptations of the outside world are even more in evidence, the scholastic system, making the fewest possible concessions to the secular world, has to contribute to preserving the separate and enclosed condition sought by the rebbe.

Moreover, this teaching places a strong emphasis on the *Halohe*,* the Jewish law that comprises a detailed guide for daily life, rather than on a highly abstract exploration of theoretical or philosophical issues. This approach is in keeping with the rejection of purely academic learning that was one of the original reasons for the popularity of Hasidism, but it also takes account of the fact that in the United States the vast majority of the students will practise secular professions. They must therefore know above all the Jewish rules concerning their social and economic activities, their family life and the observance of numerous daily rituals and the kashrut.[41] For the same reason, only the ablest students are encouraged to attend the *kolel* for recently married men, where they continue their studies for one or two years. This is in fact a recent innovation in Satmar Hasidism. This institution, which has developed considerably among many Hasidic communities in the United States, did not exist in Hungary and the rebbe resisted its creation for about twenty years.[42]

The religious teaching for boys is conducted in the Hebrew of the Torah texts rather than the modern Israeli Hebrew and in Yiddish, the language of everyday use both at school and at home. The secular teaching in English, with the boys, which is a legal requirement from the age of seven years – whereas the children are at school from the age of four – is very limited: there is a small amount of English and mathematics, some basic geography and so on. The classes, which last two hours, take place in the afternoon, when the children are already tired from a long morning and some Jewish teaching at the beginning of the afternoon. The spirit of the lessons is often foreign to them, because of both the language used and their content, which is sometimes extremely puzzling for these children. For instance, a teacher might tell some seven- to eight-year-old boys the story of a boy called Peter who made a friend by taking in a lost dog. Now for a Satmar child the dog is an unclean animal; if you touch one, you must purify yourself by washing your hands. For them the idea of having an animal as a pet is therefore shocking. The atmosphere of the classes is noisy and the children are disruptive, whereas that same morning they have been behaving very respectfully towards the *melamdim*,* the schoolmasters who teach them about the Bible and the Talmud.

Underlying the deficiencies of the secular teaching, there is the lack of motivation among the community leaders, whose main concern is simply to conform to the legal requirements and who, moreover, fear the exposure of the young people to the undesirable secular American culture.[43] This situation, observed by the ethnologist Israel Rubin in the 1960s, which still prevails around thirty years later, has therefore not evolved very much, although many parents, aware that their children must at least have a correct knowledge of English, were asking for improvements in its teaching back in the 1960s. Clearly, a form of teaching based on a substantial religious education combined with scanty secular knowledge cannot fail to impact on the professional future of the adults taught in schools of this kind.

In contrast to the boys, the girls in the Satmar schools, as in the majority of Hasidic schools of other communities, receive limited religious teaching based on Biblical parables, moral lessons and a simplified knowledge of the

Jewish laws and customs. By contrast, the girls receive a much more extensive education in English than the boys. The content of this teaching has developed in the last thirty years; mothers and daughters no longer want just to sew; they now learn how to use a computer effectively and familiarize themselves with the various activities that relate to office jobs. In the Satmar school in Borough Park, where the most prosperous followers live, Rubin observed a class of fourteen- to fifteen-year-old girls simulating stock-exchange activities on Wall Street by monitoring the progress of their 'investments' in the financial pages of an American daily newspaper. This development is linked with evident economic and professional needs. Increasingly, young girls and also married women are working in the tertiary sector. The development of female education is nevertheless less advanced in Williamsburg than in Borough Park, where the girls even receive some basic scientific education, under the heading of 'environmental studies' – 'science' is not a positive term for the Satmarer.

The cost of the academic system, from the *haider* to the *yeshive*,* as well as the *kolel*, is very high. The pupils' parents, who generally have large families and usually have modest incomes, would not be able to meet the true cost of this education. One of these schools' main administrative tasks therefore consists in fund-raising – because of their religious nature they do not benefit from any state subsidies.[44] Both the followers who are able to raise funds and the generous donors – some of whom are extremely rich – are highly esteemed by the community.

SATMAR: ZIONISM AND AMERICAN POLITICS

One of the distinctive characteristics of the Hasidism extolled by Joel Teitelbaum and by his followers is a radical opposition to Zionism. As we know, this attitude was undoubtedly almost universal in the Hasidic movement before 1945: the rebbes had opposed political Zionism from the very outset. The return to the Holy Land is a constant aspiration among the Jews and from the beginnings of the Hasidic movement, some of its followers had settled there, in particular a brother-in-law of Baal Shem Tov (see below in Chapter 6). This very limited emigration continued until the Shoah.* However, the Hasidim considered the development of political Zionism from the end of the 19th century to be a rebellion against God. In their view, a Jewish country could be established only by the will of God and under the leadership of the Messiah as his emissary. Before the Second World War in Hungary, Joel Teitelbaum had already been a fierce opponent of Zionism and particularly of the Mizrachi party, which claimed to be both Zionist and religious. However, whereas after the war most rebbes considerably moderated their opposition to Zionism, and from 1948 towards the new state of Israel (see Chapter 6), the Satmarer rebbe and his followers maintained their opposition. The extreme anti-Zionism of the Satmar is based on a passage in the Babylonian Talmud (Ketubot, 111: 1), according to which in his alliance with the chosen people God has imposed the oath never to 'force the End', therefore never to try to seize the Holy Land by force. According to Joel Teitelbaum, violation of this oath brings the worst disasters, even to those who did not participate in it. Accordingly, he explains the Nazi genocide as the punishment for the Zionists' violation of this oath.

Moreover, the rebbe accuses the Israeli government of undermining the Jewish faith, for instance by incorporating women into the army, developing a secular educational system and allowing forbidden activities on the Sabbath. Deploring the fact that the prestige of the existence of an independent State should have led a majority of Jews, even orthodox, into error, the rebbes and his followers are fully determined to resist the Zionist heresy.[45] This attitude is expressed in anti-Israeli meetings in Williamsburg but also in Madison Square Garden in New York, during marches by young Satmarer or anti-Israeli demonstrations in front of the United Nations headquarters, as well as through anti-Israeli articles in Satmar publications and advertisements in the *New York Times*.

Furthermore, Satmar provides financial support to various ultra-orthodox communities in Israel, specifically so that they can maintain their yeshives and other educational institutions, which are fully independent and do not receive state subsidies. In 1953, Joel Teitelbaum was elected chief rabbi of *Edah Haredit*,* the 'community of God-fearers', a coalition of various Hasidic and ultra-orthodox communities of varying sizes who refuse to recognize the State of Israel (see Chapter 6), mainly based in Mea Shearim, the old Jewish quarter of Jerusalem. Although Joel Teitelbaum never left Williamsburg to assume this role, his strong convictions acted as an influence on *Edah Haredit*.

The rebbe died in 1979 and his successor, Moishe Teitelbaum, upholds the same principles. On 11 February 2001, the Central Rabbinical Congress of the United States and Canada (see p. 33 above), which comprises 150 Hasidic communities, led at the outset by Joel Teitelbaum and today by Moishe Teitelbaum, published a statement in the *New York Times* entitled, 'Why are we against the Israeli government and its wars?' Among other things, it states that 'Zionism, by its very nature, rejects the concept of a divinely imposed exile [on the Jews]. In addition, it has been consistently indifferent to the sufferings and dangers to which it and its embodiment, the State of Israel, have inflicted upon Jew and Gentile'.[46] On 12 February 2002, this same institution organized a demonstration against the State of Israel before its consulate in New York, in which 20,000 people are estimated to have taken part.

However, the Satmar also participate in local and national politics in the United States. As is traditional among Jewish emigrants to the United States, the Satmarer initially voted for the Democrat party, while ensuring when the candidates were nominated at the primaries within this party that they supported the candidates who were most sympathetic to their views on specific questions. Thus, the Satmarer had long supported the non-Jewish Democrat representative in their constituency, John Rooney, who at the Congress in Washington, had facilitated the immigration of the parents and close relatives of the Hasidim who had already settled in the United States. At the primaries in 1972, they did not support a clearly left-wing Jewish candidate who opposed the Vietnam war and they again voted for Rooney, who had supported this war and who, primarily as a Catholic, opposed abortion and expressed support for an increase in aid to religious schools. Shortly before the vote, before the festival of Yom

Kippur, the day of the Great Atonement, the rabbi's spokesman announced to the thousands of followers gathered in the synagogue that they should vote for Rooney, who was elected with an increased majority.[47] However, from 1968, the Satmarer began to vote for the Republican party, particularly in presidential elections. The Democrats appeared to be too left-wing and in favour of sexual tolerance and feminism, ideas that had come from supporters of the counter-culture and the hippy movement of the late 1960s, whereas the Republicans remained the champions of traditional family values and morality.[48]

Although the Jews constitute only a minority compared with the black and Latino electorate in Williamsburg, Satmar and the other Hasidic communities in the district represent a significant political force because the Hasidim are voters who show little tendency to absenteeism and also because they are generally registered in one and the same constituency.

It is clear that this community, which aims to be very much enclosed, nevertheless participates in a level-headed way in various political struggles. As we will see later, in relation to Kiryas Joel, a Satmar settlement in the New York area, the community occasionally brings considerable political force to bear.

Furthermore, to disseminate its ideas and views, Satmar produces a weekly publication in the Yiddish language, called *Der Yid* ('The Jew' in Yiddish), which was founded in 1953 and has a print run of 30,000, with 25,000 copies being sold in Williamsburg itself.[49] This weekly also circulates a great deal of information about Hasidic community life and publishes many small advertisements. Its importance for the propagation of the Satmar political ideology and its highly diverse viewpoints is only increased by the fact that the followers refuse to make any use of television and make only limited use of radio; even reading a 'serious' daily newspaper such as the *New York Times* remains a limited activity.

THE SATMAR ECONOMY

The Satmar evidently observe the prescriptions concerning kasher food in a highly rigorous way. To this end, they buy their supplies almost exclusively from butchers, bakers and dairy producers who are followers of the movement or from other trustworthy Hasidim who belong to closely related 'Hungarian' communities. Given their massive presence and their influence, the Satmarer play a major role within the kasher food industry established by the Central Rabbinical Congress (see p. 33 above); furthermore, many Satmar followers are involved in kasher food production and trade. The various Hasidic communities, including Satmar of course, call on their followers to support the shopkeepers of their own community. Beyond a legitimate remuneration, the profits of the shops sponsored by Yetev Lev D'Satmar* are supposed to revert to their institutions.

The kasher industry and trade provide the Satmar Hasidim with various forms of economic activity, as managers of shops and businesses, and as artisans, salesmen, ritual slaughterers, restaurant supervisors and so on. The Satmar institutions themselves are another major source of work, especially in the religious sector of their schools, in which the teachers, both men and women (for the girls), are followers of the community. With the demographic expansion of the community, the Satmar educational system has as we know undergone a considerable expansion. It employs around 600 teachers – men and women – and administrators, and 200 more people in charge of administration and maintenance.[50] Because of the growth of the movement, the commercial kasher sector and the religious items sector have also expanded, opening up additional economic opportunities for the followers.

Despite everything, the 'religious' professions provide only limited openings; while 25% of former pupils of the Satmar yeshives take part in them, these activities are not highly remunerative; many teachers are employed only on a part-time basis.[51] Therefore many Satmarer, like the other Hasidim in Williamsburg, and beyond, practise 'secular' professions. Some are diamond-traders, sometimes highly prosperous, but they usually live in Borough Park, not in the district. Furthermore, since the 1970s many Satmarer, men and women, have worked in jewellery shops and shops selling electronic and photographic equipment. Others work as bookbinders, printers or electricians. Finally, and this is a new development, many followers work as computer operators, and some are even high-ranking computer professionals.

Professional activities among the Satmar women correspond to those described for Williamsburg as a whole (see p. 30); however, because of the large scale of the movement and its institutions, many of them find posts within the vast Satmar educational system. Moreover, the followers now have a nearly exclusive role in the shops and other economic activities located in Kiryas Joel, a Satmar settlement in the New York area (see below), in which the Satmarer – today several thousand – are the sole inhabitants.

Interestingly, the development of Satmar professional activities is simultaneously moving in opposite directions. On the one hand, increasing numbers of men and women are working outside the district, in trade and the tertiary sector – particularly as computer professionals, which gives them important contacts with the outside world. This tends to weaken the social control exercised by the movement and to give rise to impulses for change and deviation from its norms. On the other hand, however, more followers are working within the community, which brings them more directly under its social control.

Moreover, women are working more often than previously. In particular, mothers of families aspire to more comfort in their homes. Thus, life in a large family is facilitated by the use of recent household devices that are increasingly sophisticated, which gives rise to the need to contribute to the household income in order to acquire them. By contrast, in another new phenomenon, husbands are helping their wives with household tasks. In theory, the traditional model in which the husband is supposed to lead and the woman to follow is still in force, but in reality new norms of cooperation, mutual trust and flexibility are increasingly in evidence among spouses.[52] Certainly there cannot be said to be a feminist movement among the Satmarer, but the status of women has subtly modified to some extent. Moreover, after the rebbe experienced an extremely debilitating brain haemorrhage in 1968, the *rebbetsen*,* his wife, Feiga

Teitelbaum (1912–2001), began to play a major role in running the community (see below pp. 45–6). From then on, many followers treated her almost like a rebbe, and her house in Kiryas Joel, particularly following Joel Teitelbaum's death in 1979, had in fact become a form of Hasidic 'court'. That being said, the men continue to be the dominant players in community affairs and the almost exclusive protagonists in religious services and in the teaching of the Torah and the Talmud, which remains predominantly a masculine prerogative.

What is the economic situation of the Satmarer? On the one hand, although the followers have adopted many new professions, their rejection of any form of higher secular education means that many are closed to them, including highly lucrative professions that are practised in New York by so many other Jews: they do not work for instance as doctors, engineers, banking executives or high-ranking civil servants. Furthermore, in periods when conditions are favourable in the diamond industry, the Satmarer, like other Hasidim working in this sector, certainly turn this to their advantage; this is particularly the case for merchants and brokers, but those who work as salaried workers – mainly as lapidaries – generally only obtain modest pay rises. In Williamsburg, however, many large families belong to the economic categories that benefit from various subsidies granted by the ODA, the aid agency for 'disadvantaged minorities' (see above). In fact the richest Satmarer often prefer to live in Borough Park or in Kiryas Joel and Monsey.

Despite the low incomes of many followers, the prevalent attitude of the Satmarer in economic matters is in no way hostile to the enrichment and prosperity of some. Also, the presence of rich followers enables the community to obtain constantly higher contributions from them for the ever-growing needs of the community institutions such as schools and oratories, as well as for all the forms of *tzedoke*, good works, which then benefit the most disadvantaged. Moreover, the followers, both men and women, generally aspire to a comfortable urban middle-class existence and although in principle moderation in lifestyle is required, there are no strict rules in relation to this.

SATMAR BEYOND THE WALLS: KIRYAS JOEL

At the beginning of the 1970s, the Satmar Hasidim founded a community in a rural area, around 80 kilometres from New York. The rebbe had long cherished the dream of establishing a community far away from the city in an environment that would protect adults and children from crime, drugs and impious influences. There was another important reason for creating a satellite community: Williamsburg could not provide enough accommodation to sustain the strong expansion of the community.[53] The Satmar approach was not entirely original because, from the end of the 1950s, a community of followers of the Skverer rebbe (originating from Skvira in Ukraine) had created a Hasidic village, New Square, in Rockland County in the New York region. Some Satmar followers discreetly bought properties situated in Monroe, a township in Orange County, approximately 80 kilometres north-west of Manhattan. Other religious Jews had already settled there, particularly following the construction of a motorway linking the small town to New York. It still took at least one hour to reach the city, but the rebbe hoped that the residents would find work in the suburban areas. Furthermore, the organizer and president of the new community owned a business situated in an industrial park that was closer to the new village than New York was, and the Satmarer who worked there were supposed to settle in the new village.

From 1974, the first families settled in houses that were specifically designed for the Hasidic way of life: the kitchens were equipped with two sinks and two ovens to ensure the separation of milk-based and meat-based food.[54] The first arrivals were delighted with the new environment and the community grew at the rate of one hundred families per year. However, this growth quickly gave rise to conflicts with the Town Board in Monroe, which had ascertained that the Hasidim were contravening the local town planning regulations: some basement apartments had been converted into classrooms and places of prayer and even into food shops. Ultimately, a compromise was reached in the law courts that allowed the Hasidim to create their own town council in October 1976 in an area of 170 hectares, for which they were then able to establish their own town planning rules. The new town called Kiryas Joel, meaning in Hebrew the area or town council of Joel (the rebbe's forename).

The employment opportunities on site or nearby proved to be inadequate and most men had to travel to New York every day by car or bus. Many inhabitants had difficulty organizing their monthly salaries to fund their accommodation, educating their children and other expenses. Nevertheless, the population grew considerably; today Kiryas Joel has around 1,332 families, with an average of 5.6 people per household, so around 7,500 inhabitants; there are also a few thousand followers living close to the town.

In Kiryas Joel, there are small modest houses alongside huge luxurious ones. Highly prosperous followers and many much less prosperous ones live side by side here. Nevertheless, they all sit shoulder to shoulder in the oratories, where the followers of varying economic status – these are often old school friends – pray side by side, study the Talmud together and exchange their news and opinions in a very friendly way. As in Williamsburg, many gestures of solidarity and charitable acts are performed here. For instance, there are visits to people who are confined to their houses and the sick in hospital, and volunteers might collect gifts for a particular Hasid who is out of work or who needs help to cover medical costs. This all contributes to creating a friendly and affectionate atmosphere among the followers who live here in a context of strong mutual acquaintance. This rather idyllic situation has nevertheless greatly deteriorated following conflicts surrounding Joel Teitelbaum's successor (see p. 45).

Kiryas Joel is the site for the higher Talmudic academy, the movement's *yeshive gdole*, attended by young people from everywhere to some extent but chiefly from Williamsburg. The majority of them are happy to embrace a very different way of life in the village from the city life. The incontestable success of Kiryas Joel, which within a few years became a small town, derives from its relatively rural and peaceful nature; many Satmarer New Yorkers therefore went to settle there.

POLITICAL, JURIDICAL AND LEGISLATIVE WRANGLES

When Kiryas Joel had become an autonomous township, it had to create a mayor and deputies for the municipal elections; at the outset, the elections were only a formality because no one would have dared to challenge the list of candidates chosen by the community leaders. But today this is no longer the case because there are now two communities in Kiryas Joel who claim to be Satmarer. Thus in October 1997, the leader of a minority dissident community, Kahal Haredim,* 'congregation of those who fear God', submitted a court application for the dissolution of the township because in his view this constituted only an extension of Yetev Lev, the dominant community. The court ruled against this dissolution but decided that the municipal polling stations should no longer be located on the premises of the Yetev Lev community, as had been the case until then.[55] This matter specifically raises the problem of the creation of a township generated by a religious community that is uniform at the outset but gradually experiences schisms over the course of time.

Furthermore, the inhabitants are electors whose votes are hotly contested in many legislative and other ballots, which are sometimes marred by irregularities. Between 1989 and 1994, at least 84 young people who were living temporarily in Kiryas Joel as students at the Satmar higher Talmudic academy illicitly issued a double vote, in both Brooklyn and Kiryas Joel. What led to such practices? With 3,700 registered electors, the votes cast in the town were almost unanimous – at least until the recent schisms – in favour of a particular candidate or party that had the support of the local Satmar leaders. Now, the larger this block vote, the greater is the political influence of the village, which enables it to obtain various advantages from its elected representatives.[56]

Some legislative and juridical disputes, which reached the United States Supreme Court, have also occurred in Kiryas Joel. Until 1989, the village was included in the educational district of the state schools of Monroe-Woodbury. That year, with support from a Brooklyn congressman, the Satmarer managed to get a law passed by a unanimous vote of the legislative assembly in New York State to create a separate educational district for the village, a law that the Republican governor of the State, Mario Cuomo, promulgated on 25 July 1989. Although the Satmarer educate most of their children in their traditional private schools, for practical purposes the new district had to incorporate one particular school that Satmar had created in 1983 for around 225 disabled children (some of whom came from other Hasidic groups). This was designed to enable them to receive specific forms of assistance, in particular specialist teachers,[57] without having to attend a specialized state school outside the village that included non-Hasidic children. In the name of the constitutional separation of the Church and the State, the New York State School Boards Association challenged the law in 1990, and in 1994 the United States Supreme Court ruled that this law was unconstitutional.

Notwithstanding this, eleven days later the New York State legislators devised a more general law that would ultimately have enabled this school to be established but this new version was once again rejected by a court of appeal.

The legislature consequently passed a new variation of the law and, once again, a judge of the Supreme Court of New York State rejected it, in a decision that was confirmed on 12 October 1999 by a ruling of the United States Supreme Court. However, this was by no means the end of the saga. A fourth law that further broadened the criteria authorizing the creation of separate schools was passed ... and this time, in 2001, a court of New York State confirmed its validity. Finally, all being well that ends well, the state school for disabled children in Kiryas Joel joined the very association of state schools that had so long opposed it![58]

This sequence of events certainly demonstrates the perseverance of the Satmarer, as well as their influence with national politicians. In Kiryas Joel as in Williamsburg, they are taking part perforce in the very form of American public life from which they are trying, specifically in the case of this specialized school, to isolate themselves!

A DYNASTY IN TRANSITION

Joel Teitelbaum, who presided over the dynamic expansion of Satmar in New York for over thirty years, was undoubtedly a figure of stature. Moreover, the Hasidim attributed to him, as is customary in the Hasidic movement, all the traditional virtues of the rebbe: spiritual gifts, exemplary religiosity and clairvoyance. Also, like the other rebbes, he held audiences with his followers and prayed for God to grant the requests that they presented to him, particularly on a *kvitel*,* and so on.

With age, Joel Teitelbaum's health became fragile and his increasingly rare public appearances took place mainly on Saturday afternoons at *shaleshides*,* the traditional 'third meal' at the end of the Sabbath. A crowd of male followers in the Satmar oratory silently followed the rebbe's every gesture, particularly as he gradually ate from the sumptuous meal that had been served to him. His wife, the rebbetsen Feiga Teitelbaum, was seated beside him, which is very rare in Hasidic circles, but the few women present remained invisible, confined to a loggia. After the rebbe had finished his meal, the food on the plates was divided into small portions, as *shrayim*,* 'leftovers' that had been sanctified by the rebbe's touch, and the followers avidly seized them because they are supposed to bring various benefits (see Chapter 2, p. 20). After the commotion caused by this distribution, it was in the utmost silence that the Hasidim listened to the *toyre*,* the rebbe's teaching.[59]

However, in 1968 the rebbe suffered a disabling cerebral haemorrhage, which put an end to his participation in the 'third meal' and to his *toyres* at the end of the Sabbath, but he continued to receive individual followers, who would ask for his blessing and present a *kvitel* to him. Furthermore, a large proportion of the community matters was then managed by his wife, the rebbetsen Feiga Teitelbaum, and by the principal *gabbe*,* the rebbe's assistant. This situation produced a period of uncertainty among the Hasidim. The followers who were accustomed to receiving the rebbe's directives and guidance then found themselves without resources. Moreover, the considerable influence exercised by the rebbetsen behind the scenes became a source of confusion; here was a woman playing a major leading role in this society traditionally run by men.

In July 1979, ten years after his brain haemorrhage, Joel Teitelbaum died of a heart attack; he was 93 years old. He had an outstanding record of achievement. He had managed to create the Yetev Lev D'Satmar group, with several dozen thousand followers, from scratch, and this in the land of America, considered by the rebbes of the past as detrimental to Hasidism. Also, despite his religious intransigence and his fidelity to a consciously immutable form of both Judaism and Hasidism, he had managed to adapt the followers' ultra-traditionalist way of life to American realities, of which the movement was also quick to make the best possible use, particularly by obtaining 'disadvantaged community' status and various forms of state aid.[60] He had also contributed to creating for the group of Hasidic communities in Williamsburg the network of charitable institutions that I have already mentioned and which, along with the state subsidies, enabled the economically disadvantaged followers to live in fairly decent conditions. Furthermore, he had managed to develop his movement while supporting anti-Zionist and anti-Israeli politico-religious arguments that were totally incongruous in the context of an American Jewish community that generally subscribed to precisely the opposite views.

The rebbe had no surviving children, and he had not named a successor. A month after his death, the council of the thirteen elders of the Satmar community designated as his successor the rabbi Moishe Teitelbaum, the rebbe's nephew, who was then 66 years old. He was also a survivor of the Nazi genocide and had hitherto been the rabbi of a small community in Borough Park.[61] From respect for the deceased rebbe, as is the practice in other Hasidic movements, Moishe Teitelbaum only officially took over the succession after the traditional Jewish one-year mourning period.

This second Satmar rebbe in the United States was quickly confronted with major challenges, with the movement dispersing into two very different centres, Williamsburg and Kiryas Joel, and the increasing number of followers, today around 15,000 to 18,000 in Williamsburg and 13,000 in Kiryas Joel and the neighbouring area, in addition to those in Borough Park and elsewhere. The new rebbe did not have the extraordinary prestige of his predecessor but he nevertheless had the advantage of a 'charisma of office' and, as he proved to be a good administrator, he remained the respected leader of this vast association. Nevertheless, dissent, splits and problems quickly arose.

First of all, he had to face hostility from Feiga Teitelbaum, whose residence in Kiryas Joel had become a base of opposition: some Hasidim who rejected the rebbe's authority went there to pray and they even created, as we already know, a dissident community, Kahal Haredim, which had some 500 followers in around 1997. At the outset, there were only a few dissidents and they prayed in a room in the rebbetsen's house but they subsequently requested authorization from the village council, controlled by the new rebbe's followers, to build an oratory next to the rebbetsen's house. This was refused them and in March 1997 before a federal court in Manhattan the dissidents demanded $6,000,000 in compensation for a curb on their freedom of religious expression. Five days after the trial began, following arbitration from a rabbi, they obtained $300,000 in compensation and, above all, permission to build an oratory, along with a ritual bath, on the designated site.[62]

The splits within the movement then widened beyond the village boundaries. In fact, shortly after becoming rebbe Moishe Teitelbaum had nominated his elder son Aaron, born in 1947, as the chief rabbi of Kiryas Joel and also as director of the local *yeshive gdole*, which suggested that he would one day be his father's successor. Then in 1999, at the age of 88 years, the rebbe named his second son, Zalmen Teitelbaum, as the leader of Yetev Lev D'Satmar in Williamsburg. This choice seemed to indicate that the latter was becoming his heir presumptive. Two parties supporting one or other brother formed among the followers and their hostilities came to a head in May 2001 with the election of the council for the Williamsburg community, with each of the two factions electing a new council! Aaron Teitelbaum's supporters, mainly based in Kiryas Joel, brought the matter before the Supreme Court of New York State and since then the conflict has become entrenched. Thus, the Williamsburg community has now created a new higher Talmudic academy in Queens, another large borough of New York, whereas previously the young people attended the *yeshive gdole* in Kiryas Joel.[63] Moreover, this dispute gave rise to a considerable reduction in the community receipts. Several years earlier, the followers had collected $5,000,000 to build a new synagogue in Williamsburg, intended for 10,000 people but the construction work had to be (provisionally?) abandoned for lack of funds.[64]

Since then Satmar has had two main centres, with very different concerns. In Williamsburg, Yetev Lev D'Satmar manages the general administration of the movement as well as economic activities connected with the kashrut, including a meat supermarket. By contrast, in Kiryas Joel, which has 76% more inhabitants than in 1990, affordable housing is the prime concern for the families. It was in fact a housing matter, in which the accommodation was said to have been unfairly allocated by the local mayor, that was at the heart of the debates during recent local elections in June 2001. For the first time there were two lists of opposing candidates: the official one and another that had the support of the dissident community. The mayor's list did obtain 57% of the votes but this is a long way removed from the former unanimity in Kiryas Joel. Municipal autonomy clearly fosters these confrontations between factions, which would have been inconceivable under the previous rebbe.

Joel Teitelbaum, the dynamic and respected founder of the movement, had managed to maintain control over an increasingly vast and complex community but only a very strong personality who enjoyed such a unanimously recognized prestige – which is not the case for his successor – would have been able to hold this congregation together. Now there are various conflicts that are well-known by everyone, particularly between the followers of the two brothers, between the dissident community and Yetev Lev.

In fact, other Hasidic dynasties experience similar controversies. The diversity of the geographical and other conditions generates for the followers, especially if they exist in sufficient numbers, the aspiration to benefit from the direct presence of a rebbe and the local leaders are inclined to withhold receipts from a more or less remote authority. Thus the Vishnitz Hasidim, an important movement in Israel (see Chapter 7), have their own rebbe, but there is also a Vishnitzer rebbe in Monsey and even in Israel itself there is another 'dissident', the Vishnitz-Sereter rebbe, based in Haifa. The Skverer rebbe, master in his village on the outskirts of New York has a 'fellow rebbe', the Skverer-Borough Park rebbe, clearly based in this sector of Brooklyn. There is a Bostoner rebbe in Boston but also a Bostoner rebbe in New York! There are countless further examples of this kind.

The complexity of the Satmar group – the kasher food industry is in Williamsburg and the main *yeshive gdole* for advanced students is in Kiryas Joel – certainly makes any separation difficult and the future remains uncertain in this respect.

WILLIAMSBURG: AN ULTRA-ORTHODOX ASSEMBLY

Hasidic Williamsburg would be inconceivable without Satmar, which is certainly the Hasidism with the greatest standing and influence among the approximately 40,000 people in this 'Hungarian' bastion of the movement. From the beginnings of Hasidism in the district, the Satmar community was associated with other groups who, while they venerated different rebbes, nevertheless shared a similar culture and way of life, as well as a staunch fidelity to a Jewish fundamentalism brought from their regions of origin. In terms of the economic survival of Hasidism in Williamsburg, Satmar was a driving force in obtaining funds from the ODA and other official institutions for improving the housing conditions and renovating the property in the district, as well as for assisting the most disadvantaged Hasidim within it.

Moreover, from the late 1950s Satmar became a major player in the ultra-orthodox Jewish world in the United States, particularly with the establishment of an ultra-kasher food industry and trade, which exercised perforce an influence right across an economic-religious sector that hitherto had not been entirely mindful of the prescriptions that it was supposed to implement. Furthermore, Satmar plays an active part in American political life; the movement makes skilful use of its electoral influence to obtain financial and, as we know, legislative, advantages in pursuit of its objectives. The followers' economic activities have also developed to some extent, particularly with the diverse activities in the tertiary sector.

Finally, there have been subtle changes, as we have seen, in the role of women. In any case, over fifty years Satmar has become one of the major centres of Hasidism in the United States; it has spread to Kiryas Joel and the surrounding area. Other movements, such as the Lubavitch Hasidim, who are also based in New York, or the Ger Hasidim in Israel, may be better-known to the general public, but Satmar, often unfavourably judged for its anti-Zionist views, nevertheless constitutes a major component of Hasidism today. Satmar has at least 40,000 followers in the United States, but also around 10,000 elsewhere in the world, particularly in Israel, where it exerts a considerable influence in the Mea Shearim district of Jerusalem (see Chapter 6), and also in other countries – particularly in Antwerp, London and Montreal. Satmar is one of the largest movements, as well as one of the most extreme and most highly distinctive; the men's long sidelocks in curls hanging around their faces and their dense beards are major emblems of their extremism.

4
Borough Park: a 'Bourgeois' District

THE DISTRICT

With around 60,000 Hasidim, Borough Park is a major stronghold of the movement today; it is the district of Brooklyn with the largest number of Hasidim.[1] However, they did not arrive in mass until around the 1960s. At the beginning of the 20th century Borough Park was still essentially rural in character, but by around 1930 it had become a suburb of Manhattan, already with a sizeable Jewish population of 61,000 people.[2] In 1957, the number had barely increased, with 63,500, around 50% of the total population of the district, with only a small proportion of Hasidim. Most of the Jews there were of Polish or Russian origin and around two thirds of them by then had been born in the United States; many were orthodox Jews with a 'moderate' religiosity. The men there wore modern suits, their beards and sidelocks were very short, if they had them at all, and the children received only a limited Jewish education.

In fact, this relatively late arrival of Hasidim was in keeping with the long-established function of the district as a second or third place of settlement for Jewish emigrants or their children, who settled there to obtain better living conditions than in the poor and overpopulated areas of New York. The district was in fact extremely pleasant, with beautiful large houses, imposing synagogues and wide tree-lined avenues. It was during the 1950s that prosperous Hasidim began to arrive from Williamsburg and Crown Heights, which were certainly less attractive areas. From 1970, several more or less renowned rebbes and their followers had already settled in Borough Park. The district gradually became increasingly Hasidic and the orthodox Jews who had remained there became stricter in their religious observance. The exacting Hasidic *kashrut** prevailed, the orthodox women, following the example of the Hasidic wives, began to wear wigs and the Talmudic academies modelled their curricula on the Hasidic *yeshives*,* which placed greater emphasis on religious practice than learning and prioritized teaching in Yiddish over teaching in English. Nevertheless, in the privacy of their own homes, these long-standing residents – who still have a presence in the district – are somewhat lax in their observance: they watch television, listen to the radio and use the telephone on Saturdays and festival days.[3]

In any case, an area of less than four square kilometres was soon home to followers from around twenty more or less influential dynasties, such as Bobov, Ger, Karlin, Bratslav, Belz, Munkacs, Spinka, Vishnitz, Skver-Boro Park, Debrecin, Keresztur, Spinka, Stolin and also Satmar, with many prosperous followers having settled there. In fact, Borough Park has a very diverse Hasidic congregation, with both small and much larger communities, who pray in around 200 oratories of widely varying dimensions, ranging from small rooms to the vast temples of the Bobov and Satmar Hasidim. The Bobov Hasidim form the largest community and their rebbe, who belongs to a dynasty of Galician origin, lives in the district. Nevertheless, the 10,000 to 12,000 Bobover constitute only a minority, 15% to 20%, of the Hasidic population.

Borough Park, situated in south-west Brooklyn, has no official administrative existence and the boundaries set for it in recent sociological and demographic surveys are therefore more or less arbitrary.[4] The Jewish quarter extends from 37th Street to 60th Street on a north–south axis and from 9th Avenue to 19th Avenue on an east–west axis. 13th Avenue is the main shopping street but some other roads also have busy shops. The total population of Borough Park reached 94,652 people in 1990, 75,721 (80%) of whom were then Jews, of whom around 64,000 (85%) are Hasidim.[5] The Hasidim here also have many children and a Jewish family in the district consists of around five people on average; one quarter of the families have five or more children but the birth rate is still lower than in Williamsburg.

The above-mentioned recent surveys provide no indication of the professional activities in the district; however, it is evident that many Hasidim, as in Williamsburg, carry out religious functions there – for instance as schoolteachers or as ritual slaughterers – or work in the *kasher** food shops and the many and various shops. Some Hasidim also work in Manhattan, particularly in the diamond trade and industry. The vast majority of them have a high enough income to live in this area with rather expensive housing. Despite everything, around 18% of the inhabitants[6] do not have a high enough income and are below the poverty line defined by the administrative authorities, a percentage that is nevertheless well below that recorded in Williamsburg where one third of the Jewish population fall into this category (see previous chapter). In Borough Park, the poverty is partly due to the presence of elderly people, with relatively low incomes, as well as to the continuing influx of immigrants from Israel and Eastern Europe. Thus, since the beginning of the 1990s, the district has received an influx of Russian emigrants from the former Soviet Union, the large majority of whom are not religious. These newcomers and the ultra-orthodox residents seem to have coexisted peacefully so far.[7]

Furthermore, in Borough Park, 35% of Jewish women between 18 and 65 years of age work, and this percentage is steadily increasing. Also, many married women feel the need for a professional training and a job; economic necessities take precedence over the traditional model, in which the woman is responsible for bringing up a large number of children at home. In Borough Park, the cost of living for ultra-orthodox families can be 30% higher because of the costs of education, kasher food and innumerable compulsory community gifts and contributions.

Like Williamsburg, the district has a large number of Jewish schools, oratories, shops for religious articles and kasher food shops – butchers', bakeries, dairy produce shops –which display clearly in their windows which rabbinical authority supervises their adherence to the kashrut. There are also snack bars, sometimes with pavement stalls, selling pizzas and falafel that are clearly kasher – this type of shop is rarer in Williamsburg. There are also two supermarkets in this district that do not stock goods forbidden by the kashrut prescriptions. By contrast, the major national supermarket chains and video rental shops that are so prevalent elsewhere are absent from the essentially Jewish shopping area of 13th Avenue and 16th Avenue.

Borough Park also has a large number of discount stores, particularly for all forms of electrical equipment, such as cameras, video cameras and radios. Also, in the converted basements of many houses, there are wholesale shops, mainly run by women, selling women's lingerie, jewellery and so on. Nearly everywhere the shops have an attractive appearance and the goods on display in the window or arranged inside are of good quality.

There are many new buildings in the district – three-storey apartment blocks and modern shops with red brick facades. From 1990 to 1997, 822 building permits were issued in Borough Park, a considerably higher figure than in other residential districts of Brooklyn.[8] Twice daily, a fleet of yellow school buses, bearing the names of the schools to which they belong in English and in Hebrew characters, travels the roads of the district. Moreover, at certain times of day large numbers of young women walk along the main shopping street, 13th Avenue, accompanied by their young children. They meet at the snack bars on the corners of certain side streets, particularly at Amnon Kosher Pizza, where the women sometimes congregate in particularly large numbers to chat for a long time on the pavement. All the shops are of course closed on Saturday but Sunday, especially in the morning, is the busiest shopping day.

Borough Park is considered a highly desirable residential area by the richest Hasidim and the profusion of construction sites does nothing to reduce the high rents and housing costs there. Many large families have therefore settled in the neighbouring residential areas, mainly Flatbush and Bensonhurst, where housing costs are lower. There are also Hasidic oratories and schools in these districts.

In Borough Park, none of the dynasties plays such a dominant role as Satmar in Williamsburg, not even the Bobov dynasty, with the largest number of followers in the district. Besides, although the Hasidic population is larger there than in Williamsburg, the atmosphere is more tolerant and some Hasidim who have chosen to live there have not only been seeking attractive living conditions but also a little more freedom and aloofness. For instance, the kiosks on the main shopping street stock the secular dailies or magazines that are rather frowned on in Williamsburg and are not to be found there. The presence of restaurants of all kinds, from snack bars to restaurants offering four-course menus that guarantee 'Jewish' kasher cuisine of Eastern European origin but also Israeli and other cuisine, and the shops with electrical or other goods attract a wide and varied public that is not necessarily orthodox, especially on Sunday mornings. Also, the recent arrival of Russian Jews who are not highly religious seems to be happily tolerated. Then there is also the presence of long-standing residents who pre-date the arrival of the Hasidim, whose orthodoxy as we know is limited ... In any case, the atmosphere in Borough Park is much more cosmopolitan and more open to the outside world than in Williamsburg.

Moreover, the district has its own unique rhythm. On Sundays, as I said, there are the visitors and the regular customers of the various shops and restaurants. In the weeks leading up to the major Jewish festivals – such as New Year and Passover – there is intense activity on the main streets. Street merchants sell all kinds of goods, from ritual objects to radios. On the festival days themselves, the atmosphere is quiet. Apart from some shops at the edge of the district, all the businesses are closed. The Hasidim hasten to their oratories in their long frock coats and fur hats, anxious to be on time. After the religious services, the activity subsides. Here and there, couples walk along with their children and small groups of people stand around and talk. A few cars drive through, provoking angry looks from ultra-religious passers-by – but traffic is not prevented here as it is in the Mea Shearim district in Jerusalem and in Bene Beraq in Israel (see Chapters 6 and 7). However, at nightfall and the end of the Sabbath and festival days, there is a sudden roar of large numbers of engines starting up and restaurants such as Amnon Kosher Pizza open their doors to crowds of hungry people.[9]

Some more or less renowned rebbes have established their 'courts' in Borough Park, particularly the Stoliner, Blueshover, Munkaczer, Kapitshinitzer, Novominsker and Skolyer rebbes and, above all, the most renowned of them, the Bobover rebbe. This concentration of various rebbes – far greater than in Williamsburg – constitutes an original feature in the history of Hasidism, which is also found in Bene Beraq in Israel. This is very unlike the situation of the 'courts' scattered across many Eastern European towns and villages, which have in fact given their names to present-day 'courts' in Borough Park. By contrast, this concentration creates a mosaic of places of prayer and opportunities for meeting friends or compatriots. It also creates opportunities for the large numbers of people who come in principle primarily to visit 'their' own *tzadik*,* for venerating another rebbe, even requesting an audience with him and submitting a *kvitel*.* Moreover, all these rebbes are surrounded by an inner circle of followers who secure the power in each of the movements, acting as administrators of the oratories or the heads of various schools. Then there are also the followers who wish to live in Borough Park because they want to live in close proximity to their rebbe. They can then almost constantly imbibe the aura around him and ask him for guidance or miraculous intercessions.

COMPOSITE REGROUPING

There is therefore a diverse Hasidic environment in Borough Park, which unlike Williamsburg is not dominated by one very large community; also, this Hasidic world has more varied origins than Williamsburg. In Borough Park, the Satmarer and other Hungarian communities certainly have a presence, but Bobov and various major dynasties such as Ger and Belz have followers who are mainly of Polish origin.

On the initiative of the director of the Ger Hasidic yeshive in Borough Park (their rebbe, like the Belzer rebbe, lives in Israel, see Chapter 6), the various Hasidic communities of Borough Park, such as the Satmarer, the Belzer and many others, setting aside their various disagreements, particularly concerning Israel and Zionism, have been cooperating since 1974 within a 'Council of Jewish Organizations of Borough Park' (COJO). The prime objective of COJO is to promote economic development in the district by setting up professional training courses, an employment office, a programme of assistance for mental health, aid for the elderly and young people and so on. Over the years, this organization has managed to obtain major subsidies for its work, which at least until 1996 amounted to an annual total of $5,000,000 from organizations in the city and state of New York, as well as from the federal State. These resources give COJO an influence, particularly politically, on the individuals and institutions that it supports. Politicians at all levels, from New York City councillors to US Presidents, have therefore courted COJO for its real or supposed capacity to determine a block vote by the tens of thousands of Jewish electors in the district.

COJO's usual intermediary in its relations with the City Hall in Manhattan, with the capital of New York State, Albany, and also with the Congress in Washington, has recently been the Democrat assemblyman for the district, Dov Hikind, a practising Jew. Between 1996 and 1998, Hikind was involved in some matters relating to misappropriation of subsidies received by COJO. In April 1998, COJO's administrative director pleaded guilty to misappropriating federal funds and making illegal payments to the assemblyman. In July of the same year, a federal jury in Brooklyn found the director of COJO's department for employment and professional training guilty of corruption and other fraudulent acts but acquitted Dov Hikind of allegations of passive corruption.[10] Moreover, Hikind, still the Borough Park assemblyman at the New York State Assembly, continues to intervene politically, sometimes vociferously, on behalf of the Jews in the area. For instance, following an incident on 30 August 1999, when four policemen fired several fatal gun-shots at a madman, an orthodox Jew who had apparently threatened them with a hammer, Hikind alerted the New York press and took part in some demonstrations against the police and its chief, Rudolph Giuliani, New York's Republican mayor. The matter was badly timed for Giuliani because he was standing for election a few months later as a New York senator against Hillary Clinton, wife of the US President Bill Clinton, who was in fact finally elected in 2001.

Furthermore, the Bobover rebbe, a major religious figure in the district, sometimes uses his political influence, albeit discreetly. Rebbe since 2000, Naftali Halberstam, the son and successor of Shlomo Halberstam (1907–2000), founder of the movement in New York (see below), received a visit from Andrew Cuomo, the Democrat candidate for the post of governor of New York State, a few months before some recent elections. Although the rebbe did not openly support this political figure, the ultra-orthodox weekly *Hamodia*, published in Israel but circulated widely in Brooklyn, printed a photograph of the two men shaking hands in its 5 July 2002 issue, which certainly appeared to be an expression of support for the candidate.

The Hasidic world of Borough Park is clearly characterized by a successful combination of traditionalism and modernity. On the one hand, there are several extremely vibrant Hasidic 'courts' and ultra-orthodox communities and, on the other, many of the Hasidim work outside the district, particularly in Manhattan, while there is also a growth of economic activity in the area itself, particularly in the shops. Finally, there is also active participation – albeit sometimes questionable, as we have seen – in political life. It is true, as we have already observed in Williamsburg and Kiryas Joel, that this politicization also exists among the Hasidim who are most closeted in their extreme religiosity. As we will see, politicization is also strongly apparent in Israel.

BOBOV: THE PRINCIPAL COMMUNITY

The Bobov Hasidim constitute the largest community in Borough Park and the neighbouring areas, with 2,000 families – around 10,000 to 12,000 people.[11] Bobov also has large communities in Israel, with 1,000 families in Bene Beraq and Jerusalem, and 150 more families in its own housing estate in Bat Yam, a beach near Tel-Aviv, while the Bobov communities in Antwerp, Toronto and Montreal each have 100 families; finally, there are 400 in London.[12] Bobov therefore has approximately 20,000 followers in total, which certainly makes it a major Hasidic movement today. However, the heart of the movement is in Borough Park, where the rebbe lives within his vast community. Like Satmar, Bobov is therefore a good example of a situation that was almost non-existent in the Hasidism of the past: the rebbes now live among their followers in cities rather than in places such as Bobowa in Eastern Galicia, which had just 1,500 inhabitants before the Second World War.

It was in Bobowa that the rabbi Shlomo Halberstam (1847–1905) established this dynasty in 1893.[13] He was the grandson of Chayim Halberstam, the rebbe of Zanz – the Yiddish name for Nowy Sacz, a town less than thirty kilometres from Bobowa.[14] Shlomo Halberstam established a first yeshive in Bobowa as early as 1893. Prior to this, the Hasidim in Galicia and usually elsewhere practised *lernen*,* Talmudic study, in an informal way, without a structured programme or system, in the *kloyz*,* that is around the tables of a *shtiebl** or local oratory. The rebbe also composed some *nigunim*,* Hasidic melodies, many of which are still chanted by followers. The second Bobover rebbe, Benzion Halberstam (1873–1941), was a composer like his father; he stated that Hasidism without melodies was like a body without a soul.[15] He also established a network of forty Talmudic academies across Galicia, called *Etz Chaim* (the tree of life), which had as many as 900 pupils; to finance these schools, he set up an organization called *Tomchei Oraisa*, 'support for study', which took charge of raising the necessary funds.[16] As we have already seen in Antwerp and in Williamsburg, today the yeshives constitute an essential part of the Hasidic institutions.

During the summer of 1941, Benzion Halberstam, one of his sons and three of his sons-in-law were massacred in Lvov (Lemberg in both Yiddish and German), with 12,000 other Jews, by the Germans and their Ukrainian accomplices. Another son, Shlomo Halberstam (1907–2000) managed to flee and to survive in Rumania. In 1946, he reached London, where other survivors and followers from the dynasty agreed to designate him as his father's successor. The new rebbe emigrated in the same year to the United States; in the years that followed, he made efforts to obtain immigration visas to the United States for Bobov Hasidim who were dispersed in the displaced persons camps in Germany and elsewhere. With financial support from sympathizers and also from American Jewish charitable organizations, he managed to buy two buildings on West 85th Street in Manhattan. One of these provided a base for the residence of the rebbe – who had remarried in 1947 – but it also served as a lodging place for young Hasidim who had survived the Shoah. These included many orphans whom, during his time in Italy just after the war, the rebbe had taken under his protection in a displaced persons camp in Bari, where a yeshive was set up so that they could immediately pursue Talmudic studies. The building also contained an oratory, two dining rooms, one for men and one for women, and even a ritual bath, *mikve*,*[17] in the basement. The second building housed a vocational school in which the surviving Hasidim, newly arrived in the United States, could train in various trades, particularly as watchmakers and diamond-polishers. The rebbe also encouraged certain Hasidim to set up businesses.

Most of the followers who arrived in New York originated from Galicia or other places in Poland. Many had been followers of the new rebbe's father, but some of them had previously been adherents of rebbes who disappeared in the Shoah. As with reb Ytsekl in Antwerp, the community that formed around this magnetic leader had become a meeting-place for the 'orphans' of their disappeared rebbes. Moreover, most of the followers, old and new, had also lost their close relatives in the tragedy in Europe and the Bobover rebbe appeared in the form of a surrogate father while the other followers they mixed with every day at the oratory or at the yeshive took the place of disappeared brothers and sisters.[18] Faced with the destitution that was affecting many of the newcomers, Halberstam would personally telephone more prosperous admirers or sympathizers to ask them to help these less fortunate followers. Moreover, the rebbe did not hesitate to arrange marriages for his disciples and, when these were agreed, he would collect money himself both for the ceremony and to enable the couples to live in a correct way.[19]

This rebbe, who influenced the post-war history of the Bobov until his death in the year 2000, had shown his understanding of the importance of effective economic integration for his followers by creating a vocational school, but at the same time he provided a warm atmosphere that facilitated the psychological recuperation that was so essential for the survivors of the genocide.

However, Bobov did not have an easy beginning in New York. As one witness recalls, at the first *seder*,*[20] the ceremonial meal on the first and second evenings of the Passover, there were just twenty-five people gathered around the Bobover rebbe. None of them had a beard, apart from the rebbe. No one could afford festival garments, less still a *shtreimel*,* the Hasidic fur cap. Around fifteen years later, in Borough Park, things are altogether different; hundreds of Hasidim from the district but also beyond, wearing large beards and traditional dress, celebrate the Passover or Purim[21] with their rebbe.

Over the years, the rebbe and his community attracted men and women who until then had had only few connections with Hasidism. They appreciated Shlomo Halberstam's benevolence and lack of pretension, as well as his gifts as an untiring teller of Hasidic short stories and parables. They also liked the welcoming atmosphere that prevailed at the oratory, where chatting and the most intense prayer happily coexisted. Furthermore, while the distinctive Bobover appearance – a long beard, sidelocks (generally discreetly attached to the temples or extremely short) and frock coats – is certainly the norm for the disciples, at the same time there is a friendly tolerance towards the more modern appearance, a dark suit and tie, trimmed beards and so on. This is a long way removed from the restrictive intransigence in Satmar circles. Furthermore, although the rebbe and his followers took a somewhat critical attitude towards the State of Israel, mainly for its 'anti-religious' politics, their views on this subject remained moderate: 'We don't shout it from the rooftops', said one disciple. In fact Bobov Hasidim, in contrast to the Satmarer, fully recognize the legitimacy of the Hebrew State.

In 1954, the rebbe and his family – he had five sons and a daughter with his second wife – left Manhattan to settle in Crown Heights and many of his Hasidim followed them there. At this time, Crown Heights had become a Hasidic district but the situation changed there at the beginning of the 1960s. A large number of rather poor black and Puerto Rican families, overflowing from the neighbouring district, Bedford-Stuyvesant, had come to settle there and in a context of mutual animosity and hostility, some of the Hasidic population left the district (see the next chapter). In 1966, the Bobover rebbe settled in Borough Park, where many other Hasidim from Crown Heights had also settled. Since 1946, in twenty years, the economic situation of the Bobover had advanced considerably; many of them had prospered as *sohrim*,* merchants in the diamond trade. Living in a middle-class area such as Borough Park was in keeping with their new prosperity. Bobov became the most flourishing 'court' in Borough Park, as well as the one with the largest number of followers. The Bobov institutions – the yeshive, the oratory and the rebbe's residence – are situated on 48th Street between 15th Avenue and 16th Avenue and this part of 48th Street, with the blessing of New York City council, has since been called 'Bobover Promenade'. Some rich followers generously financed the construction of a vast new synagogue, with marble-covered walls, which was completed in 1988. It has a large hall for wedding receptions and other celebrations.

As we know, on his arrival in Manhattan the rebbe had founded a yeshive, initially intended for the young survivors of the Shoah, whose traditional education had been destroyed by the events. The rebbe engaged the best teachers, whether they were Hasidim or simply orthodox; the yeshive also accepted without distinction any young practitioner wanting to study the Torah. Today Bobov has a set of schools, from the nursery school to the *kolel*;* this institution for married men, which began with fifteen students in 1971, had more than 150 students fifteen years later. In around 1995, Bobov was educating over

2,000 pupils, boys and girls, at a cost of over $5,600,000. A fleet of eleven buses and four minibuses transports the pupils from their houses to school and back. Teaching does not stop in summer; it then transfers to vacation camps in the Catskill mountains in New York State, where many Hasidim spend the hottest months of the year. In fact, the Bobov schools have 'secular' English departments that are large enough to be recognized (and therefore subsidized) by the authorities of the official state schools. The school facilities include dining-rooms, kitchens, lodging for boarders, a library and an oratory. In the schools, the religious education is influenced by the Bobov tradition; the traditional Bobov songs and the Bobov style of prayer are learnt and fidelity to the Bobover rebbe is cultivated.

It is also clear that although the Bobover use Yiddish – with the familiar intonations originating from Poland – in everyday life as in the discussions in Talmudic study, they also use English widely; both men and women use it increasingly commonly in everyday life and many read the 'profane' American newspapers.[22] The rebbe also has a relatively tolerant attitude towards higher-level secular studies. Although he does not encourage them, he maintains contact with the male followers who choose to go to university after their studies at the yeshive. Although the young women are not shown the same leniency, some of them nevertheless decide to attend Touro College, a higher educational institution that adheres to orthodox Judaism, which runs many courses alternately for men and for women, which thus prevents any meeting in the classrooms.[23] In any case, young people have made their way as businesspeople, doctors, lawyers and accountants, while maintaining links with Bobov and supporting its activities financially.[24]

All the followers integrated into community life are supposed to make a contribution according to their income to the maintenance of the Bobov institutions. In particular there are the living costs for the rebbe and his family, and funds have to be obtained for the rebbe's charitable gifts to his most impoverished visitors. Furthermore, it is necessary to ensure the maintenance of the expensive traditional educational system. Every follower who has the means is required to meet his own children's educational costs but he also has an obligation to contribute to financing the studies of pupils from poor families.[25]

During the religious celebrations at the Bobov oratory, rich and poor, as in the majority of Hasidic communities (see p. 42 above), sit side by side on the same wooden benches in the *shtiebl*, but there are undeniable differences based on wealth. This is particularly evident in their homes, since the most prosperous Hasidim have large houses with high-quality furniture, draperies, chandeliers, silverware and so on. Many of them even have two fully equipped kitchens, one for meat-based and the other for milk-based food. Economic success is also displayed at the festivities associated with circumcisions, *bar-mitsves** and weddings, at which the level of opulence demonstrates the wealth and social position of those who hold them.[26] The poor living conditions of the past in Poland or during the immediate post-war period are no more than memories for these followers.

The Hasidim are discreet concerning the 'miracles' that the rebbe performs. As a member of his inner circle stated: 'We don't talk about miracles when we see something happen ... Our rebbe is a *tzaddik*,* whether or not he'll show me what he did ... in sickness or in business.'[27]

As with the Satmarer, a degree of nepotism prevails in the Bobov institutions. The rebbe appointed his close relatives to various positions of responsibility – the administration of the court, management of the yeshive and the *kolel*. The family's ascendancy also extends to the large Bobov community in London (400 families), whose spiritual leader is a son-in-law of the rebbe, as well as to the Bobov district, Kiryat Bobov, in Bat Yam in Israel, where another son-in-law of the rebbe runs the yeshive.

Among the specific Bobov traditions that date back to the past in Poland, there is a form of 'mystery play', the *Piremshpil*,* which is performed at Purim. At first in Borough Park, the Bobover alone observed this festival but today five communities do so.[28] It involves a theatrical production in Yiddish that is performed by some Hasidim, amateur actors, which takes place at the large community oratory, before around 1,000 spectators, including the rebbe. This takes place on the second night of the festival of Purim (or Feast of Lots), a joyous festival that commemorates the liberation of the Jews, who were threatened with extermination by Haman, chief minister of the King of Persia, Ahasuerus (from 488–465 BCE), an event that is narrated in the Biblical book of Esther. These annual mystery plays relate in verse form some more or less fictional episodes of Jewish survival through divine intervention.

This event can give rise to discussion of the period of occupation in Poland, as for example in the 1948 *Piremshpil*, in which a young Jew miraculously managed to escape from his Nazi persecutors to survive among some partisans. He then found his mother, who had believed him to be dead, to the sound of the American hymn commemorating the Liberation. Subsequently, the rebbe preferred the productions to deal with a distant past instead, even if in the minds of the spectators, these unfailingly evoke the recent tragedies. For example in 1971, but also in 1977, the 'Play of Daniel' portrayed the exile to Babylon and the faith of Daniel, Hanania, Mishael and Azariah, martyrs in the book of Daniel, under threat from King Nebuchadnezzar. When the heroes are thrown into the blaze to burn alive there, a violinist plays the *ani maamin* melody ('in absolute faith, I believe in the coming of the Messiah') until the end of the scene. Very much in the spirit of the festival of Purim, the theme of martyrdom that is accepted but followed by the miracle in which the heroes do not burn, is life-affirming in spite of failures and death. These mystery plays, which combine levity and seriousness, help members of the community, many of whom are survivors of the Shoah, and their children, to transcend this immense tragedy.[29]

Shlomo Halberstam died on 2 August 2000 at the age of 92 years. Between 10,000 and 20,000 people, Bobov Hasidim but also adherents of other rebbes, as well as various rebbes from Borough Park and elsewhere, attended his funeral. He was buried in the Bobov section of a Jewish cemetery in South Brunswick, New Jersey. The vast tombstone that was erected there is now a place of pilgrimage for the followers, particularly at the *yourzeit*,* the anniversary of the rebbe's death.

Shlomo's eldest son, Naftali Tzvi Halberstam, who is also a survivor of the Shoah, became his successor at the age of 68 years. The father and son had a very close relationship and under his governance the Bobover philosophy, style and form of behaviour seem to have remained essentially the same.

BOBOV: A MODEL

From the moment that he arrived in the United States, the rebbe undertook to create for his Hasidim or close sympathizers, first in Manhattan, then in subsequent years in Crown Heights and Borough Park, a set of institutions for connecting them with the past while also providing them with a means of adjusting to the realities of American life. As we know, Bobov had rapidly established a structure for welcoming refugees with board and lodging, an oratory with a friendly atmosphere, a traditionalist educational system that also provided some secular knowledge and even some professional training, a particularly original step for a Hasidic leader. Bobov did not implement any form of more or less systematic proselytism (unlike the Lubavitch Hasidim – see the next chapter), but the rebbe's generosity of spirit and his leniency towards non-Hasidim meant that many people, more or less strict in their practice, but also generally originating from the same regions as the followers themselves, were drawn to New York by Bobov, its melodies, the warm and informal atmosphere of the oratory, the parables told by the rebbe and so on and they joined the community.

The benevolence of the rebbe and his followers unquestionably facilitated the relations between the Bobover and a part of the Jewish world; this attitude was certainly due to Shlomo Halberstam's personality but in my view it also had some historical roots. From the beginning of the 20th century and between the two world wars, the Galician Hasidim found themselves in a weak position – many former pupils of the traditional schools, the *haider** and the *Talmud Torah*,* had abandoned the Hasidic way of life, particularly when they migrated towards the cities and abroad.[30] Even from this period, breaking with every dissident would have been suicidal for the Hasidim of this region. Also, to this day the enormous cost of projects such as the scholastic system and the construction of a vast synagogue makes the financial aid of former Hasidim and sympathetic compatriots extremely useful. As we will see (Chapter 6), Belz Hasidism, which also originates from Galicia, operates a similar policy of relative openness.

The Bobov community, with its significant minority of followers, provides through its clearly traditionalist but relatively liberal form of Hasidism a socio-cultural model that applies in general to the middle-class Hasidic population (including the Satmarer) of Borough Park.

5
Crown Heights, Seat of the Lubavitch Movement

A HIGHLY TURBULENT DISTRICT

Crown Heights, the third largest Hasidic district in Brooklyn, is inhabited today principally by the Lubavitch Hasidim, numbering around 12,000 to 16,000.[1] These figures are clearly lower than those for the Hasidic populations of Williamsburg and Borough Park, at 40,000 and 60,000 respectively. However, Crown Heights is the seat of Lubavitch, also called *Habad*,* a Hasidic movement that seeks global expansion through missionary activities (among the Jews) that often take a spectacular form, bringing notoriety to this form of Hasidism and thereby to the district among a wide public. Moreover, in 'Crown Heights South', to use the electoral and administrative term for this district of New York, the Hasidim constitute only a minority of the total population of around 100,000 people, the majority of whom are blacks (Afro-Americans in current terminology) and Puerto Ricans. The relations between this majority and the Hasidim have sometimes taken a violent turn, which has also brought some notoriety to Crown Heights in the media.

Just before the Second World War, Crown Heights was a suburb of Manhattan, with tree-shaded avenues and beautiful houses, where middle-class white people of various origins, particularly Italian but also Irish and Jewish, had settled – generally not very religious or moderately religious people – as well as a small number of black people. In fact, the majority of inhabitants were American-born and English-speaking; it was the elderly people alone who spoke only Italian or Yiddish.[2] However, there was also a small community of Lubavitch Hasidim, founded by Russian emigrants in 1925. It was in this group that the sixth *rebbe** of the Lubavitch dynasty, Joseph Isaac Schneerson, settled in spring 1940 when he reached the United States having managed to leave Europe. After the war, with the arrival of survivors from Europe, the Hasidism in the district diversified and increased substantially; we already know that the Bobover rebbe had settled there in 1954. The arrival of large numbers of Hasidim, with their highly distinctive religiosity, led, as in Williamsburg and Borough Park, to the departure of most of the non-religious or only very moderately religious Jews.

However, other more global social processes were in force in this sector of Brooklyn. In the neighbouring district of Bedford-Stuyvesant, with a predominantly black and Puerto Rican population, which was also in strong expansion, there was difficulty housing so many newcomers, many of whom settled in Crown Heights. In the intensely racist climate of the period, a black family only had to move into a house or flat in a district hitherto populated by 'whites' for the latter to move away. This phenomenon was also often exacerbated by some rather unscrupulous property dealers who bought back the 'invaded' properties to sell them back to the newcomers at inflated prices.[3] Whereas in 1950 the whites constituted 85% of the population in Crown Heights, during the 1960s three quarters of them left the district and it became 70% black. The city of New York housed many poor families in the old blocks and, with poverty, criminality also moved into Crown Heights. Some Hasidim therefore quickly left the area but for many of them such an exodus proved more difficult: the Hasidic communities had in fact invested heavily in their oratories, schools and other institutions. Nevertheless, in the mid-1960s the Bobov community sold its temple and school buildings and the rebbe and the majority of his followers settled in Borough Park.

The Hasidic fate of Crown Heights seemed to be sealed. However, one of the Hasidic communities, the Lubavitcher, refused to give way. Menahem Mendel Schneerson, the seventh rebbe of the dynasty, who had taken over the succession from the sixth rebbe at the latter's death in 1950, declared firmly to his Hasidim: 'We're staying here.'[4] To demonstrate their determination, the Lubavitcher undertook some expensive works to enlarge and renovate their main oratory. With the other Jewish communities having left the area, the council of the Jewish community in Crown Heights then came under the control of the Lubavitcher. This council decided to buy back the houses of those who were leaving in order to sell them back, usually at a loss, to Hasidim who wanted to stay in the area. Furthermore, between 1977 and 1985 the council contributed to the renovation of 600 apartments in fifteen blocks.[5] Moreover, at the end of the 1980s, Lubavitch was planning to build a major extension to its head office, as well as two new schools, one for boys and another for girls, at a cost of $20,000,000, $5,000,000 and $12,000,000 respectively.[6] Another sign of Hasidic vitality in the district was the conversion of a building into a hotel, which opened in 1984, for the numerous visitors who flocked in from all over America and abroad, particularly to attend a *farbrengen*,* a large gathering on Saturday afternoons, at which the rebbe Menahem Mendel Schneerson delivered highly acclaimed long addresses.[7]

The Lubavitcher therefore held firm despite many incidents and even something close to a pogrom in August 1991 following a severe traffic accident. A follower who was driving in a procession of cars that had accompanied the rebbe to his spouse's grave unfortunately on his return killed one child and seriously injured another, both of whom were from Guyana. Three hours later, hundreds of young blacks took to the streets in the Hasidic district, smashing windows and shouting 'Jew! Jew!' A 29-year-old Talmudic scholar was stabbed to death by a sixteen-year-old boy. Violence and pillaging continued for four days. The New York City authorities, as well as Jewish and black leaders, did their best to calm the mood for a long period but then in 1992 a Hasidic woman, a mother of four, was stabbed to death. The impact of these events and the mutual hostilities persist to this day, although incidents are now a rarity.[8]

Although, as we know, they constitute a clear minority in the district, the Hasidim nevertheless have a fairly strong presence in an area of some twenty-four blocks bounded by Nostrand and Utica Avenues to the west and east and by Eastern Parkway and Empire Boulevard to the north and south. The average-standard housing in the Hasidic district includes many English-style houses with red-brown brick facades, as well as detached houses with peristyles of columns that generally date from the 'bourgeois' period prior to 1940. These are inhabited mainly by Hasidim but there are also some apartment blocks, in which Hasidim live alongside non-Jewish inhabitants of the district. Many of these are non-Hispanic immigrants from Haiti, Jamaica and Guyana, especially since the mid-1960s.

The Hasidic area obviously has many Lubavitch institutions and there are *kasher** shops and restaurants, Jewish bookshops and shops selling religious articles, which are intended mainly for the inhabitants and possible visitors. Unlike Williamsburg and Borough Park, the district has no specifically commercial function; it is essentially a residential area. There are also several oratories, each with its own rabbi, intended for the nearby residents. Some followers work in the area, as teachers at the Lubavitch Jewish school or as employees of the movement's various institutions, but the majority work outside the area, especially in Manhattan, particularly in the diamond and textile industries and trades, but also in many other professions and jobs (see below).

In Crown Heights, with its very mixed population, and also because the Lubavitch Hasidim have a policy of openness towards Jews who are not highly religious or are non-religious, the atmosphere is in no way oppressive. Here, women who are not dressed in the traditional Hasidic style – loose-fitting clothing, dark tights, wig, hat etc. – can walk around without fear of reproach and a non-religious Jew has run a newspaper kiosk for twenty years that is open on Saturdays, only twenty metres from the rebbe's windows.[9]

Another sign of the area's openness to the outside world is the 'Lubavitch Crown Heights' visitor centre, which provides a tour of the Hasidic sites in the district conducted by a rabbi every Sunday morning. The tourists are mainly Jewish but there are also non-Jewish participants. One of the places visited is a bakery on Albany Avenue in the middle of the district, where for six months the *shmure matses*,* three 'preserved unleavened cakes' are handmade with particular care, to be arranged on a symbolic dish at the *seder*,* the commemorative meal on the first two evenings of the Passover. These unleavened breads can be bought by anyone, including the Sunday tourists, whereas most Hasidic communities reserve these special unleavened breads for their disciples.[10]

However, as in Williamsburg and Borough Park, large numbers of men can be observed coming to the oratories to pray in the morning, often very early. Then there are also the children who wait in front of their houses for the yellow school buses, and later on in the shopping streets, women can be seen with their young children here too, going to do their shopping and taking the opportunity to chat with acquaintances whom they meet here and there.

During the week, many men, most of whom travel to work outside the area, wear dark double-breasted suits, ties and black hats, which without espousing the most recent fashions, differ from the somewhat archaic style that prevails in

Williamsburg and to some extent in Borough Park. Furthermore, here neither children nor adults display long sidelocks falling in curls around their faces; also, while the beards are ubiquitous, they are well-groomed and appear in many cases to be rather short and therefore trimmed. Here on festival days and the Sabbath, the *shtreimel*,* the fur cap that is so much in evidence in most Hasidic communities is conspicuous by its absence: in fact, the Lubavitcher do not wear this at all. However, on those days they wear a black frock coat in a silk fabric, which is almost the only traditional item of clothing that they retain.[11]

Since the departure of most of the other Hasidic communities, Crown Heights has therefore been a district in which the Hasidim are almost exclusively Lubavitch followers for over thirty years. Most of the various Lubavitch institutions certainly exist there for the resident followers but they also function as a strategic nerve centre – 'the head and heart' – of a vast international Lubavitch network, also known as *Habad*. This assembly includes both communities and a large number of 'missionary' bases, from which the movement's *shlihim*,* 'emissaries' or 'delegates' seek to persuade non-religious or only moderately religious Jews to embrace the Jewish faith (see below). There are frequent exchanges between these various places and the centre in Crown Heights, with the customary presence of visitors, particularly the *shlihim*, but also of new converts who are attracted to Habad. These new converts come from all over the United States and abroad, in order to restore their spirits with a rebbe, particularly at the *farbrengen*, or for various meetings and other activities, as well as to attend courses in Judaism and Hasidism and then to propagate them in turn like their preceptors in Kiev, Johannesburg, Frankfurt or elsewhere.

This Hasidic district is therefore both homogeneous and very open to the outside world.

LUBAVITCH, A SPECIFIC FORM OF HASIDISM

Lubavitch Hasidism, which has endured for two centuries, has always been a special case within the movement. The founder of the dynasty, Shneur Zalman of Lyady (1745–1813), born in Liozno, near Vitebsk in Belarus, was a follower of the *maggid** Dov Baer of Mezhirech (see Chapter 1). He acquired a remarkable knowledge of the Talmud and the Jewish laws at a very early age, as well as a firm grounding in mathematics and astronomy, forms of knowledge that were certainly unusual among *tzadikim.** Shneur Zalman attracted many disciples originating mainly from Lithuania and Belarus, which were two countries of choice for the *misnaggedim*,* the adversaries of Hasidism, proponents of a Talmudic and rationalist form of Judaism. Shneur Zalman's thought – which is found in his posthumous work the *Tanya*, published in 1814 and still highly esteemed by the Lubavitcher today – is imbued with a way of thinking that is both mystical and rationalist, summarized by the Hebrew acronym, *Habad*, for *Hohma, Binah, Daat*, meaning 'wisdom, understanding, knowledge'. Habad is also the second name, more prevalent outside the movement, by which this form of Hasidism is known. Lubavitch itself, as with other Hasidic dynasties, is the

Yiddish name for Lyubavichi, the small town in Belarus in which the dynasty, from its founder's son Dov Baer Zalman (1733–1827) onwards, maintained its residence for over a century from 1813 to 1915.

The vicissitudes of the First World War forced the fifth rebbe, Dov Baer Schneerson (1860–1920) to leave Lyubavichi, which ceased to be the seat of Habad. Dov Baer Schneerson settled in Rostov on the Don River. However, the atheistic and anti-religious Soviet regime oppressed the Hasidim along with other religious groups. In 1920, Dov Baer's son, Joseph Isaac Schneerson (1880– 1950), became the dynasty's sixth rebbe after his father's death. He continued to conduct the mainly clandestine activities of the movement, which included maintaining *yeshives** and ritual baths. In 1927, he was arrested and after some weeks in prison, he finally received authorization to emigrate. He stayed first in Riga in Latvia, then left to settle in Otwock, a small town near Warsaw. In 1939, after the German invasion, Joseph Isaac Schneerson managed to escape from Poland and he arrived in New York in March 1940. As we know, he settled in Crown Heights, and surrounded by some followers, he ran a yeshive and a small Hasidic community. His death in 1950 marked the beginning of a new and particularly prosperous period for this Hasidic movement under the leadership of the dynasty's seventh rebbe, Menahem Mendel Schneerson.

AN ORIGINAL REBBE

In 1941, the son-in-law of the sixth rebbe, Menahem Mendel Schneerson (1902–1944), and his daughter Chaya Mushka, who were living in Paris, came to join him in Crown Heights. On the way, it was noticed that Schneerson bore the same name as his father-in-law; they were in fact distantly related. Also, a strong endogamy within an extended blood relationship has existed within the Lubavitch dynasty for several generations.[12]

The fate of the future seventh Lubavitch rebbe is an unusual one for a Hasidic leader. A rabbi's son, born in 1902 in Nikolayev in Ukraine, he had a reputation as a prodigious Talmudic scholar from the age of thirteen years. At 21 years, in 1923, he met his future father-in-law in Rostov on the River Don. He went on to collaborate there with Joseph I. Schneerson to ensure the continuation of the movement's religious activities in the face of persecutions from the Communist regime. However, in 1926 he embarked on a long period of his life that particularly distinguished the future rebbe from his peers. He settled in Berlin and studied philosophy, mathematics and physics at the university. In 1928, he married Chaya Mushka, who was one year older than him, in Warsaw, after a four-year engagement. Both this long engagement and the late age at the marriage were contrary to Hasidic orthodox practices.[13] At the wedding ceremony in the court of the Lubavitch yeshiva in Warsaw, Menahem Mendel wore the traditional Lubavitch Hasidic black frock coat under the canopy but for the reception that followed he put on a modern suit, brown shoes and white gloves,[14] sartorial finery that was rather unusual for a Hasidic disciple!

The couple, who did not go on to have children, lived in Berlin for four years to pursue studies there, then in 1932 just before the Nazis took power, they settled in the 14th arrondissement in Paris. The followers say generally with some pride that M. M. Schneerson studied 'at the Sorbonne'. He certainly seems to have attended courses at the University of Paris, but in fact he was enrolled at the higher institute of civil engineering, (École supérieure des travaux publics or ESTP) on the Boulevard Saint-Germain, 300 metres away from the Sorbonne![15] He is said to have obtained a diploma as an electrical engineer. He attended two oratories on the Rue des Rosiers in the Marais, the Jewish quarter, where he provided courses in the Talmud.[16] From 1936, he also worked on the publication of his father-in-law's 'letter' to his followers all over the world and he contributed to a Habad learned journal that was published in Warsaw.[17]

During these fifteen years in such secular cities as Berlin and Paris, Schneerson appears to have received financial support from his father-in-law, who seems to have approved of these university studies.[18] After all, did M. M. Schneerson, with his substantial 'secular' knowledge, not go on to assert on various occasions the limited nature of scientific knowledge compared with the absolute quality of the Revelation?[19] In any case, the future rebbe appeared at ease in the non-Jewish world. There are some photographs of him in Western-style clothes with a beard that seems to be trimmed, carrying some French newspapers, while his wife Chaya has a sophisticated and elegant appearance, with her hair partly uncovered.[20]

Whatever the facts of the matter, this is certainly an entirely original path for a rebbe who went on to become so influential and prestigious. As we shall see, some of his ideas, which were also original, were undoubtedly derived from this period of immersion both in learning and in the secular world.

After the German invasion of France, the Schneerson couple moved to the United States in June 1941. Menahem Mendel is said to have first used his engineering skills in a machine-tools factory. The rebbe, who gave him a very warm welcome, and who praised his piety on several occasions, gave him responsibility for various activities within the community; in particular, he put him in charge of a new publishing house, *Kehot*, which was to publish the complete works of the various Lubavitch rebbes; from 1948, he worked for Habad full-time. He had specific responsibility for the day-to-day running of the movement's activities, which did not prevent him from pursuing scholarly activities and writing religiously inspired texts.

The sixth Lubavitch rebbe died on 28 January 1950, without having given any indication as to his succession. He had a grandson and another son-in-law who was older than Menahem Mendel, either of whom could also have become rebbe. However, the Lubavitch council of elders preferred Menahem Mendel Schneerson; their choice seems to have been particularly determined by his administrative talents, amply demonstrated since his full-time work for Habad in Crown Heights.[21] Menahem Mendel acceded to their request with a degree of reticence and became the seventh rebbe of the dynasty at the age of 49 years, one year after his father-in-law's death. This one-year period, which is often observed when a new rebbe is nominated, is designed to respect the mourning period following the previous leader's death (see p. 45).

In contrast to his father-in-law and his other predecessors, the new leader sported a modern hat and a tie from the outset;[22] most of his followers did likewise. Also, unlike the Satmarer's long curls, their sidelocks – *peyes** in Yiddish – are almost invisible because they are either discreetly arranged close to the ears or they form part of the mass of hair in the beard. Moreover, as we already know, the followers wear hats and suits, usually black, but in a rather modern cut. This partial rejection of Hasidic tradition in terms of appearance accords with the highly symbolic level of self-presentation in a new chapter of Lubavitch history. In fact, from the beginning of the 1960s, M. M. Schneerson put into practice the key concept of *Ahavat Israel*,* literally love of Israel and in fact of all Jews, which involves a Hasidic mission to reignite the Jewish flame in every Jew, however remote from the faith. This plan certainly had its origin in Baal Shem Tov and Shneur Zalman of Lyady, the spiritual ancestor of Habad,[23] but Schneerson moved missionary work to the forefront of the followers' activities, so that this has now become an integral part of the image presented by Lubavitch.

This type of undertaking was rare among the Hasidim, at least until a few years ago. Certainly, the Bostoner rebbe, a long-established exception in the United States, has long practised similar activities but on a small scale.[24] Nevertheless, Lubavitch has gained something of a following among the 'rival' Hasidic communities. In fact, from 1998 in Israel, the ultra-orthodox party Agudath Israel, according to the instructions of its main religious leaders (the Gerer rebbe, the Vishnitzer rebbe and others) created two networks of schools, Nesivos Moshe, in various places in the country, for children from newly religious or non-religious backgrounds and for the children of recent Russian immigrants (see Chapter 6). However, these Hasidic movements do not make this type of task an essential priority, whereas it is the other way round for Lubavitch, which has also implemented some spectacular modern methods of achieving its objectives.

The movement's 'headquarters' in a tall British-style building with a red brick facade at 770 Eastern Parkway are the centre from which these activities have developed, ranging from isolated actions to the establishment of schools especially intended for the *baalei tshuve*,* literally the masters of repentance, the new converts who turn or return to the Jewish faith and practices.

THE LUBAVITCH ZEAL

One of the especially visible Lubavitch missionary operations is one practised mainly by the students of the yeshives, the Talmudic academies of the movement. These students invite passers-by who are thought to be Jewish – the question is put to them – to enter their truck, called a *mitsve tank*,* 'tank of prescriptions', positioned at a strategic site, for example by the New York public library at the junction of 5th Avenue and 42nd Street. The visitors are then invited to observe the ritual of putting on the phylacteries, *tfillen*,* accompanying these acts with *ad hoc* blessings and prayers.[25] The observance of this prescription provides the students with opportunities to present enlightening speeches to interested passers-by, to engage them in debate and to exhort them to return to Jewish observance. Launched in 1967, this campaign was followed by other initiatives relating to religious observance, such as encouraging every family to own a copy of the Torah and a prayer-book and placing on various house doorposts *mezuzes* (sing. *mezuze*)* – cases containing a parchment with passages from Deuteronomy.

There were further highly targeted missionary campaigns, particularly from the 1960s during the period of the hippy and beatnik counter-culture and the Eastern religions, in which many Jewish students had become deeply involved. Some militant Lubavitcher regularly took up positions at stands (among other 'competing' stands, particularly those of Judaeo-Christian movements such as the 'Jews for Jesus') on the paths of university campuses that were well-trodden by these students. For example, at the University of California at Berkeley and Los Angeles, the followers distributed leaflets and talked to the men and women whom they wanted to engage in debate, in order to dissuade them from these rather un-Jewish paths. The Lubavitch also invited young men and women to visit the 'Habad houses' that had been established at the same time close to these campuses. There, highly affable rabbis, the Lubavitch 'delegates', *shlihim*, welcomed them, explained the scriptures to them and gave them advice on how to deal with their problems or existential dilemmas. In these Habad houses, which were also created in the urban areas with strong Jewish populations, weekend gatherings were organized, with lectures, discussions, religious services on the Sabbath and suchlike. Many young people who were attracted by these activities, without necessarily embracing Hasidism, nevertheless returned to the religion ... and to a more orderly lifestyle.

In 1990, there were around 1,900 Habad houses, certainly not of equal size, but spread all over the world, particularly in the former Soviet Union, where the Lubavitcher are especially active today; there were 220 in the United States alone and 180 in Israel. In 2001, there were said to be 2,400 of these outposts worldwide, run by the *shlihim*, who are generally trained in Lubavitch institutions in Crown Heights.

As a result of their fairly efficacious 'Judaicizing' activities, combined with a highly conservative moralism, the rebbe and Lubavitch acquired a certain prestige within the Jewish institutional establishment, particularly in the United States. This is a prestige that is never accorded to other great Hasidic dynasties, whose renown remains confined to ultra-religious circles. The activities of the Habad houses also received financial support from major Jewish organizations and associations of 'Friends of Lubavitch'. Thus, in Los Angeles, 'Friends of Lubavitch' gathers together businessmen, academics and personalities from the media world. For example, at a banquet of this association held to celebrate the rebbe's 70th birthday in 1972, a doctor offered $120,000 to the movement, while the president himself had made a donation of $1,000,000![26] At a telethon held in 1981, again sponsored by 'Friends of Lubavitch', Elliot Gould, a well-known film actor who was its presenter, collected $1,000,000 for reconstructing the Habad house in the Westwood district (near the campus of California University), which had been destroyed in a fire. At another telethon in August

2000, a total of $6,000,000 was pledged in donations! The telethon's presenter, Jerry Weintraub, a film producer and a 'conservative' Jew (thus a Jew with a very different religiosity from Hasidism) stated on this occasion that the Hasidim were carrying out excellent work 'in carrying on our heritage. It's important to me to keep their light lit.'[27]

Although the educational and other programmes of Habad are not entirely to the taste of all the Jewish organizations, they nevertheless receive substantial financial and material assistance from them.[28] Thus, in Los Angeles, a city in which the vast majority of the 500,000 Jews living there are non-religious or only very moderately religious, Habad receives considerable aid, particularly from rich and famous personalities. In London, where Lubavitch is also very active, at the thirteenth banquet of the 'Friends of the Lubavitch Foundation' in 1989, £900,000 was collected to enable Habad to make contact with 20,000 children attending non-Jewish schools.[29]

There is therefore a perception among many Jewish personalities, institutions and press organizations that their own struggle for a strong Jewish identity, as well as their pro-Israeli standpoints (on Lubavitch and Israel, see below), are reinforced by the actions of the Lubavitch *shlihim*. Habad also very obligingly acknowledges these forms of support – for example, reproducing in a book about its activities a particular article from a journal of a major Jewish organization emphasizing how effectively Habad is combating assimilation and intermarriage, as well as anti-Israeli propaganda, particularly on the campuses.[30] This institutional backing for Lubavitch exists to a greater or lesser extent in many towns and countries.

The activities of the Habad houses are connected to those at the headquarters in Crown Heights. When the *shlihim* observe that someone is zealously following the path of Jewish observance, they send him to spend a few days at the New York headquarters, to become immersed in the ambience of the Hasidic world and particularly, during the rebbe's lifetime, to attend a *farbrengen*, at which the latter would discourse at length to disciples who were imbued with a sense of the merit of all his statements. Gripped by the collective fervour and thenceforth feeling able to give a meaning to the world, and having received a warm welcome from the families who gave them hospitality, many *baalei tshuve*, Jewish 'penitents' returning to the faith, then found themselves fully committed to a path of total devotion to Hasidic Judaism. It should be emphasized that the *farbrengen* were only intended for a male audience but that from 1975 – in an indirect concession to the prevailing feminism – a similar meeting took place once a year for the Lubavitch women.[31] Finally, from 1992, the *farbrengen* and the rebbe's addresses came to an end when he suffered a brain haemorrhage.

However, the influence of the Habad houses or a brief sojourn at Crown Heights were not enough to work a radical transformation of a *baal tshuve*, usually having only just emerged, especially in the 1970s, from the counter-culture, Marxist movements, the Jews for Jesus or other similar movements. From 1962, the rebbe established the first Talmudic academy in the district, which was intended specially for the 'penitents' who had been deprived of an orthodox Jewish education. A second yeshive of this kind was then created in

Morristown in New Jersey, more specifically intended for single men. For the female 'penitents' it was only in 1972 that a first form of teaching was put – or more or less thrown – together for them. Finally, a specific school and a hall of residence for repentant *baalot tshuve* (the feminine plural of *baalei tshuve*) were established in 1974.[32]

Of course, Lubavitch has a set of Jewish schools of all levels for the children of long-standing followers both in Crown Heights and elsewhere in the United States and abroad, particularly in France, with over forty in Paris, the Paris region and the provincial areas, (see Chapter 8).[33] The teaching is conducted using the most modern methods, including audio-visual techniques; this is a long way removed from the traditional model of the Eastern European *haider** or *Talmud Torah*,* as they continue in essence among the Belzer, Satmarer, Bobover and many other Hasidic communities. In general, the Lubavitch schools provide a secular education that is substantial enough to obtain state subsidies. For the girls, the secular studies are more advanced than for the boys, but for both sexes the religious instruction, which is certainly less extensive for the girls, takes precedence and, as with other Hasidim, it takes place in the morning, when the children are most attentive and receptive. The principles of Lubavitch teaching are therefore similar to those of other Hasidim. However, the fact that the Habad communities in Crown Heights and elsewhere have 'penitents' in their ranks, usually with a good secular scholastic education, often to university level, encourages the movement to provide a higher level of secular education than in most of the other Hasidic movements. This is also a highly valuable training for providing the various kinds of missionary activities – publications, lectures and debates, in all languages – that are aimed at a wide international public.

The widespread use of modern communications technology constitutes a further original feature of Lubavitch. In fact, under Menahem Mendel Schneerson's leadership, the movement had been quick to establish a telephone link to the Habad houses and other Lubavitch centres throughout the world, which enabled the followers assembled for this purpose to hear the rebbe's addresses live through loudspeakers. Many of these were also recorded on cassettes and sent to subscribers. There were also radio broadcasts and, from 1984, some Lubavitch television programmes and video-cassettes were produced. Finally, in the mid-1990s in Crown Heights and elsewhere, particularly in France, Lubavitch created some highly sophisticated and very active websites. The instigator and founder of the Brooklyn website, the rabbi Joseph Kazen, had gained the rebbe's approval for introducing this innovation as early as 1990. Whereas the other Hasidic leaders have misgivings about radio and are opposed to the use of television and the internet because of all the 'obscenities' that these media transmit, the rebbe, probably influenced by his technical knowledge and his interest in technology,[34] did not hesitate to use it for 'positive' ends.

A SPECIFIC SOCIAL STRUCTURE

Through its proselytism, Lubavitch has developed a different sociological composition from the other Hasidic movements. Whereas some homogeneity persists in the latter communities through the transmission of successive generations, with Lubavitch there is a constant influx of new blood as a result of the 'penitents', who often have highly diverse origins and outlooks. Accordingly, in Paris, where Habad is extremely dynamic, a very large proportion of the followers are of Sephardic* origin – Algerian, Moroccan and Tunisian Jews (see Chapter 8). In Israel, half of the 4,500 or so Lubavitch families in the country are 'penitents'.[35] Furthermore, many of the newcomers are university-educated and work as qualified professionals in large companies or in public service, or as doctors, pharmacists or lawyers. The range of professions in the Lubavitch communities therefore differs from that of most of the other Hasidic groups because, as we know, followers in the latter, barring a few exceptions, have essentially only received Jewish and Talmudic educations and cannot take up these kinds of profession, which require extensive periods of specialized study. Certainly, as in the other major Hasidic communities, the followers in Crown Heights and elsewhere, particularly in France, include rabbis, *kashrut** supervisors, schoolteachers (men and women) and small traders who run kasher food shops, religious bookshops and shops selling goods for ritual use (prayer-shawls, phylacteries etc.).

Nevertheless, many followers who perform religious functions practise them outside the Hasidic environment. Some of them are rabbis, teachers in yeshives, kashrut supervisors, circumcision specialists, directors of youth activities in non-Hasidic communities and even directors of halls of residence for Jewish students established on the campuses by the major Jewish organizations in the United States and elsewhere. These activities provide various followers with professional openings, but above all they accord with the missionary doctrine of the movement. Moreover, many communities and organizations do not have qualified religious personnel available themselves and they therefore do not hesitate to recruit Lubavitch Hasidim. Lubavitch therefore collaborates on important matters such as the religious life and education with many Jewish communities, often with a very limited degree of orthodoxy, whose followers and children Lubavitch representatives clearly seek to influence according to their own convictions. We shall see that this holds particularly true in France, specifically through a highly advanced Lubavitch school system. This very active involvement in wider Jewish circles again distinguishes Lubavitch from other Hasidic movements.

This dissimilarity also expresses itself in demographic terms. As for other Hasidim, the Biblical prescription 'be fruitful, and multiply' is certainly of fundamental importance for the Lubavitcher and many families in Crown Heights have six or more children. At a public address in 1980, the rebbe strongly condemned the concept of 'family planning'.[36] This warning must be understood in connection with the influx into Habad circles, especially since the early 1970s, of 'penitents',[37] who, unlike the followers of Hasidic descent, are frequently familiar with this type of practice. Furthermore, the newcomers, some of whom are already old and influenced by their previous lives, have generally until then had few or no children, while others are still single at an age at which the Lubavitcher 'by birth' are already married and are parents.

The Lubavitch groups therefore have rather fewer children than other Hasidic communities, such as the Satmarer, the Belzer, the Bobover.

KASHRUT: OBSERVANCE AND INCULCATION

Like other Hasidic communities, Lubavitch aims to secure a complete adherence to the kashrut from its followers. Moreover, Habad seeks to inculcate this observance in other Jews. Among the campaigns of the movement, there was one from 1975 for a faithful adherence to the kashrut; the movement even established a fund to help families who wanted to make their kitchen and utensils conform to the relevant prescriptions.[38]

The movement uses various methods for safeguarding this kashrut. In the first place, this is through the *bet din*,* the rabbinical court in Crown Heights, which issues certificates to butchers and other kasher shops to guarantee to customers that the products that they sell conform to the Jewish prescriptions, including for food under the supervision of other Hasidic communities. This was also the case for some Satmar products, at least until 1983, when an incident between the Satmarer and the Lubavitcher resulted in the Lubavitch movement boycotting all products under Satmar supervision.[39] From 1987, at the initiative of Aron Rubashkin, a long-standing follower and a butcher by trade, Lubavitch also set up a centre for slaughter, production and distribution of kasher meat and poultry in Postville, Iowa, a small agricultural centre in the Mid-West, which created 350 jobs in this town and led 150 followers to live there. Also, thirty Hasidim who were ritual slaughterers practised their trade there.[40] The produce of this business is distributed under three different trademarks in Crown Heights, but also in other places where there are Lubavitch communities and kasher shops run by followers.

However, in Montreal for example, the Lubavitcher sit on the rabbinical council of the united Jewish community of the town, which allows ritual slaughterers from some Hasidic communities, including Lubavitch, to affix a double identification – stamps or seals – to the pieces of meat, to indicate that the meat is kasher both according to the community as a whole and according to particular Hasidim. Some butchers are known to sell only meat slaughtered by *shohetim*,* ritual slaughterers who are followers of a particular Hasidic group; accordingly, someone who wants to consume only the meat approved by his own community can do so without the unitary system being put into question. More or less the same system operates in Antwerp, within the orthodox community and also within the Paris Consistory;[41] nevertheless, in Paris and the surrounding region, Lubavitch has organized its own ritual slaughter and a system for supervising various butchers since 1991 (see pp. 130–1). In fact, the Lubavitch Hasidim adjust extremely well to various situations because their functions within extended Jewish communities enable them to influence the organization and practices of slaughter, to appoint kashrut supervisors in various restaurants and ultimately to influence the kashrut practices of a relatively wide public.

LOCAL – AND ISRAELI – POLITICS

Lubavitch takes an active part in American political life. As we have seen, in the 1960s, when the other Hasidic communities were fleeing Crown Heights, the Lubavitcher decided to remain there, which undoubtedly constituted an important political decision in the conflict-ridden context of the period. The property renovations instigated by the council of the Jewish community in Crown Heights, from then on under Lubavitch control, along with the funds and subsidies that these operations required and security issues for the inhabitants, involved numerous contacts with administrative and political agencies.[42] In 1976, when the electoral boundaries of Crown Heights were being redrawn, the Lubavitcher took the opportunity of increasing their political influence; they asked for the southern part of the district, where the Hasidim live and vote, to become a separate electoral constituency. This division was accepted by the relevant electoral committee. Although the 15,000 or so Hasidim represented only a small minority of the 97,000 inhabitants of the new district, they managed to forge an alliance, a 'rainbow coalition', with some black groups. Accordingly, in February 1983 the rabbi Rosenfeld was elected a town councillor of the district but he then lost his seat in 1986. However, the 'rainbow coalition' remained influential in local agencies, particularly the agency that distributed various subsidies.

Lubavitch also makes its presence felt in some higher-level elections, particularly the New York mayoral election. In 1989, the Hasidim in Crown Heights, along with those in Williamsburg and Borough Park, supported the black candidate David Dinkins against Edward Koch, who was in fact Jewish, in the primaries of the Democrat party. As Mayor, Koch had blocked some protective measures for the Hasidim during the periods of tension in Crown Heights. The rebbe had received visits from Dinkins on two occasions before the primaries and before the actual election; these were clear indications of his preferences. Dinkins was then selected by the Democrats and finally elected Mayor, but he very quickly became *persona non grata* in Crown Heights because the Hasidim felt that the New York police had not intervened strongly enough during the severe racial incidents in 1991 (see p. 61 above). From then on, the Lubavitcher switched their allegiance to the Republican party and in particular to Rudolph Giuliani, who was mayor of the city from 1994 until the beginning of 2002, thus until after the terrorist attacks of 11 September 2001.

Finally, when the Republican Michael Bloomberg was elected as city mayor in November 2001, this was with the support of a Crown Heights political action committee, which in fact represented Lubavitch. A few months earlier, the council of the Jewish community in Crown Heights had 'prohibited' Hillary Clinton, President Clinton's wife and senatorial candidate in New York State for a seat that she then won, from coming to the district because of her 'anti-Semitism' and her support for David Dinkins, then mayoral candidate again in the Democrat party primaries.[43] Clearly there are numerous examples of Lubavitch interventions in various elections and, although the movement seems to have opted several years ago for the Republican party, it is the more or less direct interests of the movement and its followers that broadly determine the expressions of political support or opposition.

Moreover, the movement does not hesitate to intervene at the federal level. Still in the rebbe's lifetime, Habad had designated a rabbi as a permanent 'emissary' in Washington. This expert lobbyist intervenes with parliamentary and other government agencies, who consult him to find out the Lubavitch position on a particular law or issue. In 1992, this emissary managed to arrange, on the rebbe's 90th birthday, for a Lubavitch rabbi to open a session of the House of Representatives in the presence of many prominent figures by intoning a formal prayer in homage to Schneerson. The emissary's interventions with many political figures also resulted in the rebbe receiving the gold medal from Congress in 1994, when twenty-three people were 'nominated' for this remarkable honour.[44] It goes without saying that these 'profane' honours, highlighted of course by the media, help to promote the cause of Habad, which is unquestionably the most widely known Hasidic movement in the United States.

We know that in the past most of the Hasidic dynasties were anti-Zionist, that the Satmarer continue to be and that today other groups have conflicting views and mixed feelings concerning this 'secular' state, although they also seek to influence its standpoint on various issues, with a degree of success, particularly through the orthodox parties in Israel (see Chapters 6 and 7).

In 1899, when Zionism was first emerging as a political force, the fifth Lubavitcher rebbe, Dov Baer Schneerson, had set out the principles of the Hasidim's opposition to Zionism. He challenged the Zionist aspiration to change the Jewish condition during the Exile and the dispersal of the Jews throughout the nations of the world. He argued that the reunion of the exiled and the liberation from the 'yoke of the Great Powers' have to depend solely on the transcendental and miraculous intervention of the Messiah, the Saviour of Israel. Zionism, which seeks the return of the Jews to Israel and the political sovereignty of this country, constitutes a human endeavour to fulfil messianic expectations; it is therefore a flagrant violation of the oath sworn by the Jewish people to wait patiently for the End of Time, for a return to the Holy Land.[45] Lubavitch maintained this position for a very long time. Even in 1943, the rebbe Joseph Isaac Schneerson, settled in New York since 1940, stated: 'Many evil Israelites who have gathered together in the land of Israel seek to contaminate not only Jewish souls, but also to defile the Holy Land itself, and to infect the Hebrew language ... Those of us who are here should be thankful that we are not over there in the diaspora of the land of Israel ...'[46]

As we will see in the chapters on the Hasidim in Israel, most of the dynasties, apart from Satmar, have in fact recognized the new State, with which some accommodation has to be made in an attempt to exert some influence there. Furthermore, as early as 1949 and on Joseph Isaac Schneerson's own initiative, a village called Kefar Habad was created in Israel for Lubavitch immigrants from Russia; located not far from Tel-Aviv, it had 1,540 inhabitants by 1969 and today it has around 3,500. This village became an essential centre for Lubavitch educational and missionary work in Israel. Finally, especially since the Kippur war in 1973, Menahem Mendel Schneerson, the last rebbe, adopted some extreme positions concerning the attitude that the Hebrew State should take towards the Arabs. Although Lubavitch still refused to recognize any divine stamp on the creation of the Hebrew State, the rebbe asserted in the name of the Jewish principle of *pikuah nefesh*,* 'respect for the soul (or the life)'[47] that Israel had an obligation to annex the Palestinian territories occupied since the Kippur war.[48] He argued, in fact, that to give back the territories or even to discuss it with the enemy was to endanger the security of the Jews in the country, a tragic mistake from the viewpoint of the religious Law.[49]

Some uncompromising positions were then adopted. In 1977, the rebbe pronounced himself in favour of an intensive colonization of the Israeli-occupied territories 'in the faith that God, who promised this land to our fathers, will not allow this to cause us any difficulties'.[50] Following Anwar Al-Sadat's visit to Jerusalem in 1977, the rebbe issued a warning against any territorial concession to Egypt; he insisted that Israel should not give back the Sinai peninsula, captured during the Kippur war in 1973.[51] This extreme attitude, with its basis in religious principle, also involved political choices, sometimes with an impact on the entire country. Thus, in March 1990, the Israeli government coalition between Likud, a right-wing party, and the left-wing Labor party collapsed because of disagreements concerning peace negotiations between Jews and Arabs. The Labor party was willing to return occupied territories in exchange for peace, but Likud rejected this course of action. The following month, the Labor party failed in its attempt to establish a government that included two ministers from the ultra-orthodox party, Agudath Israel.* In fact, two members of this party who were close to Lubavitch and who had initially agreed to enter the government withdrew their support on discovering from the Habad headquarters in Crown Heights that the rebbe's position on a transfer of territories had not changed![52] The intended coalition could not be established and a government constituted by the right-wing and ultra-orthodox parties took power.

The rebbe made further interventions in Israeli politics on many other issues. From 1970 to 1980, he led a campaign for an amendment to the Law of Return, which would specify that a convert had to conform to the criteria of the *Halohe*,* the Jewish law, that is according to the interpretation of the ultra-orthodox rabbis alone.[53]

Unlike most of the other Hasidic rebbes, who are strongly opposed to military service for their followers (see Chapter 6, pp. 88–9), Schneerson allowed his followers to serve in the Israeli army, generally in the chaplaincy. Thus during the Six-Day War in 1967, but also in other circumstances, Habad followers would return to their units and practise their customary militancy there, providing phylacteries, prayer-shawls and so on to the soldiers.

Lubavitch also puts forward its annexationist standpoint in the United States, as it has done long since the rebbe's death in 1994. Thus on 4 January 2000, at the discussions in Virginia between the Israeli Prime Minister Ehud Barak and the Syrian Foreign Affairs Minister, a group of around forty followers, who travelled from the headquarters in Brooklyn in trucks covered in slogans such as 'we shall not move from Golan', demonstrated at length against a possible Israeli withdrawal from this territory occupied since 1967.[54]

In the course of his long 'reign', Schneerson, without ever having visited Israel, had nevertheless become a figure of some consequence in the political life of this country! Also, leading politicians in Israel, including ministers, did not fail to pay visits to him in Crown Heights.[55]

PERSONALITY CULT

Unbounded admiration and belief in the rebbe's superhuman powers are, as we have seen, intrinsic features of Hasidism from its beginnings and this 'personality cult' remains ubiquitous today in the Hasidic movements in general. The attachment of the Hasidim to Menahem Mendel Schneerson, which developed over the course of a particularly original and dynamic forty-three-year reign, is in no way atypical, rather the contrary.

In the style of his fellow rebbes, Schneerson held audiences with his followers, usually in the evening in his case, on Sunday, Monday and Thursday from 20.30 to 22.30 p.m. and sometimes until 2 a.m. His followers would present him with *kvitel*,* notes on which they had inscribed their petitions and requests for intercession, for instance to cure the sick or the infertile. These visitors also consulted M. M. Schneerson on the most diverse problems and his advice or opinion was generally scrupulously followed. Like other rebbes for their own followers, Menahem Mendel Schneerson was (and remains since his death) an outstanding religious figure, considered as a 'great man', the 'leader of the Jewish world' and so on.[56] However, in his case, there are several original characteristics. The prestige of this rebbe, who was also an engineer and who studied 'at the Sorbonne', as followers like to say, who could discuss the finer points of religion and science, read Proust and Hegel[57] and speak several languages – Russian, German, French and English – is reinforced by some important 'secular' qualities. These are particularly appealing to the recent followers, the *baalei tshuve*, who often have a great deal of secular knowledge themselves.

The transmission of his speeches by telephone line, radio and even television across the United States and elsewhere in the world, an activity unknown to other rebbes, also contributes in a novel way to the Schneerson cult. This method of communication, albeit essentially received by an initiated audience, contributes to reinforcing the emotional rapport of the follower hearing and watching his leader on television, which is also the case, of course on a completely different scale, for the evangelical audio-visual preachers and the late Pope John-Paul II.[58]

Furthermore, the fact that figures from the 'profane' world – sometimes highly prominent ones – would come to converse with the rebbe and often publicly praised his qualities also contributed to the cult dedicated to him.[59] The role played by the rebbe in Israeli political affairs also won him the sympathy of certain Israeli politicians, who would pay him a visit at Crown Heights when they came to New York, as some of the publications of the movement were keen to emphasize. For many followers, the tributes paid to the rebbe by many figures from the secular world – no rebbe had ever before enjoyed such recognition – further increased his prestige.

There are also large numbers of photographs of the rebbe in the living-rooms of Lubavitch followers in Crown Heights and elsewhere, as well as in their shops, booksellers and groceries and, finally, in the Habad houses. No rebbe has had an image that is so widely reproduced and celebrated.

Finally, the total adherence to the rebbe, whose authority was beyond question, pervaded the Lubavitch values system and a specific way of life, which has certainly contributed to cementing communities constituted of followers with very diverse outlooks, many of whom are recent adherents, with disparate social, cultural and professional profiles. The intense cult of Schneerson has therefore exercised a unifying function, and has continued to do so since his death in 1994 at least at an underlying level, although some serious divergences concerning the actual degree of this veneration are strongly in evidence today. In fact, some of the followers hold Menahem Mendel Schneerson to be none other than the Messiah!

IS THE REBBE THE MESSIAH?

There is certainly a constant anticipation of the Messiah among orthodox Hasidic Jews, which is expressed particularly in the major prayers of the daily liturgy that they practise assiduously;[60] however, they tend to envisage it as a remote prospect that bears little relation to the immediate future. The first Lubavitch rebbes had a similar attitude to this question. However, the sixth rebbe, Joseph Schneerson, Menahem Mendel's predecessor, following the trials that afflicted the Jews during the Second World War, had announced the proximity of the 'redemption'.[61] Now, in relation to this, a new original feature belatedly came to influence the approach taken by Menahem Mendel and, of course, by the movement: namely, since the end of the 1980s every Habad act, sermon and campaign has referred to the imminent arrival of the Messiah.

In fact, the belief of followers, but also of Jews in general, in the Messiah's imminent advent, is itself thought to have a determining influence on his coming. Thus in 1988, the rebbe declared: 'It is within the grasp of each of us to act so that the redemption will come quickly, not just tomorrow or after some time, but today, literally.'[62] Schneerson also indicated the circumstances of his arrival: 'The King Messiah can come immediately, "in a twinkling of an eye" ... And he certainly will come immediately. And as this is so, then clearly the King Messiah is already present in the world ... Moreover, he is present as a "great man (a *gadol**)" ... a king from the house of David who meditates upon the Torah and performs its commandments.'[63]

At the beginning of the 1990s, through broadcast messages as well as advertisements in the press and on billboards, Habad undertook to announce the imminent arrival of the Messiah to the public at large. Punchy slogans such as 'we want the Messiah now – we don't want to wait' were spread around, including in pamphlets and on stickers. On 11 April 1991, at the festival of Passover, the rebbe delivered an address on the subject of the redemption, which caused a great sensation among the followers; he specifically declared: 'What more can I do to motivate the entire Jewish people to clamor and cry out, and thus actually bring about the coming of Maschiach ... ?... *Now do everything you can to bring Mashiach, here and now, immediately* ... I have done whatever I can ...'.[64] From then on, the disciples redoubled their efforts in the messianic campaigns. On 19 June 1991, Lubavitch placed an advertisement in the *New York Times* announcing that certain recent events – in particular the mass emigration of Jews from the former Soviet Union and the defeat of Iraq in the Gulf war – were signs that heralded the redemption.[65] Shortly afterwards, in July 1991, the rebbe proclaimed: 'We have already seen concrete miracles witnessing that this is *the year in which King Messiah shall be revealed*, leading to *the hour that the King Messiah comes.*'[66] The intense veneration conferred on Schneerson gave rise to the conviction among his followers that the rebbe was the *gadol*, the Great One already present in the world, to whom he himself had referred some years earlier. Some even launched a petition asking people to declare that they recognized the kingship of 'his holiness, the Rebbe, long may he live, the King Messiah'.[67] In fact, the rebbe himself never stated that he was the Messiah and he seems never to have given a clear indication as to whether he rejected or acquiesced in the messianic veneration of many of his followers.

In April 1992, a group of Lubavitch rabbis published 'a rabbinical decision' proclaiming the rebbe's messianic attributes.[68] However, other rabbis in the movement expressed their opposition to this text. In any case, the followers' intense veneration of the rebbe, which developed over the course of a forty-three-year 'reign', certainly seems to have contributed to the upsurge of these messianic pressures.

At the age of 92 years, the rebbe died early in the morning of 12 June 1994 in a New York hospital, and the funeral took place that same afternoon. The news spread like wildfire within the Lubavitch communities: in Toronto, a charter plane was soon on its way to New York to transport a group of followers to the funeral.[69] A crowd of an estimated 12,000 people witnessed the coffin being taken, in a highly charged atmosphere, from Crown Heights to the New York cemetery, where M. M. Schneerson was buried beside his father-in-law, the previous rebbe. For a week, the synagogue at 770 Eastern Parkway remained full for the *shive*,* the traditional Jewish week of intense mourning.

Among many followers, this death did nothing to alter the conviction that Schneerson was the Messiah; some of them admitted that they had been mistaken as to his messianic arrival during his lifetime but stated that he would be brought back to life. In 1998, the rabbi Butman, a former colleague of the rebbe and director of the 'World Headquarters to bring the Messiah', published an article in *Haaretz*, a well-known daily newspaper in Israel. He expounds here why the rebbe is indeed the Messiah, including with reference to *gematria*,* numerology – in Hebrew, figures are represented by letters of the alphabet – a technique that is used particularly in the interpretation of Kabbalistic writings. Thus, he argues that the number 770 (the number of the rebbe's residence) is equivalent to 'Bet Meshiah', the house of the Messiah: 'This then literally shows that the house of the Rebbe is the house of the Messiah!' He concludes his article as follows:

'On this matter there is unanimity among all members of Chabad throughout the world: The Rebbe, King Messiah, will take us out of exile immediately. That is the secret of our existence and of our redemption.'[70]

This messianic belief, which a historian and rabbi, the author of a brilliant article and book,[71] condemns for its Christianizing tendency because it implies the resurrection of the rebbe-Messiah, persists among some of the Lubavitch leaders and followers.[72] Although the major Hasidic groups such as Belz and Satmar have long considered Lubavitch as a movement that is not very 'kasher' and the rabbi Schach, leader of the non-Hasidic orthodox in Israel, had condemned Lubavitch messianism at an early stage,[73] the rabbis of the American orthodox Jewish organizations were rather slow to react. In June 1996, two years after the rebbe's death, the orthodox rabbis declared that 'there is not and has never been a place in Judaism for the belief that Mashiach ben David [Messiah son of David] will begin his Messianic Mission only to experience death, burial and resurrection before completing it'.[74]

There are three possible motives for the prolonged orthodox indifference towards this 'heresy': 1. Lubavitch carries out good works (its missionary activity); 2. this messianism is only an ephemeral flight of folly; 3. community conflicts are to be avoided.[75] Furthermore, unlike the movement of the 'false messiah' Shabbetai Tzevi (Chapter 1), this messianism has not led to a rejection of the Jewish prescriptions or to sexual licence among the Lubavitcher. Moreover, apart from a vociferous minority, the followers refrain from flaunting their messianic convictions and, because of their missionary work, they also continue to be appreciated by the Establishment, which seeks the preservation of the Jewish identity. Moreover, Lubavitch has infiltrated many more or less orthodox Jewish communities to some degree; thus in England one third of them seem to have engaged Lubavitch followers as rabbis and in Russia Habad has recently managed to obtain official recognition from the authorities for the federation of Jewish communities, which the movement controls.[76] This is therefore a long way removed from a vociferous excommunication!

The movement's leaders today at the headquarters in Crown Heights certainly claim that the 'messianists' constitute only a marginal group. However, the movement distributes video-cassettes, particularly through its website, which show a Schneerson who is alive and well from some old recordings; although this posthumous audio-visual presence is ostensibly intended to preserve the rebbe's messages, it seems to me to be reinforcing through the tape the belief in his return as a Messiah.

The messianic expectation aroused by Schneerson did not develop as a reaction of hope in a situation of crisis, as is often the case for messianic movements throughout the world, including for the messianism of his predecessor. On the contrary, the rebbe and his inner circle cite positive factors indicating the proximity of the redemption, such as the liberation of the Jews of the former Soviet Union and the favourable outcome of the Gulf war. Just before the Gulf war, in January 1991, when Iraq was threatening Israel with its missiles, Schneerson declared: 'It is obvious that after the Holocaust distress shall not rise up a second time ... To the contrary, there will be only goodness and mercy, goodness that will be revealed to all the children of Israel, wherever they are.'[77]

THE MOVEMENT WITHOUT THE REBBE

More than ten years after the death of M. M. Schneerson – for whom the movement has not wanted to nominate a successor – Habad has not collapsed, far from it. From the end of the *shive*, a day of the Messiah drew several hundred followers to Crown Heights: all the speakers assured the audience of the continuing validity of the rebbe's message. Despite their excruciating pain, the followers should continue to obey his directives and the *shlihim*, the emissaries, many of whom had come to Crown Heights for the funeral, were enjoined to pursue their activities with all their former zeal.[78] Since the rebbe's death, the number of Lubavitch institutions has increased by 30%. The movement has 3,000 *shlihim* in a total of 107 countries. Thus in 1994, it already had these emissaries in eight cities of the former Soviet Union; five years later, in 1999, they had a presence in forty-five towns. The rabbis who lead the movement have therefore managed, as we will see in relation to France (Chapter 8) to pursue the tasks undertaken on Schneerson's initiative, without in fact having a new charismatic leader.

Lubavitch constitutes a major and particularly original component of the Hasidism that has revived since 1945. Under the leadership of Menahem Mendel Schneerson, Habad developed into an open, modern-style movement that is still firmly rooted in Jewish ultra-orthodoxy and in the Hasidic tradition, with a particularly intense cult of the rebbe and an enduring belief, even beyond the rebbe's death, in his powers of miraculous intercession. Accordingly, as many as four or five hundred *kvitel*,* written requests, are placed on his tomb every day – there is a special office in Crown Heights that gathers the petitions and arranges them there. Furthermore, Habad continues with the intensive expansion of its innumerable 're-judaicizing' programmes.

Despite its indisputable successes, Lubavitch today has two serious disadvantages. The first is the still very real belief in M. M. Schneerson's 'resurrection'; the continuing controversy between those who believe in the rebbe's imminent messianic 'return' and those, seemingly in the majority, who reject this idea, has created severe conflicts, particularly in the years that followed the rebbe's death. There were splits in some yeshives, and even at the Lubavitch headquarters, the 'non-messianists' and the 'messianists' occupied their own different parts of the building. The dispute between the two factions has more or less subsided today but the 'messianists' run websites and publish journals and brochures of their own invention that refer to the rebbe as a King Messiah and they collect signs that herald his imminent advent.[79]

A persistence of these messianic impulses in subsequent years would certainly seem to incur the risk of having the movement classified as one of the heretical 'pseudo-messianisms', along with Sabbateanism. Everything will depend on the way in which the current leaders express their convictions as to an imminent messianic redemption – a reason that is also given for the rebbe's lack of a successor – and finally, more particularly, on the belief held by some in the 'resurrection' of M. M. Schneerson. Nevertheless, it seems that most of the rabbis or followers who still believe in the resurrection of M. M. Schneerson, confronted with critical pressure from other Hasidic orthodox movements, generally keep their convictions under wraps. Accordingly, this messianism, supported by some secret believers, is ultimately set to wane and disappear.[80]

However, in the long term what is equally serious for a movement that has dispersed further worldwide than ever before is the absence of a rebbe, a true spiritual father and centralizing leader; undoubtedly the cult of Menahem Mendel Schneerson still performs its unifying function because it is shared by every single Lubavitcher. However, as we will see in Chapter 8, the movement in France, for example, which is relatively large, has some specific characteristics that clearly distinguish it from Lubavitch in Crown Heights. It is true that the followers constantly refer to the rebbe's innumerable 'speeches', printed or recorded on audio or video cassettes and to his letters and his texts, which are used in determining major standpoints within the movement in Paris as in New York and elsewhere, as well as for taking the appropriate decisions that are inevitably required by the day-to-day running of his institutions in a particular place. However, these references to the disappeared leader in no way preclude differing interpretations as to these standpoints and decisions. Furthermore, Habad today has a collegial form of management, which is unusual within Hasidism. It might be possible for some of the leaders in the long term, while being part of Lubavitch, to generate new regroupings,[81] particularly on various issues, including of course the belief in Menahem Mendel Schneerson's 'resurrection', as occurs in other Hasidic movements, as we have already seen in relation to Satmar, which is not an isolated example.

It remains to be seen what will become of this highly remarkable and original movement.

6
Jerusalem

HASIDISM IN THE HOLY LAND

After the Second World War, the State of Israel became another centre of contemporary Hasidism. There are Hasidic communities more or less throughout the country, but two cities in particular have the largest number of followers: Jerusalem and Bene Beraq, which forms part of the suburbs of Tel-Aviv. These two cities have around 600,000 and 140,000 inhabitants respectively. Once again, there are no demographic data that relate specifically to the Hasidim but it can nevertheless be estimated that they account for half of approximately 128,000 ultra-orthodox Jews in Jerusalem, 64,000 people, and two thirds of the 120,000 *haredim** in Bene Beraq, 80,000 people, giving a total figure of 144,000. There are also several thousand Hasidim in some other towns, such as Ashdod, Arad, Bat Yam and Natanya, as well as a few thousand in Kefar Habad and Nachalat Har Habad, two Lubavitch villages. Furthermore, there are also some Hasidim in certain towns in the occupied territories, such as Emmanuel in the West Bank. In fact there are said to be 200,000 Hasidim, including men, women and children, in Israel.[1]

I shall attempt to present the movement in Israel by describing the largest and most influential communities in Jerusalem and Bene Beraq, in which almost 70% of the Hasidim in the country live. However, first let us examine the form in which Hasidism existed in the past in Palestine, before the creation of the State of Israel and before the Shoah.

During the 18th century, there was an influx of Jewish emigrants from Eastern Europe, including some Hasidim, into Palestine. In 1747, a brother-in-law of Baal Shem Tov settled first in Hebron and then in Jerusalem.[2] In 1777, 300 people, following two leaders of the movement that was then emerging, settled in Galilee, particularly in Safed and Tiberias. A certain amount of Hasidic immigration continued into the 19th century. There were various reasons for this: there was of course the importance of the Holy Land in the Jewish religion, with its additional mystical motivations for the Hasidim: some Kabbalists had settled in the country, particularly in Safed. Some leaders also seem to have wanted to create a Hasidic centre in the Holy Land, while fleeing the persecutions of the *misnaggedim*,* the adversaries of Hasidism, as well as the meagre living conditions that prevailed in Eastern Europe (see Chapter 1). The number of followers in the Israeli land certainly remained small, however, at just a few thousand. Nevertheless, in 1876–1877, just over 2,000 of approximately 16,000 Jewish inhabitants of Jerusalem were Hasidim. This presence, which persisted throughout the decades to come, was in no way connected with Zionist political activity;[3] as we know, the Hasidim were strongly opposed to this.[4] Nevertheless, the ultra-orthodox in Jerusalem, Safed or Tiberias constituted a core of the Jewish population that provided the Zionists, even socialists and atheists, with very useful evidence of an enduring Jewish presence in the holy city.[5]

At the beginning of the 20th century, the Hasidic movement was still opposed to the Zionist project. In Poland, the Agudath Israel* (Union of Israel) party (see Chapter 1), broadly influenced by the Hasidim, discouraged any impulse among its followers to leave for Palestine. However, after 1930 some of the members of Agudath Israel in Germany and Poland, with more realistic views, particularly confronted with the economic difficulties and the rising anti-Semitism in Eastern Europe, settled in Palestine and did not hesitate to cooperate with the Zionists.[6] These included the Ger Hasidim in particular; furthermore, at the beginning of the Second World War, the Gerer rebbe, Abraham Mordecai Alter (1866–1948), leader of this major Hasidic movement in Poland and an eminent figure in Agudath, managed to flee occupied Poland and, accompanied by his son-in-law, Yitzhak Meir Levin, he settled in the Holy Land in 1940. Levin, who was very close to his father-in-law, became leader of the Agudath Israel party in Palestine in 1947 and in 1948, as one of the thirty-seven members of the Jewish People's Council, the vast majority of whom were Zionists, he signed Israel's declaration of independence.[7]

The positive attitude thenceforth adopted by Ger and Agudath Israel towards the new State, shared by the rebbes of various other Hasidic dynasties, encouraged their followers to emigrate to Israel after the Nazi genocide. From 1948 to 1951, 685,000 Jews flocked to Israel, around half of whom were survivors of Hitler's genocide.[8] These included some Hasidim, particularly from Belz and Vishnitz, whose rebbes had themselves settled in the country either before or after its accession to independence.

Even some followers of the strongly anti-Zionist Satmarer rebbe settled in the country, particularly in Jerusalem, where they found allies who had long since settled there, particularly the ultra-orthodox in the old community of the city, who were strongly opposed to Zionism.

MEA SHEARIM AND ITS ULTRA-ORTHODOX

Hasidism is indisputably flourishing in Jerusalem: around thirty more or less well-known rebbes, along with their followers, live there today: in 1996, the city had 602,000 inhabitants, including 175,000 non-Jews, mainly Arabs.[9] At least 30% of the 427,000 Jews – 128,000 people – are *haredim*, ultra-orthodox, half of whom are Hasidim, and they are increasing in proportion within this population.[10]

The historic heart of Hasidism is in Mea Shearim ('a hundred gates' in Hebrew), a district situated near the ramparts of the ancient old town, not far from the Mandelbaum gate that was the only route between Israel and the Arab part of the city between 1948 and the Six-Day War. Mea Shearim was created from 1874 by some ultra-orthodox Jews, mainly Hasidim from Eastern Europe. After the war of independence in 1948, some *haredim** who were living in the old town, which fell under Jordanian control, settled in Mea Shearim and nearby.

The district and its immediate surrounding area have 20,000 inhabitants today.[11] These are mostly descendants of the ultra-orthodox who had already settled in Palestine before the Second World War. It is above all here that an ultra-orthodox group developed from the 1920s, called *Edah Haredit** ('community of those who fear God'), which comprised Polish and then Hungarian Hasidim – who arrived later – and non-Hasidic orthodox. This group separated during the 1930s from Agudath Israel,* which had established ties with Zionist organizations (see above). Agudath* and Edah* shared the same way of life and religiosity but Edah remained faithful to 'the traditional attitude of non-cooperation with the Zionist parties'.[12] This schism persists to this day and the district remains a form of enclave that rejects its connection with the State of Israel as far as this is possible.

The urban environment in Mea Shearim is somewhat oriental in character, and the district was created during the era of Ottoman rule in Palestine. The few thousand inhabitants of this enclave, consisting of little more than a few streets and blocks of houses, with many Talmudic academies and oratories and gates that it was possible to close until 1911,[13] still live in an area with a very particular character, with its labyrinths of narrow streets, its passageways and dead-ends, its more or less dilapidated houses and its paved courtyards. In one part of the district, Batei Ungarin, situated around a vast courtyard, there is a permanent presence of wooden sheds backing on to the houses, where during the festival of Sukkot,* just eight days at the beginning of the Jewish year, the followers take their meals and even spend the night;[14] this is a highly distinctive feature of this place.

In Mea Shearim, there are over fifty oratories, some ritual baths (*mikves**), religious schools for all levels, *haidarim*,* schools for children, *yeshives*,* Talmudic academies, *kolelim*,* schools for young married men belonging to various communities. Finally, as in other ultra-orthodox districts there are numerous shops for *kasher** food, religious articles, (silver candelabra, prayer-shawls etc.), Hasidic clothes (fur caps, frock coats etc.), religious books that are often bought by tourists with varying levels of religious observance but also by Hasidim visiting Jerusalem. In the roads and alleys of the district, some inhabitants dress in a casual way that is found nowhere else among the Hasidim. Accordingly, followers leaving the ritual bath before the Sabbath can be seen wearing the strangest outfits, long johns and vests, covered with the *talles katan*,* the garment with ritual fringes that every Jew is supposed to wear – but not necessarily in such an obvious way. In this district, Yiddish is the main language used; the modern Hebrew used in the State of Israel – certainly rather different from the sacred language, *loshn koidesh*,* that is used for prayer and Talmudic study – is avoided there as far as possible.[15]

To all appearances, the inhabitants of Mea Shearim have a fairly low standard of living. It is true that a substantial number of the inhabitants do not work and devote themselves to extensive Talmudic studies, if only to avoid military service in the Israeli army (see below). Jerusalem is the city in Israel with the greatest number of people in need: one third of the inhabitants have an income below the official poverty line. The Arab district in the city is certainly severely affected by poverty but this is also the case for the ultra-orthodox population, especially in Mea Shearim.[16]

Life in the district has been strongly influenced by the activity of a militant organization founded in 1935, 'Neture Karte',* the 'guardians of the city'; their leader, Amram Blau (1894–1974) and his partisans wanted to create an orthodox community that was totally separate from the 'Zionist' Jews. The Neture Karte* were passionately anti-Zionist from the outset, and so they remained, refusing to recognize the State of Israel and its institutions.[17] Furthermore, they are also militants who are committed to defending the ultra-traditionalist way of life in the district; they march through Mea Shearim carrying placards proclaiming that the 'daughters of Israel' should dress in a decent manner and before the beginning of the Sabbath they block the entrances to the district to prevent cars from crossing it throughout its duration. Sometimes their actions are more spectacular and more violent, with stones being thrown at transgressors. In 1953, the movement had appointed the Satmarer rebbe, Joel Teitelbaum, as its spiritual leader, who as we know was the leader and proponent of religious anti-Zionism.[18] Today the Guardians of the City seem to account for a few hundred at most of the 20,000 or so inhabitants of Mea Shearim. Furthermore, the Satmar Hasidim, despite their radical anti-Zionism, have a strong presence themselves in Jerusalem and in the town of Bene Beraq (see below). In Jerusalem, they have a Talmud Torah, a primary school for 800 children, a Talmudic academy with around 200 students and a kolel.* Satmar even has a housing estate, Satmar Shikun, for several dozen families in the Katamon district. Mea Shearim is not their principal place of settlement.

BRATZLAV: THE 'DEAD HASIDIM'

Mention should also be made of the presence of an unusual Hasidic movement, Bratzlav Hasidism, in Mea Shearim. The movement was established in Mea Shearim well before the Second World War by some followers from Ukraine and Poland and it had a yeshiva there, founded in 1937, and a synagogue. The disciples maintain a fervent cult around a rebbe who died nearly two centuries ago: Nahman of Bratzlav (1772–1811), a *tzadik** from Podolia in Ukraine, an original spiritual figure from the beginning of the Hasidic movement. Bratzlav has a few thousand followers worldwide, especially in Israel, the United States, particularly in Borough Park, and Great Britain; some have dispersed to live as hermits in various places. The great-grandson of Baal Shem Tov, Nahman was well-known for his gifts as a story-teller, his advocacy of an affective and mystical religiosity based on the Kabbala and, finally, his claim to be the only true *tzadik*,* rebbe, predestined to be the redeemer of the Jews, if not the Messiah himself.[19] These messianic attributes, which his followers still recognize in him, have led them to reject the idea of giving him a dynastic succession, which is why this movement has not had a rebbe for two centuries.[20] As we know, the Lubavitch Hasidim, who are also generally persuaded of their last rebbe's messianic attributes, also reject the idea of giving him a successor (see p. 79). The Bratzlav followers are nicknamed *toite Hasidim*,* 'dead Hasidim', because they remain faithful to this one leader, whose teachings – published from 1808 by one of his followers – they continue to study.

The synagogue in Mea Shearim possesses, near the holy Ark containing the Torah scrolls, a decorative armchair brought from Ukraine, which is said to have belonged to the *tzadik*.[21] This place of prayer attracts a remarkable variety of visitors: immigrants from the former Soviet Union, *haredim* from Israel who tirelessly visit the tombs of holy figures and young *baalei tshuve*,* American 'penitents'. The disciples meet daily to read and re-read texts by and about Nahman; in their view, the very act of opening the books that contain his writings immediately invokes his 'presence'.[22]

Like the Lubavitch Hasidim, the Bratzlav Hasidim hold annexationist views and some followers, mainly *baalei tshuve*, have settled in towns in the occupied Palestinian territories. The movement also has a *kolel**and a community in Bene Beraq, as well as in Safed; the Bratzlav centres in Jerusalem and Bene Beraq are in dispute, which is not particularly surprising given the absence of a rebbe or any other prestigious living leader to arbitrate in conflicts. Nevertheless, all the Bratzlav followers in the world today have a place of assembly in the small town of Uman in Ukraine, where Nahman had settled in 1810 shortly before his death and where he is buried. At Roshe Shoune,* New Year, in particular, the pilgrims – between 3,500 and 4,000 in 1995 – usually having arrived on charter planes, assemble in a synagogue founded in 1994 in a former factory. There is already a plan for a much larger synagogue. Around the tomb of the *tzadik*, the fervour is great, especially at two o'clock in the morning, when the second day of Roshe Shoune is approaching, because this is the moment when Nahman pleads for the lives of his followers.[23]

The followers, who believe that they are still in communion with the soul of their one and only rebbe, want to preserve and disseminate the heritage of their spiritual father: the publication of their intellectual master's teachings and other works about him is the principal activity of the Bratzlav centres. The disciples therefore carry out some missionary work;[24] their yeshive and the Bratzlav community in Borough Park have attracted some 'penitents' of both sexes, many of whom are university-educated. In 1979, the followers in New York also set up a research institute that now has a website and publishes books and cassettes. The followers of the Bratzlav movement devote considerable intellectual activity to a leader who in fact specifically rejected reason and Jewish philosophical works (such as Maimonides' *Guide for the Perplexed*) as a means of access to the faith.

TOLDOT AHRONOT, A DYNASTY OF THE DISTRICT

In addition to Bratzlav, many Hasidic communities, such as Belz, Ger and Satmar, have a presence in Mea Shearim, where they have their own oratories and schools. However, the district has its own recent Hasidic dynasty, Toldot Ahronot: its followers are generally known as the *reb Arele Hasidim*, 'the

Hasidim of reb Arele'. Arele is the familiar diminutive form of Aron Roth (1894–1947), the founder of the community, who came from Hungary to Jerusalem in the mid-1920s; at the end of a four-year stay, he returned to Europe but he then came back to Jerusalem in 1940. At his death, he had few more than thirty followers, including their families. He was succeeded by his son-in-law, Avraham Y. Kahan (1914–1997). He was a close friend of the rabbi Amram Blau, the leader of the anti-Zionist Neture Karte, and he issued some extremely strict religious decrees,[25] to which the followers have to sign their allegiance every year. For instance, unless they live too far away the disciples are supposed to participate only in the Toldot Ahronot religious services; in any case they are required to attend the community worship on the Sabbath, for which punctuality is obligatory and talking is forbidden while it is in progress. Also, married women have to shave their heads and cover them with a black scarf, not a wig; a man and his wife may not walk along together in the street – the husband walks along in front of his wife; and the men are supposed to purify themselves every morning in the ritual bath.[26] The community has its own ritual bath, *mikve*, to which only the followers from the community are admitted; it is also a place in which the men can converse and exchange news and discussion of the Torah is explicitly forbidden there.[27] The religiosity of the reb Arele followers is affective and mystical in nature; more than with other Hasidim it is characterized by long periods of prayer and spiritual meditations accompanied by intense bodily movements.[28] For the followers, daily Talmudic study is a mode of liturgical fervour rather than a quest for learning. Contact with the secular world is avoided as far as possible and the followers stay within the boundaries of Mea Shearim.

Despite this strictness, under Avraham Y. Kahan's long reign the community has grown considerably; today it has some 300 to 350 families, around 1,500 to 2,000 people.[29] They all live in the district or the neighbouring area because according to another community prescription, the followers who live in the Holy Land must live in Mea Shearim or nearby.[30] The reb Arele followers had an oratory at the very centre of the district, but the expansion of the group required a larger building, situated at Batei Ungarim. There is a yeshive there, attended by some eighty to ninety pupils. The community has a *haider*,* with 200 pupils,[31] and the girls have their own school, which provides three hours of religious instruction and two hours of teaching in secular subjects. Officially, the girls attend from the age of three years to the age of seventeen but the parents often take them out of school as early as thirteen years, so that they can help with the household tasks. The girls primarily have to learn to become *yiddishe tochter*,* Jewish daughters who will want to marry an *erlicher Yid*,* an honest, that is to say, a religious Jew.[32]

The demographic expansion of the community is probably sustained by its role in the Mea Shearim economy. The followers work in professions that do not require secular learning but generally demand some practical experience, particularly in crafts and business trades, usually associated with religious knowledge and prescriptions. They run various shops in the district and nearby; many sell and produce articles of worship, such as *guertel*,* ritual belts worn by

Hasidim during prayer,[33] and phylacteries. Some run small shops selling religious books and items. There are also the scribes who inscribe the calligraphic texts on the parchment of the phylacteries, Torah scrolls and so on, working in their own homes. Furthermore, the clientele for all these activities extends beyond the local population. Jewish tourists from all over the world know that trustworthy goods can be found in the district.

Since, as we know, many of the young men in Mea Shearim, despite often being fathers of families, continue to study the sacred texts in one of the *kolelim* of the district, particularly to avoid Israeli military service (see pp. 88–9), and the above professions are not very lucrative, it is not surprising that many families in Toldot Ahronot have difficulty making ends meet. These certainly account for a large proportion of the inhabitants of Jerusalem whose income is below the essential minimum (see above).

It is therefore not surprising that the community has a set of associations, *hevres*,* 'circles of friends', which operate rather like health insurance companies and mutual assistance societies. Other groups provide interest-free loans; one helps to finance wedding expenses and another deals with expenses connected with births. The followers, of course, are called on to contribute to financing these various associations, but other people are as well; groups of five to ten pupils from the yeshive therefore regularly do the rounds of the oratories and synagogues in Mea Shearim to collect contributions for the association for marriages.[34] All these actions of mutual aid operate in a traditional way; as we will see, the Belz and Ger Hasidim in Jerusalem also have their institutions for mutual aid and assistance but being more numerous and with some rich followers in their ranks, the charitable activities are considerably more extensive and diversified.

The movement which, in this connection, follows the rules formulated by reb Arele in a book entitled *Shulhan HaTahor*, the table of purity,[35] also requires an asceticism of its followers that is unusual in other Hasidic circles: thus, the men limit their sleep in order to devote themselves to Talmudic study and the family food is deliberately austere. Sometimes the men study during the meal, setting aside their fork and spoon from time to time and neglecting the food left on their plate.[36] Their houses are also very modestly furnished: sofas are rare and tables and chairs are basic in their construction.

Although this asceticism derives from spiritual considerations, it is nevertheless in keeping with the standard of living of the followers, who earn very little, study for long periods into adulthood and bring large numbers of children into the world. Here too, the rebbes set the example: Jacob Shmuel Kahan, the community's current leader, born in 1940, has fourteen children; his brother and rival (see below) has sixteen! Furthermore, because they do not wish to owe anything to the 'Zionists', most families do not receive either maternity benefits or allowances from the Israeli social security system.[37]

However, neither the followers' generally modest incomes nor the quests for charitable donations in Mea Shearim are enough to meet all the community needs, particularly the essential maintenance of the traditional schools, from the *haider* to the *kolel*, which naturally refuse any form of official subsidy, which would inevitably involve a certain amount of control from the Israeli authorities. How do these schools manage to survive in such conditions? It is mainly through assistance from Hasidic circles in New York and elsewhere; it is here that the Neture Karte movement plays its role, particularly through its ties with the powerful and sometimes rich Satmar Hasidim based in Brooklyn. Moreover, the Toldot Ahronot leaders, particularly the rebbe, make periodic visits to the United States – of course to Brooklyn – to collect major donations that enable their institutions to survive. In fact, there is a centuries-old tradition in Jewish circles in many towns of the Diaspora of visits paid by emissaries of Hasidic institutions and other ultra-orthodox groups from the Holy Land in search of financial aid for their educational and other institutions.

During the week, the men wear vertically striped grey-and-white kaftans like those worn by the ultra-orthodox in Jerusalem before the Second World War. Another particular custom of the 'reb Arele' is for boys to wear a *shtreimel*,* a fur cap, on the Sabbath and festival days from the age of thirteen, their *bar mitsve*,* the rite of passage that marks the adolescent's attainment of 'majority', whereas in other Hasidic communities this is worn only by married men.

Avraham Kahan died in 1997, having suffered a brain haemorrhage in 1995. From this moment, his elder son Jacob Shmuel Kahan, born in 1940, took over the running of the community and at his father's death he obtained the support of the majority of families in the movement, while another son, David Kahan, born in 1942, won the adherence of a smaller proportion of the followers. In fact, in addition to whatever private conflicts may exist between the two brothers, there are religious and political divergences. Whereas the younger brother is a Satmar disciple, sharing its staunch anti-Zionist stance, Jacob Shmuel is more of a 'moderate', who studied at a yeshive belonging to the Vishnitz Hasidic movement, which has a much more favourable attitude to the State of Israel, and seems to have an advantage in relation to an inevitable process of integration into Israeli society.[38] To take language as an example: officially, Yiddish remains the language used by the reb Arele followers, whereas the *loshn koidesh*, Biblical Hebrew, is used exclusively for prayer and study. However, many followers today use Israeli modern Hebrew, which is undoubtedly necessary since in the State of Israel, bus drivers, postal workers and government officials all speak Hebrew, but some speak it even among themselves, including at the end of the Sabbath, at *shaleshides*,* although this is a religious celebration.[39]

Furthermore, reb Arele's followers, Neture Karte and other related ultra-orthodox groups cannot completely detach themselves from surrounding Israeli society despite their rejection of Israel. There is certainly no question here, as in Brooklyn, of voting and getting involved in local politics but in any case the inhabitants of Mea Shearim in general make use of the water supply, electricity, rubbish collections, postal services and public transport that are provided for them by the municipal and State authorities. Moreover, on the vital question of the exemptions from military service, the ultra-orthodox of Mea Shearim claim the same legal advantages that are accorded to all the other ultra-religious groups. When they reach the age of military service, ultra-orthodox young men can enrol as full-time Talmudic students with a state-accredited association of yeshives. Nevertheless, some young men in Mea Shearim do not even trouble to use these procedures, for which they sometimes go to prison.[40] As for those who apply, if their files are judged to be in order, they benefit from a deferral of enlistment, on condition that they do in fact study the Torah without carrying out any paid employment for a three-year period, the legal duration of military service; this amounts in fact to an exemption.

Moreover, in Israel, women also are supposed to do military service, but the young orthodox women are likewise exempted. The ultra-orthodox, and particularly the overwhelming majority of Hasidic dynasties (with the exception of Lubavitch – see the previous chapter), consider that the religious studies of their young people are as important as military service because they safeguard the spiritual and moral defence of Israel. The anti-Zionist Hasidim of Mea Shearim certainly do not regard themselves as defenders of the country but, just like the other *haredim*, they benefit from these exemptions, which were granted as early as the war of independence in 1948–1949, and which, barring a few exceptions, have continued since then in a country that is in an almost permanent state of war.

On this matter of vital import for the followers' lives, the isolationism of the reb Arele followers is therefore only very limited. Ultimately, they benefit from the struggle between the ultra-orthodox and Hasidim connected with the Agudath Israel* party and the other ultra-religious political forces,[41] which consistently oppose any attack on the privileged status of the students in their yeshives. Despite their desire for a state of maximal retreat, reb Arele's followers participate in everyday life in Israel, sometimes to their advantage, as in relation to military service, but also sometimes more tragically to their disadvantage because despite their rejection of Zionism, there have also been some recent Palestinian attacks on Mea Shearim.

In the final analysis, in the Mea Shearim district, which is somewhat reminiscent of the ghettos, or – and why not, given its 'oriental' architecture – the mellahs of the past, most of the communities seek to preserve a way of life that if not analogous to that of the Hasidim in Eastern Europe is at least close to a situation that pre-dated the existence of the State of Israel. The Toldot Ahronot community is certainly one of those that are most strongly attached to this past.

Mea Shearim is in some sense a place of conservation, almost a museological collection, and this impression is neatly reinforced by the attraction that it exerts over its many visitors, who also contribute to supporting it by their purchases and their small donations or gifts to this or that yeshive or other institution. The self-imposed confinement of Mea Shearim is therefore distinctly limited in every domain.

MANY COMMUNITIES: BELZ, ONE OF THE LARGEST

It is not possible here to describe all the many communities, with their oratories, schools and other institutions across various parts of Jerusalem, including districts of relatively recent construction. In 1965, the Klausenburger rebbe (see

Chapter 7) sponsored the construction of a district in the north-west of the town, Kyriat Zanz. Other ultra-orthodox districts then established links with this centre; Shikun Habad (a Lubavitch settlement), Itri, Unsdorf, Mattersdorf, Ramat Yerushalaim and Ezrat Torah, which constitute an area with 3,000 ultra-orthodox families, each with five to ten children on average.[42] Since then, Jerusalem has also become the place of residence for various *admorim** – the title often used in Israel by the Hasidim themselves – these are more or less well-known or influential rebbes, such as those from Talnoye, Rachmistrivka, Karlin, Biale, Biale-Peschischa and Nadvorna. Finally, it is in the holy city that two particularly powerful rebbes, the Gerer and the Belzer rebbes, maintain their 'courts'.

I have already described the Belz Hasidic community that has flourished so strongly in Antwerp since 1945. The Belzer are the disciples of a Hasidic dynasty that emerged in Belz in Galicia at the beginning of the 19th century. The influence of this dynasty, whose followers lived mainly in Polish Galicia, also spread to Hungary because, at the beginning of the First World War, the third rebbe, Issachar Dov Rokeah (1854–1926) left Belz, which was on the battlefield between Russians and Austrians, and fled to Hungary where he remained until 1922. He had some success in Hungary and left a following there.

During the Second World War, the fourth rebbe, Aaron Rokeah (1880–1957) managed to flee Poland for Hungary in 1941. He was accompanied by a half-brother, the rabbi of Bilgoraj (a town in Poland), but he had to leave behind his wife and his seven sons and daughters, who were all assassinated by the Nazis. He lived in Budapest until 1943, then in 1944 the two brothers again managed to escape the persecutions and take refuge in Palestine. The rebbe settled in Tel-Aviv, remarried in 1947, divorced, and then married again in 1949. He encouraged the establishment of a Belz yeshive in 1952 in the Katamon district of central Jerusalem, which started with only eight students. However, shortly afterwards the community acquired 5,300 square metres of land on Agrippas Street, in the Mahane Yehuda district, relatively far from Mea Shearim and its neighbourhood. It was there that in 1954 a vast oratory, a large Talmudic academy and a hall of residence for 200 students were constructed. Students came from all over Israel, but also from Belgium, the United States, Canada and elsewhere. From then on, the rebbe divided his time between Tel-Aviv and Jerusalem, but the seat of the community was then situated in the holy city.

Following his arrival in Palestine, the rebbe moderated the traditional anti-Zionist stance of the movement; from 1949, he encouraged his followers to vote, at the elections of the first Israeli parliament, for the United Religious Front, an alliance incorporating Agudath Israel and some Zionist religious parties.

Since 1945, the dynamic resurgence of Belz Hasidism in Antwerp, New York, Montreal and elsewhere has been remarkable. As we know, at the beginning of the 1960s the Antwerp community had 74 families, more than 400 people, two thirds of whom were children; today it has trebled in size – despite the split from a group that also claims to be from Belz, it has more than 250 families (see Chapter 2)! In Montreal, Borough Park and Williamsburg, but also in London and elsewhere, the Belz communities with their oratories and yeshives have undergone a strong expansion. At the outset in Israel, the followers' economic situation was less favourable than in the above communities. The construction of the large modern yeshive on Agrippas Street was therefore largely funded by followers in Antwerp, New York and elsewhere. Moreover, the Belzer, unlike the anti-Zionist communities in Mea Shearim, have not hesitated to accept, immediately following the founding of the State of Israel, subsidies and other public funds, particularly for their schools.

In any case, the educational network developed and with it the number of adherents also continued to grow; families who did not necessarily adhere to Belz Hasidism at the outset found that they were able to educate their children in favourable conditions in its scholastic institutions and joined the movement as a consequence. It should be noted that the language of instruction in the Belz schools is Yiddish at every level, but modern Hebrew is also taught there for one hour a day.

BELZER REBBE AT THE AGE OF SEVENTEEN

Reb Aaron died in 1957 at the age of 79 years. He had no descendants and the elders of the movement therefore designated his nephew, Issachar Dov, more informally known as Berele, as his successor. He was the son of Aaron's half-brother, the rabbi of Bilgoraj, and was born in Tel-Aviv in 1948; he was therefore only nine years old when the rebbe died and was unable to assume his role for many years. Under the supervision of the elders and the personal guidance of two rabbis from the community, Berele received a special education. While waiting to have a new *admor** to venerate, the followers maintained the cult of the deceased rebbe, particularly by visiting his tomb at the cemetery at Mount Menuchot in Jerusalem. Thus, on the anniversary of his death, on the 21st day of the Hebrew month Av, in August, thousands of followers from all over the world made their way there as pilgrims. Gathered around his imposing funeral monument,[43] they recited psalms, *tilem*,* and placed *kvitel*,* notes with requests for intercession, there in a ceremony that continues to this day.

In 1965, at the age of sixteen years, Berele married Sarah, who was eighteen years old, the daughter of the Vishnitzer rebbe, the leader of an influential Hasidic movement established in Bene Beraq (see Chapter 7). It was in this town that a grand wedding ceremony was held, attended by thousands of people.[44] This matrimonial alliance with a powerful dynasty reinforced the rather weak position of the future rebbe, particularly confronted with the other Hasidic leaders, who were mainly very advanced in age, but also with certain Belzer, especially the oldest, who had known and venerated the previous rebbe and who displayed a certain disdain for the young man. Berele continued for a while with his studies in Bene Beraq and one year later at the decision of the elders of the movement, he became the fifth Belzer rebbe, at the age of seventeen years, an exceptionally early age for this responsibility. He was also the first rebbe to have been born a citizen of the State of Israel.

While demonstrating his fidelity to the traditions and customs of the dynasty, the new rebbe quickly proved to be energetic and dynamic and, over the years, he managed to establish an important position for Belz within the Hasidic movement. Moreover, in contrast to the older opponents, the young generation of Hasidim venerate him unreservedly. Belz also has a presence elsewhere in Israel, particularly in Tel-Aviv and Haifa, somewhat secular cities, and also in Ashdod, where the community was created only in 1979, and of course in Bene Beraq. In all the towns where it has a presence, the movement has a set of schools for boys and girls that educate 6,000 children in total. The budget for these schools exceeds $20,000,000 per annum.[45]

COMMUNITY EXPANSION AND MUTUAL ASSISTANCE

In Jerusalem, the community has expanded considerably; accordingly, in 1977 the foundation stone was laid for a vast housing project, a new estate called Kiryat Belz, to which 400 families of followers, at least 2,000 people, moved to live in a suburban environment. Of course, there are already oratories and schools there; the rebbe travels there to conduct religious services and other ambitious projects have been achieved: a house for the rebbe, community centres, schools, a shopping centre and a large Talmudic academy; a vast synagogue that can accommodate 5,000 followers was also recently completed. This housing estate officially constitutes a 'world centre' of Belz Hasidism and, as such, it has obtained large State subsidies since 1985.[46]

Study programmes have also been created relatively recently in various towns in the land for the *baalei tshuve*, the 'penitents', particularly for the Russian immigrants.[47] Have the Lubavitch missionary ambitions perhaps set an example for Belz? As we already know, the Belzer are not the only Hasidim in Israel to have adopted measures of this kind.

Belz has many relatively impecunious followers, particularly – as in other Hasidic communities – among large families, sometimes with eight or more children, and young couples where the husband is pursuing Talmudic studies at the *kolel* after marriage and the schoolteachers and other religious officials, who are often low-paid. The movement has therefore set up a network of institutions for community mutual aid that meet many needs: for example, one of them provides financial assistance to young couples for buying an apartment; another allocates financial subsidies for *bar mitsve* celebrations and weddings; yet another contributes to funding medical expenses.

Other Hasidic movements, such as the Gerer (see below), also have complex networks of mutual assistance associations. Furthermore, the Hasidic districts generally have at least one 'discount' price supermarket, which is accessed by presenting cards that are issued to large families, with four or more children. These are generally warehouses with limited stock but well supplied with various goods, particularly food labelled kasher by the Hasidic authorities; there is also clothing and even furniture there, all sold at cost price. The start-up capital for these establishments comes from legacies or a charitable founder; the shop then has to become self-financing as a non-profit-making enterprise.[48] The Hasidic communities, including Belz, also use their community centres to enable impecunious Hasidim to celebrate weddings, circumcisions and *bar mitsves* at a moderate cost.

Like the other communities, the Belz Hasidim have many other methods of helping disadvantaged families, in particular a system of interest-free loans provided by non-profit-making foundations administered by volunteers, called *gemahim*,* an abbreviation of *gemilut hasadim*, literally 'giving favours, "goodwill"'. Furthermore, the Hasidim also have their own informal system for buying and selling second-hand goods. Like other Hasidic groups, Belz has set up a form of cooperative economy that enables them to alleviate the financial difficulties that many of them experience. In the Belz communities, as in all the Hasidic communities, there is also a complete system of permanent mutual assistance, which also often operates during daily religious services in the oratories – with collections for specific purposes, to help a particular family in difficulty following illness, to provide funds to impoverished young girls when they are getting married and so on.

BELZ AND POLITICS

Admittedly, all these methods combined are not enough to provide decent living conditions and the wide range of State subsidies and funds is also very valuable. This makes it important for Belz, as for the majority of the Hasidic communities in Israel, apart from the minority of hard-liners in Mea Shearim, to participate in political life and if possible in the governmental, parliamentary and municipal agencies and various institutions that enable them to obtain various kinds of allowances.

Moreover, the Belzer have gradually asserted themselves as a political force over the years. It should not be forgotten that Issachar Dov, born in 1948, was a very young member of the somewhat gerontocratic learned assembly of Hasidic ultra-orthodox leaders and, even today, although he is over 50 years old, he remains one of the youngest among them.

Until the 1970s, Belz and its followers were accustomed to voting for the ultra-orthodox Agudath party; nevertheless, the movement continued to belong to the anti-Zionist Edah Charedit* association (see p. 83 above). However, in around 1980, the rebbe asked Edah to recognize the manifest expansion of his communities and to appoint a Belz figure to the rabbinical court, *bet din*,* of this association but this request was rejected. The rebbe therefore left Edah* in 1980, created his own rabbinical court and set up his own organization for an ultra-strict ritual slaughter, *glatt kasher*.* This latter initiative provided jobs for Belzer as ritual slaughterers, *kashrut** supervisors and butchers, as well as substantial incomes from taxes levied on meat and so on.

Following this break with Edah,* Belz approached the Agudath Israel party and Issachar Dov was made a member of its ruling council, Moetzet Gedolei Hatorah,* the Council of Torah Greats.[49] However, the honeymoon period between Agudath and Belz was short-lived. In fact, the Belz *admor* took the view that his movement did not receive a fair share of the State subsidies granted to Hasidic institutions; moreover, Belz did not succeed in calling elections to nominate the members of the central committee of Agudath Israel, which was strongly dominated by the Gerer rebbe's partisans.[50] Finally, the party had not allocated them a favourable enough position on its candidates' list to enable them to elect a representative to the Knesset, the Israeli parliament.[51] On the eve of the parliamentary elections of 1988, the Belzer rebbe joined forces with the rabbi Eliezer Schach (1898–2001), the spiritual leader of the non-Hasidic orthodox, based in Bene Beraq, to found a new party, Degel Hatorah,* 'the flag of the Torah'. This time, along with a dozen or so leaders of major yeshives and non-Hasidic rabbinical judges, Issachar Dov became the only rebbe within the Council of Greats of the new party. Both Schach and the *admor* were 'doves' on the question of the occupied territories: they regarded the fate of these territories as less important than the survival of the Jewish people and the religious tradition.

Furthermore, back in 1981, the rebbe had strongly criticized the extremist policies of the Begin government and he had expressed support in around 1995 for the peace process with the Palestinians and the Oslo Accords.[52] In an address in 1996, the rebbe strongly condemned Benjamin Netanyahu's government for acts of bloody repression against the Palestinians. He explicitly stated that living by the sword was a privilege accorded to the descendants of Esau rather than the sons of Israel. The spokesman for the Belz Hasidim recalled on this occasion that the *admor* supported the peace process instigated the previous year and that this viewpoint conformed to the haredi tradition of not provoking the 'Gentiles'.[53] By contrast, the Gerer rebbe and, as we have seen, the Lubavitcher are 'hawks' on this question.

However, at subsequent elections – in 1992 and 1999 – Agudath and Degel Hatorah formed mainly for electoral purposes an alliance called 'United Torah Judaism'. In 2001, the Councils of Greats of Agudath and Degel Hatorah, united once again, called on their electors to vote for Ariel Sharon, the leader of Likud, the right-wing Israeli party, as Prime Minister, a figure whose deeply intransigent political stance towards relations with the Palestinians is well-known. The Belzer rebbe therefore at least tacitly approved this standpoint. Sharon was elected Prime Minister and this led to an agreement with the government that provided the ultra-orthodox with deputy ministerial posts for housing and the educational sector in charge of religious schools; also, some representatives from the coalition were to oversee the financial committee of the Knesset.[54] For the ultra-orthodox, including the Belz Hasidim, the possibility of providing their followers and their institutions with financial, educational and other advantages certainly played a part in this turnaround.

BELZ, A SUCCESSFUL MOVEMENT

In just over a half-century, Belz has become a major Hasidic movement in Israel; it is also strongly established in the Diaspora, particularly in Antwerp, but also in Williamsburg, Borough Park and elsewhere. Issachar Dov Rokeah, who initially faced a difficult task given his youth, has managed to lead a vigorous congregation in the country and abroad. He has also succeeded in making his mark in the political constellation of the *haredim*, the ultra-orthodox Israelis, and Belz plays an active part in the country's political system. Although he is ultra-orthodox, the rebbe is 'tolerant', or better put 'indifferent', towards the non-religious Jews; in fact, Belz in Israel as elsewhere lives and operates among other Jews who are non-religious. Many of the Belzer practise 'profane' professions among secular or only moderately religious Jews and at least some of them live in predominantly secular towns such as Tel-Aviv, where Belz runs a Talmud Torah,* a yeshive for novices and even a *kolel*, all under the direction of an uncle of the rebbe. The Belzer are certainly much more numerous in Bene Beraq, an ultra-orthodox town near Tel-Aviv, where they have five places of prayer.

However, particularly since the end of the Second World War, Belz has been able to take advantage of support and solidarity from more or less religious Jews, some of whom came from their own schools before the war. This support is given primarily in the form of financial aid, such as for their schools or for building or renovating their places of prayer. Belz certainly adheres to an extreme religiosity and to the traditions of the movement that were practised in the past in Galicia, but it therefore displays a certain indifference towards the 'deviant' behaviours of other Jews, provided only that these do not jeopardize their own way of life.[55] We already know that in this sense there is a wide variation in the behaviour of the various Hasidic movements: Satmar operates a form of withdrawal and (albeit relative) isolation, whereas Lubavitch opts on the contrary for a policy of 'love' expressed in missionary activity towards the other Jews. In any case, the strategy of the Belzer has turned out to be 'profitable' in both senses of the word.

GER, A MAJOR HASIDIC MOVEMENT

I mentioned Ger at the beginning of this chapter in relation to its rebbe's role in the initial expansion of Hasidism in the emerging State of Israel, and also within the Agudath, the ultra-orthodox political party, which signed the country's declaration of independence.

Just before the Second World War, Ger was the largest Hasidic movement in the world, reportedly with 100,000 disciples, mainly in Poland. Many of them perished in the Shoah but Ger rose from its ashes to become one of the major Hasidic movements in Israel today; it claims the allegiance of 4,000 families,[56] which represents at least 20,000 people including children. Around 8,000 followers (many of whom do not customarily live in the holy city) attend its religious services in Jerusalem for the major festivals of New Year and the Day of Atonement, at the beginning of the Jewish year. The movement is currently constructing a new oratory in Jerusalem – at a cost of $16,000,000 – that will be able to receive even more people. From the arrival of Abraham Mordecai Alter, then the Gerer rebbe, in Palestine in 1940, it was in the holy city that the dynasty was established; since 1948, the rebbe's house and also the Ger synagogue have been in the central district of Gueula, a place of assembly for all the followers in Israel and elsewhere. Ger in Jerusalem, however, constitutes only a part of the movement in the country. There are many disciples in Bene

Beraq; there is also a housing estate on the periphery of Tel-Aviv, but situated near Bene Beraq, with 400 Ger families. Finally, there are also Ger communities in Ashdod, a port in the south of the country, in Arad in Neguev and in Hatzor Haguelilit in Galilee.

A RESOLUTE DYNASTY

The Ger dynasty was founded by Isaac Meir Rothenburg Alter (1799–1866). A disciple of various well-known *tzadikim*,* he became a prestigious rebbe himself from 1859, settling first in Warsaw and then in Ger, Gora Kalwaria in Polish, thirty kilometres from the Polish capital. This small town, with just over 6,000 inhabitants, 50% of whom were Jewish, was the citadel of the movement until the Second World War. Rothenburg Alter was the author of *Chiddushei ha-Rim*, 'news from Rim' (an acronym formed from his initials), a six-volume collection of commentaries that were published in 1875 after his death, which have since been the reference work in Hasidic yeshives for the dialectics, *pilpul*,* of Talmudic commentary. In fact, for this influential rebbe, Talmudic study was an essential component of Hasidic piety and this conception spread throughout Polish Hasidism at that period.[57] This is a measure of how far Hasidism had evolved over a century from a fundamentally affective religiosity towards a practice much more based on reasoning, akin to that of their adversaries, the *misnaggedim*.

Isaac Meir demonstrated strong political commitment as an implacable champion of the traditional Jewish way of life. He was at the forefront of the opposition to the government regulations that sought to impose a more modern form of dress on Jews, for which he spent a short period in prison in 1851. The regulations were repealed shortly afterwards.[58] He also led a largely successful campaign against the State's requirement, supported by the *maskilim*,* adherents of the Jewish Enlightenment movement, for the schoolmasters, *melamdim*,* in the traditional schools to take official examinations.[59] Religious intransigence combined with political involvement has characterized the activities of this dynasty ever since.

At Isaac Meir's death in 1866, his grandson, Yehudah Leib Alter (1847–1904), who was also known as Sfas Emet, succeeded him. Under his influence, Polish Hasidism rejected Zionism. Yehudah Leib was succeeded by his eldest son, Abraham Mordecai Alter (1866–1948), also called Imre Emes. An orderly man, he imposed the recitation of morning prayers at the prescribed times, which is sometimes still far from being the practice today among other Hasidim. He was a skilful organizer, who established a structured framework for the movement. He was one of the founders of Agudath Israel in 1912. The Gerer rebbe, who shared Agudath's hostility to Zionist goals, nevertheless visited the Holy Land on several occasions from 1921. Aware of the intense poverty that prevailed among the Jews in Poland after the First World War,[60] he did not discourage his followers from settling there, which some of them did from the mid-1920s. He supported housing projects, such as the founding of the town of Bene Beraq from 1924. The Ger Hasidim who emigrated to Palestine created communities that became centres of the movement's revival after the Second World War.

In 1936–1937, the rebbe spent eight months in Palestine and he returned only reluctantly to Poland in order not to desert his many followers in this land.[61] Three years later, the German invasion in September 1939 sealed the tragic fate of Polish Judaism: the overwhelming majority of Ger Hasidim and their families were assassinated by the Germans.

However, the rebbe and his family, through the intervention in the United States of a committee of rabbis, supported by some eminent secular figures, managed to arrange for him, his wife, and his children and sons-in-law to leave Poland and settle in Palestine. We know that in 1948 his son-in-law, the rabbi Isaac Meir Levin, was going to support Israel's declaration of independence. However, a few weeks after the creation of the State of Israel, on 6 June 1948, Abraham Mordecai Alter died. His third son, Israel Alter (1895–1977) became the dynasty's fourth rebbe and it is to him that the arduous task of developing the movement fell. Reputed to have a very quick mind, he welcomed into his home, twice a day, countless visitors of every kind – religious and less religious – who came to him for advice on all sorts of questions. However, in accordance with Ger tradition women were not admitted into his presence; also, the rebbe did not accept small donations, *pidyen*,* at the submission of *kvitel* during these visits, which did not prevent followers and sympathizers from contributing frequently and generously to the maintenance of many institutions – places of prayer, yeshives and other educational institutions of the movement.

As a member of the Council of Torah Greats in the Agudath party, Israel Alter played an active role in this party, and was in the government from 1949 to 1952. Moreover, his son-in-law Isaac Meir Levin was its minister for social affairs; both the spiritual interests of the ultra-religious and the material and financial support for their educational and other institutions were therefore furthered by an eminent Ger figure at the highest level. Furthermore, Levin did not hesitate to declare that the State of Israel had been established through manifest miracles and that the hand of divine Providence was guiding its path. Ger had therefore entirely abandoned the Hasidic anti-Zionism of the past and these declarations attracted the censure of Neture Karte and Edah Haredit in Mea Shearim.[62]

After his death, on 2 February 1977, Israel Alter, who had lost his only son in the Shoah, was replaced by his brother Simhah Bunem Alter (1898–1992), until then a renowned Talmudic scholar but also a businessman who had amassed a fortune in property. It was at the request of a delegation of leading figures from the movement that he agreed, at the age of nearly 80 years, to become the fifth Gerer rebbe. Despite his age, he proved to be a good administrator and he made a great contribution to the movement's geographical expansion in Israel, to Arad, Ashdod and the outskirts of Tel-Aviv.

After seven years of illness, which prevented him from carrying out many of his functions, the rebbe died in July 1992. The Ger elders designated as the sixth Gerer rebbe his half-brother, Pinhas Menahem Alter (1926–1996), the director of the movement's largest yeshive* in Jerusalem. This rebbe was one of the most political; already a member of the Agudath* Council of Torah Greats in the previous rebbe's lifetime, he was its man of steel and its leading personality. Alter also contributed frequently to *Hamodia*, the party's journal, expressing very uncompromising views. He fiercely condemned the assassination of Yitzhak Rabin in 1995, but he was also opposed to the 1993 Oslo Accords. He specifically asserted that 'Just as a *Sefer Torah** [the Torah scrolls] becomes invalid if one letter is missing, so it is wrong to deprive the Holy Land of any of its territories.'[63] Pinhas M. Alter reigned for only a few years until his death in 1996. He was succeeded by his son Jacob Arie Alter, born in Poland in 1939, who was also a rich property dealer.

TRADITIONALISM WITHOUT CONFINEMENT

As a Hasidic movement, Ger is particularly attached to maintaining the Hasidic traditions of the past. The Gerer celebrate the Friday evening *tish halten*,* the mystical meal with the distribution of the *shrayim*,* the remainders of the dishes begun by the rebbe, with great intensity, with the audience thronging and jostling around the banquet table, particularly when the rebbe is speaking.[64] The submission of *kvitel*, with requests for miraculous intervention, forms part of the ritual of the audience surrounding the rebbe. The Gerer traditionally wear a *spodek*,* a tall and narrow fur cap, unlike the *shtreimel*, the flat hat worn by other Hasidim. The veneration and cult of the rebbe are also strongly apparent among the followers.

Mainly at the instigation of the fourth rebbe, Israel Alter, Ger demonstrates great prudery in sexual matters. The movement's rabbis remind the young married men that sexual intercourse once a week is enough and that they do not have to prolong the sexual act for the pleasure of their spouses ... which in no way prevents the Gerer from raising large families.[65] As with the reb Arele Hasidim, husband and wife may not walk side by side in the street, and in the discount supermarkets run by the Gerer there are separate opening times for men and women. Moreover, the women, especially the youngest, are not supposed to work for non-*haredim* employers; their only permitted activities are religious instruction, participation in family life and the education of young children, or office work carried out at home.[66]

Furthermore, the modern media, particularly television and video, are strongly condemned, although use of the internet and email is permitted.[67] It is true that, although they are consciously ultra-traditionalist, at the same time the Gerer often have secular professions – two of their recent rebbes have been successful businessmen – and for these disciples the internet has become a necessity. In Israel, the Gerer are stereotyped as the 'Polish traders' because they have a reputation as practically minded people with a good position in the local economy.[68] They therefore combine traditionalism with a strong involvement in the secular world, particularly in the economic but also, as we shall see, in the political sphere.

From 1974, Ger more or less forced young couples among their followers to settle in new housing estates, inhabited almost exclusively by the movement's disciples, situated in various towns in Israel, particularly in Ashdod, on the coast, in Hatzor Haguelilit in Galilee and in Arad in Judea. This was part of a housing development programme that, with the support of the Agudath Israel party, had obtained mortgages from a state source at advantageous rates. The rebbe Israel Alter was seeking to provide lower-cost housing for young married people who were often impecunious because the husbands were generally still studying at the *kolel* and so on. They were individually ordered to live there for at least five years, away from Bene Beraq, Jerusalem and the centre of Tel-Aviv, where housing was expensive. Nevertheless, many 'exiles' considered this relegation as a test to be endured temporarily.[69]

Furthermore, to help the disadvantaged families, the Gerer have seven discount supermarkets across the country. As we already know, they have different opening times for men and women; the supermarkets in the 'secular' towns are open to 'correctly dressed' non-orthodox customers.

Moreover, the fifth rebbe, Simhah Bunem Alter, Israel Alter's successor, imposed some moderation on the richest followers. He ordered that the weddings, *bar mitsves* and so on – often an occasion of sumptuous festivities for Hasidim – should be conducted in a more modest way and that the young married people should live in smaller flats, including in the above-mentioned new housing estates.

MISSIONARY WORK

With the housing estates in Ashdod and elsewhere, Ger had created some centres of orthodoxy, including oratories and yeshives, at the very heart of populations that were not highly religious.[70] Moreover, the Gerer in these towns have since engaged in missionary activity. In association with some other Hasidim,[71] from 1997 they created a set of schools, for boys and for girls, called *Nesivos Moshe*, intended mainly for children from non-religious families. More secular subjects are taught there than in the traditional schools themselves and the teachers show relative leniency towards behaviour at home that is not very religious. The main objective is to influence the children, and through them the parents, to make them into *baalei tshuve*, penitents. In 2001, there were twenty of these schools, with 2,500 pupils; a remarkable success in four years. This scholastic system is mainly financed through donations, which come above all from America.[72] Another programme of this kind, called Shuvu, 'repent', particularly targets the children of recent Russian emigrants. In total, Nesivos Moshe and Shuvu educated 7,000 children in 42 schools and 72 nursery schools in 2001.[73] Reportedly around 1,000 people today are working for the various institutions of this kind and many volunteers have travelled the country to encourage parents to have confidence in them. Furthermore, Agudath, the party mainly controlled by Ger, now prioritizes missionary work and considers the activities for young people as one of its most effective methods.[74]

Ger and other Hasidic movements therefore concur, albeit less ostentatiously, with the Lubavitch-style proselytism (see previous chapter), which certainly also exists in many Israeli towns. Furthermore, these schools also provide vital openings and (modest) incomes for the teachers, often wives of students at the *kolel*, where studies provide an opportune reason to avoid military service ...

Moreover, political considerations are not alien to the missionary involvement for, of course, if Jews are brought back to the path of righteousness, in time, voters are also gained for the ultra-orthodox parties ...[75]

GER AND POLITICS

As we already know, since the beginnings of the dynasty in Eastern Europe the Ger rebbes have manifested a strong political commitment and this continues today in Israel, particularly through the intervention of the Agudath Israel party.

Ger is the predominant faction, particularly on the Agudath Council of Torah Greats, and it holds the reins of its administration and its journal, *Hamodia*.[76] The Gerer rebbes and the party are strong champions of the entire Hasidic and ultra-religious Ashkenazi* world, particularly in the domain of housing and education. To this end, the followers take an active part in the election of representatives from Agudath Israel, since 1992 actively involved with Degel Hatorah in the United Torah Judaism coalition. As we know, the ultra-orthodox have participated in or supported cabinet coalitions since 1948, and this was still the case for United Torah Judaism in the first Sharon government, which was in power from 2001 to the end of 2002. This ultra-religious coalition, which brings together mainly Ashkenazi Jews, confronted with the Sephardic ultra-orthodox party Shas,* does not set out, in principle, to hold ministerial portfolios as such, but it has obtained deputy ministerial posts for housing and education in this government and finally chairmanships of influential parliamentary bodies, such as the finance committee. These are key posts for obtaining advantages and subsidies that enable them to tackle the housing needs of Hasidic families and their many children, as well as for the schools and many other ultra-orthodox institutions. After recent general elections, at the beginning of 2003, United Torah Judaism[77] was voted out of the second Sharon government in favour of the secular party Shinui, which is strongly opposed to the ultra-orthodox, and this new situation, carries the risk of negative consequences for the Gerer and the *haredim* in general, but since January 2005, the orthodox coalition has once again been part of the government with two deputy ministers in Sharon's third administration.

Ger and Agudath Israel are also strongly opposed to military service for young Hasidim who, regardless of their talents, continue to study for the requisite years in the yeshives in order to avoid it (see pp. 88–9 above). Furthermore, protests and pressure from a wide Israeli public repeatedly raise the issue of conscription for the ultra-orthodox. Thus, again recently, in July 2002, the Israeli parliament, with support from the ultra-religious parties, approved a law that, despite some restrictive amendments, maintains the exemptions for ultra-orthodox students.[78]

Moreover, Ger and Agudath belong in the ranks of the 'hawks' on the question of the occupied territories, on the right to settle wherever they choose in the Holy Land, on the danger in which the peace initiatives before the second Intifada (2001) placed the country and so on. Accordingly, for them the small town of Emmanuel (3,614 people), founded in 1981 in the heart of the occupied territories, and there are many others, is an entirely legitimate settlement, supported by the Gerer rebbes. Whereas the rabbi Schach, spiritual leader of the non-Hasidic orthodox, had strongly opposed the settlement of the haredim in this town, Pinhas Menahem Alter, a major Ger figure at the time and later the sixth rebbe of the movement, implicitly assented to the creation of this town by declaring in 1981: 'The Torah doesn't say anything about Green Lines [the internationally recognized boundaries that divide the State of Israel from the occupied zones]'.[79]

A major Hasidic movement in Israel, Ger is therefore deeply rooted in Israeli political society, just as Belz is, as are many minor Hasidic groups that necessarily leave the political initiative to the more powerful movements ... along with most of the useful official posts. Apart from the reb Arele group and the Satmarer in Mea Shearim, the Hasidim in Jerusalem are active contributors to the life of the holy city from every viewpoint – political and economic as well as religious. We also know that the ultra-orthodox proportion of the Jerusalem population is rising and in recent years there has been an increasing possibility of having an ultra-orthodox mayor there. At the beginning of June 2003, this was achieved: with 52% of the votes, the rabbi Uri Lupolianski, aged 51 years, father of twelve children, founder of a large charitable association, Yad Sarah (see next chapter), supported by Agudath and Degel Hatorah, was elected mayor of the holy city. Today, therefore, Jerusalem and Bene Beraq, the second Hasidic citadel in Israel, are run by *haredim* who, if not Hasidim themselves, at least have the vital support of the principal Hasidic movements and are therefore in a position of strength.

7
Bene Beraq and Other Locations

BENE BERAQ, ULTRA-ORTHODOX CITADEL

Whereas Jerusalem, despite its tens of thousands of ultra-orthodox of every kind, remains a city in which they form a minority, Bene Beraq, with approximately 145,000 inhabitants, Israel's tenth largest city by head of population,[1] is a true citadel of the 'men in black', who represent 85% of its residents – around 120,000 men, women and children. The only exception to this general situation is a fairly secular district, Pardes Katz. No other town in the world, apart from small places such as Kiryas Joel in the New York region (see Chapter 3), or certain settlements today in the Palestinian territories or those created by Habad (see pp. 115–16), has such a large proportion of ultra-orthodox inhabitants. Furthermore, contemporary Bene Beraq is situated a few kilometres away from the ancient Bene Beraq of Biblical times, which was eight kilometres east of the port of Jaffa (now incorporated in southern Tel-Aviv).

However, religious life in Bene Beraq is not exclusively Hasidic. There are also many *misnaggedim*,* orthodox, often of Russian or Lithuanian origin, who were formerly adversaries of Hasidism – and they often remain opposed to it today – all led until his recent death by the rabbi Eliezer Menachem Schach, as well as a minority of Sephardic orthodox Jews.[2] Bene Beraq is one of the ten towns that belong to the suburbs of Tel-Aviv, which has 1,140,000 inhabitants,[3] 353,000 of whom are in Tel-Aviv itself. Bene Beraq, situated approximately five kilometres from its centre, has strong economic links with Tel-Aviv and many of its residents travel there to work every day.

In 1922, the rabbi Isaac Gerstenkorn (1891–1962), from Poland, visited the Holy Land and in conjunction with an association that wanted to create a religious settlement in Palestine, he bought a plot of land of 1,044 dunams or around 104 hectares,[4] which belonged to an Arab village in the Tel-Aviv area. It is there that Bene Beraq was founded in 1924; led by the rabbi Isaac Gerstenkorn around thirty ultra-orthodox families from Warsaw settled there in an initiative supported by the Ger *rebbe**. In 1950, the year in which Bene Beraq officially attained the status of an independent township, it occupied 7,100 dunams, or 710 hectares. Gerstenkorn chaired the committees that ran the town from 1924; he was also its mayor from 1950 until his death. He worked persistently to develop the town, travelling to the United States and South Africa to obtain financial aid because at the beginning, between 1924 and 1928, Bene Beraq had experienced many difficulties following a strong economic downturn in Palestine.

At Gerstenkorn's invitation, the ultra-orthodox rabbi Joseph Tzvi Kalish (1885–1957) became the new town's spiritual leader; he managed to gain the support of Hasidim from all the dynastic allegiances. After Gerstenkorn, a Ger Hasid,* Reuben Aharonowitz (1903–1975) became mayor. The administrative and political management therefore remained ultra-orthodox and specifically Hasidic. In 1937, the town had 4,000 inhabitants. The population, which was ultra-orthodox – except in the north of the town, in the Pardes Katz district, created under the auspices of Histadrut, a major secular socialist trade union organization – grew exponentially. In 1948, there were 8,800 inhabitants; in 1955 there were 25,000; and in 1968 it was the eight largest town in the country, with 64,700 inhabitants; currently it has nearly 145,000. This remarkable dynamism is due to the contribution that Tel-Aviv makes to its development by providing it with many jobs; also, Bene Beraq has developed some industry of its own. Some food companies and a cigarette factory were established in Bene Beraq; in 1969, the town had 150 factories and many workshops that employed 8,000 workers. Bene Beraq is surrounded by some fairly secular towns (Ramat Gan, Petah Tiqwa, Givatayim).

Now an ultra-orthodox bastion, Bene Beraq has hundreds of oratories, synagogues and *yeshives** of all kinds and affiliations. It is one of the very few towns in Israel in which almost all the roads are closed to traffic on the Sabbath and festival days. The major roads are named after the great sages and scholars of ancient times, such as the rabbi Akiva (45–135) and Yochanan Ben Zakkai (1st century), but also more recent famous figures such as Noam Elimelech – this is Elimelech of Lyzhansk (1717–1787), disciple of the *maggid** Dov Baer of Mezhirech, a major instigator of the cult of the *tzadik** – or figures such as Sfas Emes (1847–1904), the second Ger rebbe's pen name, or Chazon Ish, the name by which a great Talmudic scholar, Avraham Karelitz (1878–1953), who lived in Bene Beraq, is known.

There is little available land in Bene Beraq and the three- and four-storey buildings, cubic in shape, with grey facades, are extremely closely packed together. Many of the facades are chipped and the roads are full of potholes. It is true that the town has a long history of problematic municipal administrations characterized by a great deal of waste. Many yeshives never paid their electricity bills and cars could be parked anywhere, with no fear of the slightest fine. Large-scale corruption, lobbying and nepotism were also prevalent there. The municipal deficit had rapidly deepened, while nearly half of the population was not paying any community taxes. The municipal services, particularly the collection of household waste, had greatly deteriorated and the roads and pavements were in very bad condition. The confrontations over obtaining favours, jobs, funds and power, mainly between the rabbi Schach's disciples and the Gerer rebbe's followers, finally led to the town council being discredited.

In June 1995, having assessed the local conditions, the minister of the interior deposed the mayor and he nominated an official[5] to be provisionally put in charge of running the town. At the beginning of 1998, the rabbi Mordecai Karelitz was elected as mayor with 87% of the votes cast; aged 46 years, he was close to the rabbi Schach, and was put forward by a coalition of Degel Hatorah* and Agudath Israel,* which has seventeen of the twenty-five seats on the town council. These town councillors, some of whom are businessmen, teachers and social workers, all Israeli-born,[6] have put an end to the disorder of the past and since their election the deficit in the municipal budget has been reduced by two thirds.[7] The town has been cleaned up and the police have begun to record the offences of reckless drivers – Bene Beraq, with a large number of children and elderly people, had until then had the largest number of accidents involving pedestrians of any town in Israel. On a further sensitive matter, the new town council put an end to the illegal construction of buildings in protected zones or in contravention of the strict safety regulations.[8] These illegal practices were certainly fostered by extreme poverty in relation to housing and the very high housing costs. Also, residential buildings were built no more than six storeys high, because the law requires taller buildings than this to have lifts, which the Haredim do not use on the Sabbath and most of the Jewish festivals.

The presence of many impoverished yeshive students – particularly those who reject military service – as well as the many large families (see below), all of whom pay very few taxes, undoubtedly contribute to making the budgetary balance of the town extremely unstable. However, the flagrant abuses of the past seem to have come to an end.

Of course, there are many strictly *kasher** food shops, traders in religious goods and so on in Bene Beraq but since 1995 there has also been a large supermarket called Shefa Mehadrin, which is part of Co-Op Blue Square, a supermarket chain that is present elsewhere in Israel, but which is entirely aimed at ultra-religious buyers here. At each entrance, a uniformed guard checks that the visitors are correctly dressed and he even has a supply of long jackets and scarves for shoppers who have arrived in shorts and tee-shirts.[9] Inside the plain interior, there is a wide range of goods, including religious items (skull-caps, prayer-shawls etc.) and strictly kasher food, all at moderate prices, mainly as a result of the savings on the presentation of the merchandise. At the meat counter, the purchaser, as a follower of a particular rebbe, is able for example to buy veal labelled 'rabbi Landau' or 'rabbi Rubin' and so on, sponsored by various religious authorities.

As in Mea Shearim there are signs cautioning women against wearing immodest clothing. As in Williamsburg, the shopkeepers – particularly in kasher food – advertise on their shop fronts their connection with this or that rabbi or religious movement. Moreover, the local pizza-maker only does home delivery, to prevent groups of adolescents of both sexes standing around in front of his stall. The newspaper stands do not stock the secular press and the roads are closed to traffic during the Sabbath and festival days (except in the non-religious district of Pardes Katz). The television aerials that are such a common sight elsewhere are absent from the houses and buildings of orthodox Bene Beraq.

Moreover, and this is a problem that is specific to an ultra-orthodox town, Bene Beraq has recently introduced a new computer-operated water supply system, which makes it independent of the national network that is run by Jewish workers on the Sabbath and festival days, which is prohibited by the Jewish prescriptions. In the beginning and until the 1930s, Bene Beraq had reservoirs that it could control according to its own rules, but with its expansion these became inadequate. Many inhabitants had therefore installed their own (not very attractive) tanks on the rooftops. These have since become unnecessary from a religious perspective.[10]

EXPANSION AND POVERTY, BUT ALSO SOLIDARITY

Bene Beraq has long been known as the poorest Jewish town in Israel;[11] 28.5% of its inhabitants have incomes below the poverty line and therefore receive state benefits.[12]

According to data from a recent statistical survey (2001), a typical household there spends NIS 2,504 ($575) per month, which is half the amount spent by a family in the neighbouring town of Ramat Gan. Religious values can broadly be said to be at the root of this situation. In Bene Beraq, many families apply the precept 'be fruitful, and multiply' as far as possible; most of them have at least four children and the majority of these have six or seven, or many more.[13] On average, a family there has five or more children, as against the national figure of 2.9.[14] Young people of under seventeen years of age therefore represent 41% of the population. Moreover, many fathers of families continue Talmudic studies for many years (as we know, to avoid military service) and they have nothing to live on but meagre bursaries that are allocated by the yeshives. Many women do not work because they have to take care of their many children. Some young girls study to become primary school teachers but the number of available posts is small. In Bene Beraq, the average number of active people, supporting families, is 0.87 per household as against 1.2 on average in the country as a whole.[15]

However, to alleviate poverty, the town has a highly advanced system of mutual assistance, known as *gemahim*,* charitable organizations – the Hebrew abbreviation for *gemilut hasadim*,* to do charitable works (see also the previous chapter). The 'yellow pages' section of the telephone directory in Bene Beraq has no less than 700 telephone numbers available for people who need aid, and this is free. These numbers arranged by subject – over more than twenty pages – cover the most diverse needs: one family provides beds or children's clothes; certain services supply wedding dresses and babies' clothes for circumcision ceremonies and another even offers to measure blood pressure; others provide blankets, plates and saucepans, mobile phones and so on. The list of services is endless.

Bene Beraq also has an informal system for buying and selling all kinds of items, particularly clothes: these transactions often take place discreetly at the back of shops, which also makes it possible to avoid the value added tax, which is very high in Israel.[16]

Assistance to the sick is also highly advanced in Bene Beraq; two organizations, one called Ezra Mitzion and another called Yad Sarah, which have dozens of volunteers, provide medical supplies to individuals in need. Health is in fact a major preoccupation among the Hasidim, in Bene Beraq and elsewhere, and although they certainly appeal to the *kvitel** and the rebbe's miraculous intercession, they do not hesitate to take advantage of modern medical care. Moreover, certain well-informed rebbes also indicate to their visitors the doctors and hospitals where a particular illness can be treated. Sometimes patients have to be sent abroad, particularly to the United States where medical costs can be extremely high. The rebbe then intervenes with the *gemahim* or other philanthropic organizations, or alternatively with particular sponsors, to request financial help so that the sick can obtain treatment.[17]

Furthermore, hundreds of women, who already have many mouths to feed, do a great deal of cooking for two organizations that distribute meals and cakes in the hospitals. At least two organizations regularly provide hot meals to the poor and the elderly in Bene Beraq. One of these, Beit Hatavshil, in addition to 700 home-delivered meals, provides complete meals daily in its restaurant for around 200 people at a nominal cost (around 0.25 dollars), except on the Sabbath when it is free, and this is mainly to preserve the dignity of the supplicants. Some of them even travel from Tel-Aviv; many are recent immigrants from the former Soviet Union. For these activities Beit Hatavshil uses the vast renovated community centre of the large former synagogue in Bene Beraq – this is mainly a relic of the past because the inhabitants prefer to pray in small oratories or with their rebbe. Beit Hatavshil is run by the followers of the Lelover rebbe, Avraham Shlomo Biderman, based in Jerusalem, but he has a good understanding of the difficult conditions in Bene Beraq because he was rabbi there for a long period. The director of the institution collects around $1,500,000 annually from thousands of donors. Very often parents who are celebrating the marriage of one of their children wish to make a charitable gesture to treat people in need; it costs them around $600. On the blackboard in the canteen it then states that the meal of a particular day is dedicated, for example, to the marriage of Eliezer Shlomo and Rachel – the surnames are not mentioned.[18] In accordance with Hasidic rules, men and women are required to sit in separate areas.

According to certain studies, 473,000 people do voluntary work in Israel, but the prize goes to the ultra-orthodox Jews in the country; nearly 45% practise this as against 15% of secular Israelis. Nowhere is the spirit of voluntary aid more in evidence than in Bene Beraq.[19]

As we already know (see previous chapter), in Hasidic circles there are *hevres*,* associations and committees that grant interest-free loans for specific needs over a short-term period. There are also some foundations, generally created by families who want to honour a deceased relative, and the capital often initially comes from the legacy of the deceased. The loans are interest-free but the repayment rate is linked to the price of the dollar or the Swiss franc to protect the foundations against inflation. Suspect debts are seemingly rare but, equally, sometimes a debt is repaid by creating a new debt with another institution. 'It is always the same 1,000 dollars that circulates', runs the joke in Bene Beraq.

The foundations have certainly experienced setbacks following non-repayments during periods of economic crisis and appeal is then made to rich ultra-orthodox philanthropists from abroad to cover the deficits.[20] Among the great sponsors of Hasidism and ultra-orthodoxy in Israel, but also elsewhere, were the three Reichmann brothers, ultra-religious Jews, magnates in Canadian and British real estate.[21] They nevertheless experienced severe financial difficulties at the beginning of the 1990s and went bankrupt in 1992.[22] A major source of donations to the Hasidim and other ultra-orthodox in Israel had therefore dried up. The Reichmanns had therefore been forced to abandon a construction project for a housing development in northern Jerusalem with 2,200 accommodation units intended for ultra-orthodox Jews; a foundation designed to finance mortgages for young orthodox couples also went under.[23]

Solidarity and charity, *tzedoke** in Yiddish, are of course extremely ancient Jewish traditions but they are particularly in evidence in Bene Beraq, where the very survival of many inhabitants would otherwise be extremely difficult.

PRINCIPAL RELIGIOUS CONSTITUENTS

Bene Beraq is a citadel of both *misnaggedim*, the non-Hasidic orthodox of mainly Lithuanian and Russian origin, and Hasidim. The heart of the non-Hasidic ultra-orthodox world is the yeshive in Ponevez. This was established by the rabbi Joseph Shlomo Kahaneman (1888–1969), known by the title '*Ponevezer ruf*',* the rabbi of Ponevez, a town in Lithuania (its Lithuanian name is Panevezys), where he had established a large Talmudic academy in 1919; at this time, one third of its 20,000 or so inhabitants were Jews. In 1940, when Lithuania became a Soviet republic, Kahaneman went abroad to raise funds for his yeshive. He settled in Palestine and in 1944 he bought a large plot of land in Bene Beraq; he opened the new Ponevez yeshive in a dilapidated building with just seven students. Today, its headquarters are situated in a building constructed on a hill in 1950; its facade is bare of any decorative element but its principal oratory has a holy Ark in the Italian Renaissance style. The yeshive forms part of a complex of eighteen buildings, called 'Kiryat Ponevez', constructed on two hectares; the complex includes the halls of residence where the students live and a vast library. The yeshive receives more than 1,200 students from all over Israel and elsewhere; it is reputed to be the best institution of its kind in the world, 'the Oxford university of yeshives', where the sharpest mental agility is developed through the interpretation and application of the texts to the realities of life. Moreover, 800 married men attend the *kolel** of this elite assembly.

After Kahaneman, it was the rabbi Eliezer Menachem Schach, whose major political role as well as the struggle against Lubavitch messianism I have already emphasized, who until his death in 2001 was the *rosh yeshive*,* the revered director of the institution, but also the spiritual leader of all the non-Hasidic orthodox Jews of Ashkenazi origin.[24]

The presence of the prestigious Ponevez yeshive and some other similar educational establishments in the town provides non-Hasidic orthodox with great influence. Moreover, while the current ultra-orthodox mayor of the town, Abraham Karelitz, is not a Hasid, it is undoubtedly the Hasidic world that predominates in terms of the number of its followers and institutions, as well as the presence of at least forty relatively well-known rebbes who are based in the town.

Ger, the most powerful Hasidic movement in Israel, whose rebbe lives in Jerusalem, has no less than twenty-one oratories in Bene Beraq, two yeshives, a Talmud Torah* and a primary school based in three buildings, with 1,000 pupils. Ger therefore has a strong presence here. Belz Hasidim is also well represented, with six oratories: the principal one receives 250 followers on the Sabbath. Belz also has a Talmud Torah for 300 children and a kolel for fifty students. The Satmarer have a presence, particularly in their own housing estate, Shikun* Yoel; they have a girls' school, a Talmud Torah, a yeshive and a kolel there. By contrast, the Lubavitcher have a smaller presence in Bene Beraq but they nevertheless have three Habad houses, including one in the non-religious district of Pardes Katz; one of their principal objectives is to proselytise among the recently arrived Russian Jews.

NUMEROUS REBBES

There are also many rebbes from more or less well-known or obscure dynasties living in Bene Beraq. Some of the dynasties whose leaders live here are as follows: Alexander, Beregszasz, Biala, Bohush, Chernobyl, Eger, Kalev, Kasan, Komarno, Machnovka, Ottynia, Ozarov, Radzyn, Shatz, Slonim, Spinka, Strikov, Tolna, Zutske.

The Alexander dynasty (from Aleksandrov in Poland), founded in 1866 by the rabbi Chanoch Henich (1798–1870), has a few hundred followers in Bene Beraq. There are also Alexander communities in Borough Park and Antwerp. Their current rebbe, Avraham Menachem Danziger, born in 1921, is on the Agudath Council of Torah Greats in Israel, and the community has a yeshive and a kolel in Bene Beraq. However, the Alexander community is a mere shadow of its former Polish incarnation, when the dynasty rivalled Ger; many towns in Poland had Alexander communities and oratories. It was in Lodz, a town near Aleksandrov, with an industrial textiles centre and 665,000 inhabitants, one third of whom were Jews just before the Shoah, that the dynasty was most influential: there were thirty-five Alexander oratories in this town. The movement also played a political role – there were Alexander representatives on the local council of the town and its Jewish community, which was chaired in 1927 by an industrialist who was a follower of the dynasty. The proprietors of the textile industry, many of whom were rich followers and well-known figures in the Aleksandrov movement, lived in palatial houses;[25] there was also a large Jewish worker population in Lodz that supported the communist party or Jewish socialist organizations, such as Bund in particular (see Chapter 1).

From the occupation of the town on the 8 September 1939, the Germans began to annihilate all the Jews in Lodz, as elsewhere in Poland: at the end of the war, there were 900 survivors in what remained of the ghetto established by the occupying forces.[26] Why did Alexander Hasidism not manage, unlike Ger, Bobov or Belz, other major Polish Hasidic dynasties, to recover its former dynamism? This is probably because their rebbe, Yitzhak Menahem Danziger, his sons and sons-in-law, were all assassinated by the Nazis in 1942 and in the crucial immediate post-war years there was no dynamic leader to take over. The new *admor*, Yehuda Moses Tieberg (1898–1973), a Talmudic scholar, distantly related to the deceased rebbe, had settled in Palestine in 1934 having worked as a diamond-polisher; until 1947, he had refused to assume the leadership of the movement. Perhaps there were not enough other dynamic survivors to infuse the movement with new life? This remains an open question.

Bene Beraq is also home to Menachem Nahum Twersky, rebbe of the Chernobyl dynasty, a town in Ukraine;[27] born in 1942 in Jerusalem, he is an unassuming man who avoids public life, but he is held in great esteem by his own Hasidim, as well as by some followers of other rebbes. He runs a yeshive that has 200 students. There are also two oratories with his followers in Jerusalem and Ashdod. We should also mention the Slonim dynasty, which started in Belarus, founded in the 19th century. Slonim still has two rebbes; the more influential one, Shalom Noah Brosovski, has settled in Jerusalem. In Bene Beraq, a number of Hasidim are associated with Avraham Weinberg, born in 1945, rebbe since 1981, and cousin of his rival in Jerusalem. Weinberg set up various scholastic institutions in Bene Beraq, including a *yeshive gdole*,* a higher Talmudic academy, with 300 students and a *kolel*. He also had a vast Slonim centre built there, comprising a synagogue, a study room, a *mikve** and a library. The rebbe also has communities of followers in Brooklyn, London and Antwerp.

These are just a few examples that give some idea of the multiplicity of the dynastic courts in Bene Beraq, which, as happens elsewhere, often arise from schisms. The followers of the various communities that result from this are generally small in number but, like the Slonim followers, they nevertheless succeed in maintaining yeshives or kolelim because of the many students who come from all over Israel and abroad.

Bene Beraq therefore has an entire mosaic of groups, which are nevertheless connected, and somewhat dependent on the major dynasties, particularly Ger, which unites all the communities more or less closely around common demands through the Agudath Israel party, particularly in relation to state contributions and financial subsidies towards their various activities and educational or other institutions. Moreover, family ties unite many rebbes through marriages between their children or grandchildren or other close relatives; and these unions, which are concluded during negotiations between the dynasties,[28] also indicate convergences, if not religious and political alliances. Furthermore, the festivities at these weddings, *bar mitsves*,* circumcisions and so on with their descendants and their close friends and family, are the occasion for an intense social activity that brings together the representatives of the various dynasties, both the minor and the more powerful ones.[29] Among these is the Vishnitz dynasty, whose rebbes have been based in Bene Beraq for nearly half a century.

VISHNITZ, A MAJOR DYNASTY

One of the first, possibly the very first, rebbe to leave Tel-Aviv for Bene Beraq was the Vishnitzer rebbe in the early 1950s; along with Ger and Belz, the Vishnitz dynasty is one of the largest in the country and it has many followers in Bene Beraq. The Vishnitzer have given their name to a district of Bene Beraq, Kiryat Vishnitz, with 6,000 inhabitants.

The dynasty's name, Vishnitz, comes from the small town of Vizhnitsa, in the province of Chernovtsy today in the republic of Ukraine; the town belonged to the Austro-Hungarian Empire from 1774 to 1918, to Rumania between the two world wars, and then Ukraine within the former Soviet Union.

The dynasty began to expand in the 19th century. Vizhnitsa, a small town attractively situated between lakes, hills and valleys, had many Jews, many of whom worked in the timber industry and trade. Menahem Mendel Hager (1830–1885), the grandson of rebbes based in Kosov in Ukraine, had become the rabbi of the Jewish community in Vizhnitsa. He gained a reputation as a miracle-working rebbe who gave amulets and made charitable gifts. He had a luxurious residence built for himself, surrounded by gardens and orchards, beside a vast oratory. This dynasty has a well-known taste for pomp and splendour; it also prides itself on having created a rich tradition of Hasidic melodies.

Barukh Hager (1845–1893), the son of Menahem Mendel Hager, succeeded him but died at the age of 48 years after a brief eight-year reign. He had twelve children and one of his sons, Israel Hager (1860–1936), succeeded his father in 1893, when he was 33 years old. He created a Talmud Torah and a yeshive in Vishnitz; he was very popular among his thousands of followers. During the First World War he left Vishnitz to take refuge in Nagyvarad (Grosswardein in German) in Hungarian Transylvania, then he decided not to return to Vizhnitsa, which had been comprehensively destroyed. His son, Eliezer Hager (1891–1946), replaced him there in 1922 and established a yeshive called Bet Israel Damasek Eliezer (Eliezer of Damascus House of Israel).[30] Eliezer survived the anti-Semitic persecutions during the Second World War and he settled in the Holy Land in 1944. In Tel-Aviv he established an oratory and once again a Talmudic academy but he died without issue shortly after his arrival in 1946.

His elder brother Hayyim Meir Hager (1888–1972), born in Vizhnitsa, then became rebbe. Like his brother, he had experienced the persecutions of the Hungarian fascists and had survived the German extermination campaigns in 1944. After the end of the war, he made an unsuccessful attempt to rebuild a community in Nagyvarad in Hungary. After a year in Antwerp, he settled in Tel-Aviv in 1947; he had many followers there and in 1950 he acquired an abandoned orange grove on an area of 33 dunams, 3.3 hectares, which was to become Kiryat Vishnitz, in south-east Bene Beraq. The foundation stone was laid in 1950 and, two years later, the rebbe settled there when just two houses had been completed. In 1973, more than 1,000 families were already living in the district, and today its total population numbers over 6,000.

Hayyim Meir Hager died at the age of 84 years in 1972. A vast crowd of 50,000 people from all over Israel is said to have attended his funeral. He was succeeded by one of his sons, Moses Joshua Hager, born in Nagyvarad in Hungary in 1916. In 1937, still a young man, he had already been rabbi in a small settlement and then in his native town. In 1943, he managed to return to the Holy Land and he lived in Tel-Aviv. He took part in setting up Kiryat Vishnitz in Bene Beraq. He plays a prominent political role in the Agudath Israel party: he is a member and president of its Council of Torah Greats, in which he expresses strongly traditionalist viewpoints.

THE VISHNITZ WAY OF LIFE

With more than 6,000 residents, Kiryat Vishnitz constitutes a true enclave in Bene Beraq. The streets bear the names of rebbes from the Vishnitz dynsty and that of Kosov from which Vishnitz originated. In a sign of continuity with the past in Eastern Europe, the yeshive was built on the model of the one that existed in Vizhnitsa and was destroyed by the Nazis; it also bears the same name, Eliezer of Damascus. It has around 300 students. Kiryat Vishnitz has a complete set of schools for boys and girls that make the district self-sufficient in terms of Jewish education. There are three nursery schools and the Talmud Torah educates 2,000 boys. The school has a residence with fifty beds for children who live outside the district. There are also several *kolelim*.* Bursaries and help from parents but also work carried out by wives, often as primary school teachers and secretaries, make it possible for the men to study for these extensive periods. The graduates of these schools hold posts as rabbi in various countries.

The district has its own *bet din*,* rabbinical court, and no less than thirteen ritual baths, *mikves** (which open at three o'clock in the morning); the Hasidic adult men are supposed to bathe there daily and they are certainly attended by over a thousand people every day. Kiryat Vishnitz is well-provided with institutions that provide social assistance. The district also has a house of retreat, Beth Shalom, for more than a hundred people; various *gemahim*, charitable organizations, provide interest-free loans to the needy, people in difficulty, impoverished Talmudic students; yet another *gemah** facilitates the purchase of apartments at advantageous interest rates and so on. There are many other organizations that provide followers in need with essential items such as phylacteries, furniture and medical supplies. The mutual assistance system here also alleviates the difficulties that stem from the extensive studies conducted by the young men, the predominance of large families and so on.

In fact, the district is undergoing an intense demographic expansion: there are many families with six children, and ten or twelve are not unusual. Of course, sexual segregation begins at the earliest age; boys and girls play separately and later there are almost no chance meetings between young men and women at festivities such as weddings, where the male and female guests are seated separately. As in the other Hasidic communities, the marriages are 'arranged' by *shadhenim*,* professional marriage-brokers, or by close relatives or friends of the young people.

The district has a hotel, *Malon Vishnitz*, with sixty-eight rooms, for the many visitors who come to restore their spirits in the Vishnitz atmosphere. There is also some economic activity in Kiryat Vishnitz: a diamond-polishing centre, a printing works, a bakery and other food shops. Vishnitz has also created its own method of ritual slaughter of livestock.[31]

While Vishnitz Hasidism began as the movement of people originating from the borders of Bukovina, Transylvania and Hungary, today many of the followers were born in Israel. Also, although Bene Beraq constitutes a vast Yiddish-speaking environment, a language to which the Vishnitzer remain loyal, many followers also use Israeli Hebrew, alongside the sacred Hebrew language, as a result of the many forms of contact with people from Tel-Aviv and participation in everyday Israeli life, which is not avoided as it is in Mea Shearim.[32]

Like Ger, Vishnitz has created outposts beyond Bene Beraq, particularly since 1980, around thirty kilometres from the town, in Rechovot, where several hundred Vishnitz families now live. More recently the movement has established an outpost in Elad, in the occupied territories (see p. 118).

THE VISHNITZER REBBE TODAY

The rebbe is of course the key figure in the Vishnitz community. As in all the Hasidic communities, his authority is absolute; like Belz, Bobov and Lubavitch, Vishnitz has no democratically elected assemblies that are forums for expressing opinions and casting votes. Also, the current Vishnitzer rebbe does not appreciate dissent and he tends to surround himself with men who always agree with him.[33] Moreover, the power is largely gerontocratic; the current rebbe was born in 1916 and his predecessor died at the age of 84 years. The situation today is not very different among other Hasidim, apart from the Belzer, where as we have seen Issachar Dov, born in 1947, has been rebbe since the age of 17 years!

Like his fellow rebbes, the Vishnitzer rebbe receives visitors who ask him for advice and miraculous interventions. Every Friday evening he conducts the service at the synagogue and when he leaves over a thousand followers are waiting to greet him and exchange the traditional *guit shabbes*,* 'good Sabbath', wishes. Moreover, that same evening he holds *tish** – the meal with the distribution of *shrayim** (see p. 20 and p. 98), parts of the dishes served to the rebbe – in a building adjoining the synagogue constructed for this very purpose, with financial assistance from rich followers in Europe (particularly Antwerp) and the United States.

The building incorporates a gallery with five to six raked rows for the audience, mainly young people who are anxious not to miss the slightest gesture of their charismatic leader. The section closest to the rebbe is for the choir, with its conductor and composer, who give harmonized interpretations of songs and hymns from the Vishnitz tradition.[34] Holding a silver or gold goblet of wine, the rebbe begins by reciting prayers from the *Kiddush*,* blessing the Sabbath. He then ritually washes his hands in a bowl that is presented to him and he cuts an enormous loaf of plaited bread that is placed in front of him. Some assistants complete the task by distributing small pieces of this bread to the large numbers of people present (only of the male sex). Then an enormous stuffed carp, the traditional Sabbath dish in central Europe, is brought on a large plate from the kitchens. Having started the dish, the rebbe distributes parts of it on small plates to his close relatives and to prominent Hasidic figures seated near to him. Then some assistants carve the fish from the dish and, as with the bread, pass pieces of it to the people seated around the table and in the galleries.

Today plastic plates and cutlery provide a means of overcoming the logistical, aesthetic and hygiene-related problems of the meal, whereas in the time of the previous rebbe the assistants literally poured ladles of soup into the mouths of the assembled Hasidim! In the Vishnitz tradition, joy combined with fervour is considered to be a fundamental principle of Judaism. This is certainly present during the meal, particularly at the passing of dishes, through the singing, accompanied by swaying movements from the chest, of traditional Vishnitz melodies on texts by the Kabbalist Isaac Luria – particularly *Kol mekadesh*, (those who sanctify), or *Bene hechale* (members of the palace). After the feast, the rebbe gives a *toyre*,* an address in Yiddish, which he frequently combines with some *gematria** (interpretation of words by their numerical value in the Hebrew alphabet) and hermetic abbreviations for the secular Hebrew or Yiddish expressions. This Vishnitz *tish* has many elements in common with those of other dynasties but, as with other Hasidim, it has its own specific characteristics, here in particular the presence of a choir.

CONFLICTS AND RIVALRIES

Relations between Vishnitz and other dynasties, and its own internal relations, are often difficult. As we know, one of the daughters of the rebbe Hayyim Meir Hager married the young future Belzer rebbe in 1964 at a grand ceremony in Bene Beraq that was attended by thousands of Hasidim, followers from both dynasties. Despite this alliance, the relations between the two movements are somewhat distant; they belong to two different political groupings, Degel Hatorah and Agudath Israel.

However, even within its own group, Agudath, there have been difficult moments in relations between Vishnitz and Ger. In 1998, the Vishnitzer rebbe accused Ger of monopolizing the key positions in the party. The rebbe even resigned from the Agudath Council of Torah Greats and made an approach to the rabbi Ovadia Joseph, leader of the Sephardic ultra-orthodox party, Shas. This party and Vishnitz had in fact already formed an alliance at the local elections. Ovadia Joseph even travelled from Jerusalem to Bene Beraq on 9 November 1998 to visit Moshe Hager, the Vishnitzer rebbe. This visit was a public display of a more enduring desire for collaboration. However, this new alliance did not last; scarcely a fortnight later, three months after the beginning of their conflict, the Vishnitzer rebbe, then aged 80 years, went to visit the Gerer rebbe, aged 58 years, in Jerusalem, for a reconciliation. This visit paid by the older *admor** to the younger one indicated a form of capitulation to Ger by Vishnitz.[35]

Moreover, there have been discords and schisms at the heart of the Vishnitz dynasty for several decades. The elder son of the current rebbe, Israel Hager, born in 1948, reputedly a great scholar, was in charge of the financial and religious administration of Kiryat Vishnitz for six years, but he was summarily dismissed and almost excommunicated in 1983 following a series of disputes and quarrels. In fact the rebbe had to reimburse large debts caused by his son's imprudent financial management on several occasions.[36] After that, one of his brothers, Menahem Mendel Hager, became his presumptive heir. Nevertheless, there has recently been a reconciliation; Israel Hager is rabbi again in Kiryat Vishnitz and he runs a yeshive in the movement. Perhaps he will become his father's successor after all ...

Moreover, Barukh Hager (1895–1964), the brother of Hayyim Meir Hager, the rebbe who created Kiryat Vishnitz, arrived in Israel in 1947, also having survived the German persecutions. He settled in Haifa, where he created a Hasidic housing development, the Seret-Vishnitz *shikun*,* which has the usual various scholastic institutions of a Hasidic community as well as a vast synagogue that can accommodate 600 men and 400 women. There is also a discount supermarket especially designed for large families. Seret-Vishnitz also provides a Jewish education in specific schools and youth clubs for Jews who have recently immigrated from Russia. Barukh Hager died in 1964 and two of his sons shared his succession. The elder son, Eliezer, became the rebbe and his younger brother, Moshe, who died in 1999, became the director of the yeshive in Seret-Vishnitz. There is also a 'Monsey-Vishnitzer' rebbe, with many followers, based in Monsey in the suburbs of New York. For many decades, Antwerp has had two Vishnitz communities who claim allegiance to the rebbe in Bene Beraq, but one of these is consciously rather modern while the other is traditionalist. However, disputes, rivalries and conflicts do not preclude the possibility of reconciliations and alliances. In December 2000, a granddaughter of the Vishnitzer rebbe married the grandson of the Seret-Vishnitzer rebbe at an impressive wedding ceremony in Bene Beraq. The high point of the festivities was the traditional *mitzve tanz*;* this is a dance that is performed to a Hasidic melody by the bride and various men from the immediate families and also between the latter; each of the partners is linked to the other by a napkin, so there is no physical contact. These dances began after the wedding feast, at around half past two in the morning; the Vishnitzer rebbe and the Seret-Vishnitzer rebbe were observed dancing this *mitzve tanz** together, wearing their *shtreimel** and their frock coats in rich silk materials with decorative brocaded patterns.[37]

The diversity of the rebbes and groups who claim allegiance to the Vishnitz name demonstrates the historical importance of this dynastic family in contemporary Hasidism. Although Bene Beraq cannot be considered a location exclusive to Vishnitz, with its thousands of followers and the rebbe's presence in their own district, this movement is certainly a major centre of the Hasidism in the town.

VARIOUS HASIDIC CENTRES: TEL-AVIV, A SPECIAL CASE

There are Hasidic communities in many towns or settlements in Israel: in Ashdod, with its Ger district; in Bat Yam, a town adjoining the Tel-Aviv suburbs, which has a housing estate called Kiryat Bobov with around a hundred families who are followers of the Bobover rebbe, and in Rechovot, with a Vishnitz housing estate. There are so many places with more or less developed Hasidic communities of every persuasion that it would be tedious to enumerate and deal with them all. I shall therefore restrict myself to describing some places that are important for various reasons.

Tel-Aviv constitutes a special case in relation to the presence of the Hasidim. The city was an essential rallying-point after the Second World War for around twenty rebbes of various allegiances who came from Europe, which turned it into a major Hasidic centre in Israel.[38] The Gerer alone had more than ten oratories in the town and the Vishnitzer and Belzer rebbes had settled there; however, as Bene Beraq expanded, Tel-Aviv lost most of its admorim* and most of their followers. In around 1997, only four rebbes from lesser-known dynasties remained in the city and only two were planning to stay. It is true that these two, the Kozhnitzer and the Bitchkover rebbes, are involved in missionary work, which requires a proximity to the Jewish public at whom their efforts are targeted. Tel-Aviv is not and never has been a 'holy' city; the streets are not closed to traffic on the Sabbath and its population has the reputation of being irreligious or at most only very moderately religious.

However, in the early post-war years, the rebbes based in Tel-Aviv showed no inclination to cut themselves off from the rest of the population. The Belzer rebbe, Aaron Rokeah, who lived there until his death, is said to have declared that the residents of every town with a Jewish population ought to know what a Jew with sidelocks wearing a *shtreimel** looks like.[39] Moreover, Belz still runs oratories and educational institutions there. The movement also sponsors a dairy there with produce that is guaranteed to be perfectly kasher. Other movements also have a presence with their *shtiebleh** and the Slonim dynasty, based in Jerusalem, has maintained a Talmud Torah in the city since 1983.

The Hasidic ultra-orthodox district was located in the city centre, around Sheinkin Street. Today, this is a 'trendy' Bohemian area, with many cafés and restaurants, frequented by young people from the media industry. There are still *haredim** who live in certain neighbouring streets but, necessity knowing no law, there is no friction or cultural conflict in this district between the ultra-orthodox and the non-religious majority who frequent the area.

Not surprisingly, Habad-Lubavitch has a presence in this city, where there are undoubtedly potential 'penitents' for its missionary work. The movement has a synagogue there, as well as five Habad houses and schools, from the kindergarten to the kolel.

LUBAVITCH SETTLEMENTS

Several decades ago, in a characteristically original move, the Lubavitch Hasidim created two villages: Kefar Habad, between the international airport of Ben Gurion and Tel-Aviv, with around 3,500 inhabitants, and Nachalat Har Habad, forty kilometres south of Tel-Aviv, with several hundred families.

Kefar Habad was created in 1949, with seventy-four families who were occupying the houses in Safarya, an Arab village with thirty-two hectares of land that had been abandoned in 1948, like many other towns and villages, by their Palestinian inhabitants fleeing from the first Arab-Israeli war. The site was allotted to the new inhabitants by the Jewish national fund, which cleared the land, built some roads and arranged for agriculture to be taught to newcomers within a cooperative village, *moshav*.*[40]

Kefar Habad provides an interesting example of economic trends within Hasidism. At the beginning, according to the fifth rebbe's wishes, the plan was certainly to create a cooperative village with an agricultural function. However, in the 1960s, just thirteen of the 170 families in the village (7.7%) were occupied in full-time agricultural work.[41] The Hasidim had quickly ascertained that this was insufficiently profitable and with the city of Tel-Aviv only around ten kilometres away, they chose to return to their previous professions – teaching, trade and crafts, which were more usual in Hasidic circles. Some schools were established and the village has a *yeshive gdole*, a higher-level Talmudic academy that accepts students from all over the world. Moreover, with the help of non-Hasidic American and international institutions,[42] a modern printing works was established, which produces innumerable publications for circulation to a wide readership, in accordance with the Lubavitch 'missionary' calling. Some vocational schools have also been created for carpentry, locksmithing and even agriculture. In fact, although the original *moshav* failed, turkey and goose farming have since developed, with the production of goose liver paté. Despite everything, the dream of an essentially agricultural village has survived.

In 1992, the community had a replica built of the rebbe's residence in Crown Heights. It contains a large library and some conference rooms. But Menahem Mendel Schneerson never in fact visited Israel …

The second village, Nachalat Har Habad, founded in 1969 near Kiryat Malachi, around forty kilometres south of Tel-Aviv, was created more specifically to accommodate Jewish immigrants from the Soviet Union, in particular from Georgia. This time any agricultural impulse was resisted; instead, a diamond-polishing centre and a textile factory were constructed so that the inhabitants could find employment on site. Some apartment blocks and a shopping centre were built and, of course, there are Jewish schools at every level. The students participate in missionary activities in the surrounding areas.

Like Crown Heights, in fact, these two Lubavitch villages are centres that form both a place of residence for a community and a base for missionary work.

NATANYA: A COMMUNITY AND A HOSPITAL

Near Natanya, a town north of Tel-Aviv with 132,000 inhabitants, there is a Hasidic district, Kiryat Zanz, which houses around 400 families – 2,000 to 3,000 people. This district was founded in 1956 by the Klausenburger rebbe, Yekutiel Yehuda Halberstam (1904–1994). Before the Second World War, he was a religious leader in Cluj, also known as Klausenburg, a town in Transylvania. The name of the district itself refers to the dynasty of the Galician town of Zanz (in Polish, Nowy Sacz), from which the rebbe was descended.

It should be emphasized that the Klausenburger rebbe, a dynamic personality who supported the Hasidic revival, also played a significant role in the rebirth of Hasidism after 1945 (see Chapter 1, pp. 13–14). Having worked hard for this in Europe, in 1947 he settled in Williamsburg, where he stimulated the development of a flourishing community. Yekutiel Halberstam, who had lost his wife and eleven children in the Shoah, remarried in New York and became a father again, going on to have two daughters and five sons.

He then sought to continue his constructive work in Israel; he managed to obtain a plot of thirty hectares in Natanya that was to become the base for his community. The development of the district began with a group of fifty emigrants from the United States. The rebbe himself handled the negotiations with the architects, contractors and engineers and he took an interest in all the details of construction. Having settled in Kiryat Zanz, Halberstam provided all the rebbe's usual functions – the *tish*, with the distribution of *shrayim*, audiences where he received the *kvitel*, petitions from visitors and so on. He died in 1994 and was buried in the Zanz section of the cemetery in Natanya. One of his two sons, Shmuel David, born in New York in 1957, became his heir in Israel, while the elder son, born in 1953, assumed the position of Zanz rebbe in the United States. The two brothers have been observed presiding jointly over a Friday evening *tish* in Natanya, which is an exceptional occurrence in Hasidic circles.

Kiryat Zanz has all the usual institutions of a Hasidic settlement: a large synagogue and traditional schools at every level. Moreover, there is a diamond-polishing centre, a shopping centre, a bank, a post office and also a hotel, because, as a seaside town, Natanya has many tourists. The district has separate beach facilities for the use of men and women. Some of the inhabitants, including many retired people, come from the United States. The inhabitants are not all Hasidim but they are all practising Jews.

A particularly original feature of Kiryat Zanz is Laniado hospital, where Jewish laws are strictly observed. The hospital, controlled by the ministry of health in Israel but not state-subsidized, opened in 1975 and has developed considerably since then. The American government contributed a subsidy of $400,000 to its creation.[43] The hospital has 400 beds at present, including 130 in a geriatric unit; it also has a nursing school. It is the only hospital in Natanya and it treats 42,000 to 45,000 patients annually; it therefore serves a wide constituency, regardless of the religious affiliation of those receiving treatment.

Klausenburg certainly remains a Hasidic movement of a relatively modest stature; however, its achievements under Yekutiel Yehuda Halberstam's leadership constitute an example of the energy that inspired some survivors of the genocide of the Jews in bringing about a revival of Hasidism after 1945.

OCCUPIED TERRITORIES

The presence of Hasidim should also be examined in the Palestinian territories that are still occupied and increasingly being colonized by Israel since the war of 1967 – territories that the Israeli annexationists call 'Yesha', an acronym for Yehuda and Shomrom, Judea and Samaria. However, the various Hasidic movements have widely ranging attitudes towards these settlements.

We know (see pp. 73–5) that the Lubavitcher, according to the last rebbe's directives, support the annexation of the occupied territories. It is therefore no surprise that there are Habad houses and schools in the Jewish towns that have been created there. Examples of this are Beitar Illit, a town constructed from 1990 near the 'green line' dividing Jerusalem from the occupied territories, with more than 11,000 inhabitants in 2001; Efrat, with 5,446 inhabitants; and Maleh Adumim, with 25,422 inhabitants. Moreover, although Habad is not officially established within Hebron, among the 400 *haredim* living within this Palestinian town of more than 60,000 inhabitants,[44] the movement is visible behind various activities in the town, including a Schneerson centre for elderly people and a 'Gutnick visitor centre'; Joseph Gutnick is a rich businessman and a follower of Lubavitch Hasidism.[45] Moreover, during the 1996 negotiations between the government of the Israeli Prime Minister Netanyahu and the Palestinians at Wye River, under the auspices of President Clinton's administration, Habad organized a demonstration before the vault of Patriarchs, a holy site for both Jews and Muslims, to prevent the Israeli soldiers from leaving the city.[46] Finally, as we know, the Bratzlav Hasidim have also settled in occupied territories.

Some of the new villages and towns in these territories have a large ultra-religious population. At the 1999 general elections, United Torah Judaism – the alliance between Degel Hatorah and Agudath Israel – won large majorities in Betar Illit (51%) and Maale Amos (65%), whereas Shas,* the Sephardic ultra-orthodox party obtained 42% of the vote in Betar Illit and 51% of the vote in Emmanuel, an ultra-orthodox town with 4,000 inhabitants,[47] the site of a Palestinian attack in December 2001 in which ten people lost their lives.[48] There are, for example, seventy-five oratories in Betar Illit, including ten belonging to various Hasidic dynasties, such as Karlin-Stolin and Zhvill, which certainly have illustrious origins but have no great influence.

Many ultra-orthodox, both Ashkenazim and Sephardim, have chosen to live in the occupied territories in recent years, often for economic reasons. At least partly because of substantial subsidies from the ministry of housing and construction, spacious and comfortable accommodation can generally be found much more cheaply there than in Israel itself. To this day, the government continues its policy of providing incentives to settle in occupied territories; it provides tax credits and mortgages. The colonies are known to receive much larger subsidies than the developing towns situated in Israeli territory as such. Moreover, the ministry of housing gives major subsidies to private security firms for the inhabitants of the towns created near Jerusalem, such as Betar Illit, or in Eastern Jerusalem.[49]

In one of these new towns, Elad, only around fifteen kilometres away from Bene Beraq, the Vishnitzer have recently established their own district, Kiryat Chassidei Vishnitz. However, the other major Hasidic movements that have settled in Israel play only a limited role in the colonization of the occupied territories. This applies both to Belz, which is reputed to be anti-annexationist and Ger, which opposes any renunciation of control over 'Judea Samaria' by the State of Israel through the Agudath Israel party, as well as to Bobov and more particularly Satmar, which is strongly opposed to Zionism. None of these movements has built large yeshives or sponsored housing projects, which might have encouraged their followers to settle there.[50] Some, such as Ger, which in fact initially supported the creation of the town of Emmanuel (see pp. 100–1), take a cautious rather than a disapproving attitude towards this colonization.

In the final analysis, apart from the small Toldot Ahronot community and the Satmarer, who are radically opposed to the Israeli expansion into the occupied territories, most of the Hasidic movements, although they may avoid creating large institutions or openly encouraging their followers to settle there, have nevertheless supported the annexationist policy of the first Sharon government, particularly through the representatives of the United Torah Judaism party in the government and in the Knesset. Finally, some movements, such as Vishnitz and Lubavitch, have a visible presence in these territories.

Hasidism in Israel, which is very vibrant and undergoing a great expansion, particularly since the creation of the State in 1948, has a particularly strong and powerful presence in Jerusalem and Bene Beraq, but it is also increasingly widespread throughout the country, as well as in the occupied territories. It is extremely diverse, ranging from the isolationists of Mea Shearim to the militant Habad missionaries. Finally, in conjunction with the non-Hasidic *haredim*, particularly through two parties, Degel Hatorah and Agudath Israel,* today in coalition, and more distantly with Shas, the Sephardic ultra-orthodox party, the Hasidim play a significant political role in the country.

8
Lubavitch in France

A HIGHLY DISTINCT FORM OF HASIDISM

Before putting forward an overview and general analysis of the Hasidic movement today, I shall discuss in this chapter a very specific form of Hasidism that has developed since the war in France, more particularly in Paris and the surrounding region.

France was not a country of choice for the Hasidim, either before the war or after 1945. Surprisingly, it was in around 1960, with the mass arrival of Sephardim,* Jews from North Africa, that it became an important settlement for one particular Hasidic movement, Lubavitch, which spread throughout the country, particularly in Paris and the surrounding region, developing a vast network of places of prayer, schools and so on. In comparison with what we have seen in the previous chapters, there are two distinctive interrelated features: the domination of a single Hasidic movement in one country and its influence over an environment that is generally alien to Hasidism, as a movement that has been almost exclusively Ashkenazi* for more than two centuries.

Today in France, there are said to be around 10,000 to 15,000 followers of Lubavitch Hasidism, including men, women and children. In reality this is a group that includes, as well as genuine followers, some more or less close 'sympathizers' who attend the Lubavitch oratories or synagogues. There are also many more or less religious families who send their children to the movement's schools; the children therefore receive a Hasidic education, which often brings the parents closer to Habad.* The boundary between these various types of adherence is difficult to draw and no one, not even its leaders, knows exactly how many people belong to the movement. However, with the figure of 10,000 to 15,000 disciples or sympathizers, Lubavitch would represent 2% to 3% of the 500,000 Jews in France,[1] which is certainly a small percentage, but it should be emphasized that before 1950 the movement had little more than a few dozen families in the country. More strangely still, in this branch of Hasidism today there is a strong majority – at least three quarters – of followers or close sympathizers of North African origin. These are the second and particularly the third generation, the children and grandchildren of the immigrants who came to France in the 1960s, after the end of colonization in Tunisia, Morocco and then Algeria. Let us examine how Lubavitch has developed over half a century, and in particular how and why the movement has become this Sephardic stronghold.

HISTORICAL OUTLINE

Before the Second World War, Hasidism did not have much of a presence in France. There were certainly some devout individuals among the immigrants from Eastern Europe who came to Paris, many of whom assembled in two oratories, at 17 and 25 on the Rue des Rosiers in the 4th arrondissement, the historic heart of Parisian Judaism.[2] As we know, Menahem Mendel Schneerson, the future Lubavitch rebbe, who lived in Paris from 1932 to 1941, provided instruction in the Talmud in the synagogues on the Rue des Rosiers.[3] At this period, there was certainly a small group of Lubavitch followers in Paris, but there were no Lubavitch oratories or institutions.[4]

Shortly after the end of the Second World War, some Lubavitch Hasidim, who had hitherto lived in the Soviet Union, benefiting from a relatively liberal attitude on the part of the Soviet authorities, managed to leave the country. Some of them stayed in Paris for a considerable time, but for most of them, as for the Hasidim in Antwerp, this was a transitional stage on the way to other destinations, particularly Brooklyn, London and Montreal. In fact, 'the form of Jewish observance that was upheld in these [Hasidic] families was more or less unknown to the Jewish community in this country [France]'.[5] However, at the request of Joseph Isaac Schneerson, who was then rebbe of the movement, around thirty families nevertheless remained there.[6]

At the beginning, the Lubavitcher assembled and lived near the two synagogues on the Rue des Rosiers and others nearby, particularly in the Rue Bourg-Tibourg and Rue de Turenne. They usually lived in very basic small hotel rooms. JOINT, the abbreviated name given to the American Jewish Distribution Committee, a large Jewish American philanthropic organization, and COJASOR,[i] a French organization founded in 1945, met these families' housing costs as well as providing modest supplies for an initial period.[7] At the time, the Lubavitch families, who spoke little or no French, lived in an enclosed circle; proselytizing among other Jews was the least of their concerns at that time.

The Lubavitcher in Paris, like the Hasidim everywhere else, have specific religious needs and these were met on a minimal basis at the time. There is certainly a *mikve*,* a ritual bath, in the Marais at 9 Rue de Villehardouin; this seems to have been the only one in Paris![8] Furthermore, the city had only one *glatt kasher** butcher and one trustworthy patisserie. Gradually, the Lubavitcher established their own ritual baths and shops; some followers worked as ritual slaughterers, particularly for the butchers who were sponsored by the Consistory of France, the 'official' institution of the Jewish religion,[9] which lacked specialists in this field. Others provided tuition in orthodox Judaism for religious families. The followers therefore had some professional openings available to them.

In the immediate post-war period, survivors of the Shoah who were followers of various dynasties attended the place of worship at 17 Rue des Rosiers, but gradually most of them left Paris. The oratory came to belong to the people who remained there; that is, to the Lubavitcher who are still in charge of it today. Invisible from the street, the oratory, which occupies an apartment over a courtyard, on the first floor[ii] of an 18th-century building, is said to date from 1879 and not from the 1780s as is claimed in some quarters.[10] The principal room

---

i COJASOR: 'Comité juif d'action sociale et de reconstruction' – Jewish organization for social work and reconstruction (*Translator's note*).

ii The first floor in British English or the second floor in American English (*Translator's note*).

serves as a place of prayer; near the entrance, a screen and curtains separate off the smaller area reserved for the women. The furniture is extremely simple; there are some wooden benches, tables and shelves with books and, of course, a holy ark with the Torah scrolls. This is a place intended as much for study as for prayer, as is entirely in keeping with the Hasidic *shtiebl*.*

Moreover, just after the war, Lubavitch began to establish its own set of educational establishments. The first major institution, created in 1946, was the Tomchei Tmimim Lubavitch *yeshive** in Brunoy, a few dozen kilometres from Paris, located in a verdant area that is said to have belonged to 'Monsieur', the brother of Louis XVI![11] The purpose of this Talmudic academy was, and remains, to train rabbis, ritual slaughterers and teachers for Lubavitch in France and elsewhere. The subjects taught essentially comprised a course of study of the Talmud and *Hessides*,* in this case study of the Tanya, the work by the Lubavitch founder, Shneur Zalman of Lyady (see Chapter 5) but also some speeches and letters, published in volumes, by the various rebbes of the movement, in particular the last rebbe, Menahem Mendel Schneerson. Most of the pupils were boarders and some came from outside France. Although the youngest received French lessons there, the commentaries on the Talmud and the Tanya were conducted in Yiddish, as they still are today.

From 1950, in addition to young people from Ashkenazi families, the yeshive received young Moroccans who had been educated in various Lubavitch institutions that existed then in Morocco – another place where some followers had settled after the Shoah.[12] This formed the still modest beginnings of the great Lubavitch advance in France among the Jews of the Maghreb.

The yeshive in Brunoy also sent its oldest pupils to provide teaching in *Talmudei Torah*.* In fact, unlike the schools of this name that we have encountered elsewhere, these did not operate full-time but provided classes on Sundays and Thursdays. These were attended by boys aged seven to fourteen who were educated at the secular state school before any full-time Lubavitch religious schools had been established. During the first few decades after the war there were twenty of these centres, mostly in the Rue des Rosiers, in the 18th and 19th arrondissements, in Montreuil, Aubervilliers and Les Lilas. However, in the 1960s, in Aubervilliers, some Lubavitch rabbis, in collaboration with a Sephardic community originating from Ghardaia, Algeria, founded a full-time Talmudic school, called Chné Or ('two lights', meaning those of the two communities involved).

From 1947, Lubavitch created a school for girls, Bet Rivakh (House of Rebecca) in Montmorency. It later relocated to a site in Yerres, near Brunoy. In around 1975, there were approximately 150 pupils; today there are around 600. The school has a complete primary-level and secondary-level course under contract with the State, and it is therefore subsidized. However, it also has a nursery school and a seminary with boarding facilities, established in 1958, which are not under contract and therefore do not receive state subsidies; clearly, the religious teaching is much more substantial there than in the section approved by the State. Furthermore, at present the young girls who are admitted to the seminary (sixty places) are required to have the diploma from the first stage of secondary education, the BEPC (Brevet d'études du premier cycle) or the baccalaureate and teaching is even provided there for the first university diploma (DEUG – Diplôme d'études universitaires générales) in languages.[13] In the Lubavitch context, as in many other Hasidic circles, the girls, including future religious instructors, receive a more advanced 'profane' education than the boys.

The seminary has since trained many teachers, most of whom are employed in the Lubavitch schools or other religious schools in France and beyond. I shall return later to the remarkable development of the Lubavitch scholastic system, which in France even more than elsewhere, forms a major component of the movement's expansion.

A SPECIFIC FORM OF EXPANSION

Some major historical events in North Africa were to contribute to the major transformation of Lubavitch. Following decolonization and the accession to independence by Tunisia and Morocco in 1956, then by Algeria in 1962, many Jews left these three countries and some of them went to France – Algerian Jews had in fact been French citizens since the Crémieux Decree of 1870.[14]

Some Jews from Tunisia and Morocco were already familiar with Lubavitch Hasidism (see above). In 1951, Menahem Mendel Schneerson had sent some *shlihim,** representatives, to open various religious schools in these countries; these accepted working-class children and they established a first important link between Sephardic Jews and Lubavitch.[15] Some young girls educated by Lubavitch in Tunisia then continued their studies in the movement's schools in Crown Heights and went on to become teachers in Lubavitch schools in Paris. Nevertheless, for the majority of North African Jews, Lubavitch was until then an unknown world. Also, the first generation of adults who settled in France seem to have been relatively impervious to its influence; most of the Algerian and Tunisian Jews identified with the secular values of the French republic and modernity; they wanted a secular education for their children that would provide them with a good level of social integration. They certainly also saw themselves as more or less traditionalist Jews, hence the value for them of the 'Sunday schools', some of which as we know were Lubavitch. Many Moroccan Jews had a strong attachment to their Sephardic religious identity of the past and they persevered in this without being very much influenced by Lubavitch Ashkenazi Hasidism, apart from the minority who had already encountered this in Morocco.

However, the transplantation to France was a painful experience for the majority of these Sephardim. The previously very close networks of extended families were dispersed across many locations in the country, but also in the United States, Canada and Israel. Although there was not much nostalgia for the North African past, many of these immigrants felt that it was difficult to lead 'truly Jewish lives'. Gradually, the Lubavitcher, at the instigation of the rebbe, who as we know had initiated missionary campaigns from the early 1960s, took stock of this situation and organized meetings for these uprooted people.

Certainly, the followers at the time were few in number; moreover, they were Yiddish-speaking and spoke the hesitant French of Russian immigrants.

However, unlike the French Jews, whom the most traditionalist Sephardim perceived as cold and 'almost goyim',* the Lubavitcher were felt to be warm and responsive to the questions and problems that were presented to them; they advised, listened and engaged with genuine concern. The Lubavitch rabbis and emissaries were therefore particularly responsive to the practical concerns of the most traditionalist Sephardim, who often felt the need to be in contact with a rabbi, particularly in order to conform to certain Jewish prescriptions. One woman reported that she had telephoned the Consistory many times to find out how to make her crockery kasher, but the explanations she received concerning its obligatory soaking[16] struck her as extremely deficient. From an acquaintance, she obtained the telephone number for Lubavitch and, on the very same evening that she telephoned, two followers appeared at her door to carry away her crockery and to carry out the prescribed ritual immersion in an appropriate form of fresh water! As for the *mezuzes** that have to be fixed to the door-posts of houses, the Lubavitcher were not only able and willing to provide them, particularly during a campaign for the observance of this prescription, but they also obligingly came to install them in people's homes.

Nevertheless for these first-generation Sephardim settled in France, the Lubavitcher were too rigorous; they did not adopt very many of their practices.[17] The break with the religiosity of the past took place mainly after 1965; on both sides, it has been an encounter between people from new generations. The Lubavitcher rabbi Shmuel Azimov, former student of the yeshive in Brunoy, and therefore already brought up in France, became the principal director of missionary activities among the Jews in France in 1965 at the rebbe's request. From then on, young *shlihim*, representatives of Russian origin, but born and brought up in France, therefore speaking French as well as Yiddish, extended their proselytizing activities particularly among the young Sephardim, who were of course all Francophone. From 1967, the Six-Day War stimulated a quest for identity, often religious in nature, among many Jews in France, Sephardic and others.

Finally, like the counter-culture revolution in the United States, the events of May and June 1968 affected many young Jewish men and women. Lubavitch sought to reach these various audiences; Habad houses were established (see Chapter 5); in 1966, at 44, Rue Vieille-du-Temple, in 1972 at 8, Rue Lamartine and others followed. The adherence of the *baalei tshuve*,* the penitents, and their incorporation into the Lubavitch movement were generally gradual; each 'penitent' found his own way of integrating that accorded with his personal concerns and tastes; there is no rite of passage for the integration of newcomers. However, when a young man is asked to conduct one of the daily evening services in a Lubavitch oratory – which requires a good religious education – this sends a strong positive signal concerning his degree of integration.

The encounter between the Lubavitch efforts and external circumstances was to yield results that exceeded all expectations: Lubavitch Hasidism in France expanded and in particular it became 'Sephardized'; the Ashkenazi of Russian origin were soon in a small minority.

LUBAVITCH IN FRANCE AND SEPHARDIC CULTURE

The second- and third-generation Sephardim of Maghreb origin who belong to Lubavitch no longer speak Arabic, or the Judaeo-Arabic spoken by their grandparents and sometimes their parents. Born and educated in France, they use French; moreover, many of them speak Yiddish to a greater or lesser degree, which is used particularly in studies at the Talmudic seminary in Brunoy and of course in Crown Heights, which many of them visit for longer or shorter periods. Belonging to Habad entails a rejection of many North African customs. Accordingly, the new followers no longer celebrate *Mimouna*, a traditional meal at the close of Passover, which is not recognized by the Hasidim.[18] In fact, the converts tend to eradicate their ancestral Judaeo-Arabic past in order to adopt customs borrowed from another culture and to take on a legendary and mythologized past associated with the Hasidic world of Eastern Europe.[19] One of the major vehicles of this transformation is the assimilation of the *Hessides*,* the Hasidism of the Lubavitch tradition, which is instilled in the movement's yeshives (see p. 122 above).

Furthermore, the married Lubavitch women, who have to cover their heads (which are generally shaven), rarely sport the knotted scarf worn by Muslim women; they usually wear wigs, often indistinguishable from natural hair, enhanced by very stylish caps and small hats. They also dress in an increasingly Western style; thus, many Lubavitch women and sympathizers, particularly the mothers of children who attend the Habad schools, especially the younger ones, instead of wearing dark tights and loose-fitting dresses that are below knee-level, now wear long narrow dresses that resemble those currently in fashion. In fact, in many cases the female Hasidic appearance is difficult to identify.

In fact, according to my recent observations, Lubavitch Hasidism in Paris has acquired some specific characteristics. First of all, various oratories that I visited have little in common with the Hasidic *shtiebleh** because they have rows of seats, like the classical synagogues, instead of the tables surrounded with benches used for studying the large volumes of the Torah. Moreover, at the Sukkot,* the mingling of women and men in the *Sukkah*,* the house in which they live and take meals during this festival, is unusual among the Hasidim but seems to be more or less tolerated, particularly at *Hol-Hamoed*,* the semi-festival days in this period. In the *shtiebl* as well, the *gabbe*,* the follower in charge of the distribution of honours during the reading of the Torah and the morning service, does not hesitate to ask a particular unknown visitor who may not look at all Hasidic in appearance, to read out the blessings that accompany this ceremony. Furthermore, during these daily acts of worship (except for the Sabbath) no one takes offence at the sound of mobile phones ringing and the conversations that ensue. It is true that the Lubavitch Hasidim are generally more tolerant than other Hasidim, but among many Sephardic followers there is a natural leniency[20] that is part of the North African way of life and therefore owes nothing to the missionary tactics. Habad Hasidism in France has undoubtedly undergone a form of 'Sephardization'.

Mention should also be made of a *minek*,* a specific local custom, that is practised by the Lubavitcher in France, of which they are very proud. Around thirty years ago, during a visit to Crown Heights by a group of followers from France, at a religious service with Hasidic dances, the rebbe intoned a series of liturgical verses to the tune of the Marseillaise! Since then, the Lubavitcher in France have observed this custom, which in some sense symbolically contributes to 'Gallicizing' their dual Ashkenazi and Sephardic origin, which is such a distinctive feature within the movement.

LUBAVITCH INSTITUTIONS: THE EDUCATIONAL SYSTEM

Today Lubavitch has no less than seventy *shlihim*, or representatives, running its various institutions in the Parisian region. In Paris itself, Habad synagogues and houses are particularly in evidence in Eastern Paris, with four in the 19th arrondissement and four in the 20th arrondissement, where many followers, as well as other religious Jews predominantly of Sephardic origin, have lived for several decades. Of course, there is the oratory in the Rue des Rosiers and also the movement's administrative building in Rue Lamartine in the 9th arrondissement, which also serves as an oratory and a place of study for adults (see p. 128 below). In the suburbs there are around twenty Habad houses and Lubavitch oratories. However, the movement does not neglect other neighbourhoods in which there are fewer religious Jews; although it does not have oratories or synagogues everywhere, there are *shlihim*, based in the other Parisian arrondissements and in various districts in the suburbs of Paris (Pontault-Combault, Maisons-Laffitte, Poissy etc.). They can easily be contacted by telephone and, from then on, more or less close relations with Lubavitch can be established. Furthermore, given the geographical dispersal of the Jews in the Parisian region, with around ten million inhabitants in 379 districts, it is not possible for all the 'sympathizers' or followers to live near a specifically Lubavitch place of prayer; they therefore attend oratories or synagogues with other affiliations.

As we know, from the immediate post-war period, various schools were set up by the Lubavitcher. In all there are said to be around 7,000 pupils today in the various Habad institutions of the Parisian region, and more than 1,500 pupils in the institutions of the eight provincial towns, in particular Cannes, Dijon, Grenoble, Lyon, Marseille, Nice, Strasbourg and Toulouse.[21] This remarkable development stems in part from the usual demographic expansion in Hasidic circles – there are many large Lubavitch families in France[22] – but it is also due to two other interrelated factors. On the one hand, the Lubavitch schools, unlike other orthodox schools in France, accept pupils from families that are not very religious, on condition that they observe the rules in force there (for example, the boys must wear a skull-cap); this policy obviously corresponds to the spirit of openness and missionary vocation of the movement.[23] Moreover, in many more or less traditionalist Jewish households in France, there is a definite disenchantment today with the secular state schools. This is mainly because of the various recurrent problems – violence, drugs, extortion – that are affecting many state schools and also, particularly since the intensification of the Middle East conflict, because of anti-Semitism among many Muslim pupils, which sometimes takes an extreme form.

Lubavitch has various large groups of schools in the Parisian region. In the suburbs there are of course the yeshive and the *haider** in Brunoy, with 400 pupils, the school and the seminary of Bet Rivakh with 600 girls in Yerres, but also the Chné Or school in Aubervilliers (see p. 122 above), which has 500 pupils, as well as schools in Sarcelles, Fontenay-sous-Bois, Massy and Villeneuve-la-Garenne. There is also a *kolel,** a Talmudic academy for married men, with thirty to fifty students, in Yerres, which was established in 1999.

In Paris, the 'Cité de l'Éducation Sinaï' for girls opened in 1990 in the 18th arrondissement, which has 1,200 pupils, ranging from the crèche to the final year of secondary education in a professional and technical lycée, with spacious premises and modern equipment. There is also the 'Cité de l'Éducation Heikhal Menachem' for boys, which opened in 1995 in the 20th arrondissement, a school development with two five- to seven-storey buildings that contain a nursery-school, a *haider* and a vocational and technical secondary school, as well as a library, a gymnasium and a synagogue. Finally, there are the Bet Chaya Mushka and Bet Hana schools, based in Rue Petit in the 19th arrondissement. A school development for girls has been established under contract in a large modern building on several floors with 18,000 square metres of working space. Around 2,000 pupils, from the nursery-school to the last year of secondary school, attend these establishments in the seventy-five well-lit modern classrooms with large windows. There is also a crèche with eighty cradles, a library, a kitchen, a refectory and a gymnasium. This is said to be the largest orthodox Jewish school development in Europe and only a small proportion of the pupils are from Lubavitch families; there are even children from non-religious families; it is therefore very much in keeping with the missionary vocation and spirit of openness that characterizes Lubavitch in France.

The school has a community hall and a synagogue that occupies around 250 square metres, with a raised vault and walls covered in stones from Hebron; two grey granite curtain walls surround the holy Ark containing the Torah scrolls. There is a mezzanine for the women with a tulle curtain that is intended to hide them from men's view. This building, which has replaced various others scattered across a range of sites, was constructed from 1995, opened for the beginning of the school year in 1999 and was officially inaugurated on 19 November 2000. The pupils seem to receive a good education there because the school results, particularly in the baccalaureate, in scientific, economic and social subjects, are excellent: the pass rate is getting closer to 100% every year.

At the formal inauguration of the Chaya Mushka development, the chief rabbis of France and Paris, the presidents of the Paris Consistory, the Central Consistory of the Jews of France and the CRIF (Conseil répresentatif des Institutions Juives de France), and the director of the FSJU (Fonds social juif unifié), attended the ceremony, as an inscription on a plaque that appears in the entrance attests. This school development is therefore recognized by the Jewish Establishment, which clearly increases its prestige among the 'clientele' of non-Hasidic parents.

Furthermore, there is an 'annexe' for boys, with 700 pupils, situated in the 20th arrondissement: there is a primary school and a secondary school (up to the age of 16 years); the course of secular teaching there is shorter than it is for the girls. As with other Hasidim, the girls have greater access to secular teaching than the boys.

Moreover, Lubavitch continues to run schools on Wednesdays and Sundays and in the evenings, which today are aimed primarily at adults, and the teaching takes place in various Habad oratories and sites, particularly at the Lubavitch administrative headquarters in Rue Lamartine, with courses for example in the Tanya for 'ladies and young girls'. On a regular basis, 500 courses for adults are run in the Paris region. There are only a few Talmudei Torah for young boys. For children and young people, Lubavitch devotes most of its educational efforts to the full-time Jewish schools.

The various school developments belonging to the movement include nursery schools, which provide the basis for a Jewish education. The movement has around a dozen of these nursery schools in Paris and the surrounding region, which take several hundred children. They are not subject to school legal requirements and Lubavitch can educate the children according to its own theories.[24] Instruction in reading the prayer book, in Hebrew, is therefore conducted at an early stage here. In fact, these pupils learn using several languages. When these nursery-schools were created, from 1975, those in charge wanted to remain faithful to the methods of the traditional *haider* and they did not want any literacy tuition in French. However, the parents considered their attitude too uncompromising and in time – in the space of five years – French teaching featured in the afternoon curriculum, while Hebrew occupied the morning hours, certainly more favourable because the children are still receptive then. Hebrew is in theory the sacred language of prayer and reading of the Torah, *loshn koidesh*,* for the Lubavitcher, as for other Hasidim, but modern Hebrew appears in the nursery-school, particularly with the use of Israeli books but also because some teachers and pupils have lived in Israel. Moreover, although Yiddish is not spoken (many Sephardic children do not know it), its vocabulary regularly appears in the young children's language with expressions such as *guit shabbes** (good Sabbath) or *guit yontef*, for a happy festival, *Yourzeit*,* on the anniversary of the death of a close relative, and many others besides.

Thereafter in the classroom and beyond it, including at home, the children speak French among themselves; Yiddish remains a foreign language for the Sephardic children, who are in a large majority, and Hebrew is essentially the sacred language. Certainly, as they progress in their studies, these two languages play an increasingly important role; at the yeshive* in Brunoy, the teaching is conducted in Hebrew and in Yiddish. After all, Yiddish is the language that was spoken by the rebbe and it continues to be used a great deal in Crown Heights!

As I have demonstrated in the various chapters of this book, while all Hasidic movements everywhere attach prime importance to an education in their own schools, the children who attend them are generally already receiving a Hasidic education at home, which is far from the case with the children educated in Lubavitch institutions in France. With the influx of so many new followers of Sephardic origin into Habad communities, the Lubavitch schooling clearly plays a particularly important role in educating and socializing their children according to the model of the movement. This is not always appreciated in traditionalist North African circles: 'We do everything possible at home to pass our traditions, our customs and our education on to them', a woman from Djerba told us, 'although our children go to the Sinaï school [a Lubavitch school]. It is not always easy. We try as hard as we can to make them understand how ancient, rich and vibrant our culture is, so that they do not forget where they come from and so that they do not believe that they are from Eastern Europe.'[25] There are other reactions of a similar kind to what is sometimes perceived as a devaluation of Sephardic Jewish religion and culture.[26] Nevertheless, the movement's schools are indisputably undergoing a period of expansion. In around 1990, there were 3,317 children being educated in Lubavitch institutions in the Paris region:[27] today, there are 7,000, more than double that figure!

FINANCIAL DIFFICULTIES: PROFESSIONS

The Lubavitch schools are heavily subsidized by the State, particularly the schools under contract, or by the town councils, in the case of crèches, but there are still substantial costs involved for example in the construction of school buildings, maintenance and staff salaries, particularly for the teachers in the religious sector. The parents are supposed to pay the schooling costs but their contribution is not nearly adequate. Today, national Jewish institutions, particularly the FSJU, which coordinates social, educational and cultural activities for the maintenance of the Jewish way of life in France, certainly contribute to the running of these schools, but in an entirely inadequate way. It is therefore necessary to raise funds and to approach donors on behalf of the schools, as well as for other purposes such as the support and maintenance of oratories. Furthermore, the financing of Habad in France, as elsewhere, does not receive any kind of subsidy from the headquarters in Crown Heights. Fundraising is therefore a major activity for some followers. In any case, the movement seems to manage to obtain funds from its disciples and sympathizers by one means or another. An annual charity gala that is aimed at a wide public is one of the fundraising methods; the tickets for the gala on 9 December 2003 cost €500 per couple – in 2001, they cost FF 2,600 (€400)! Furthermore, 'Beth Loubavich' (the Lubavitch house), the movement's official organization run by the rabbi Shmuel Muchka (see above), which sponsors the Chaya Mushka school development on the Rue Petit, is 'an association of recognized public benefit that is authorized to receive donations and legacies'.

Are there enough rich people to provide financial support for the movement? This is certainly the case among the doctors, dentists and other professionals, businesspeople, engineers, computer scientists and so on, whether they are followers of 'the inner circle' or sympathizers.[28] Nevertheless, the movement in France has a large number of followers who work in professions related to the religion. There are of course the *shlihim*, the ritual slaughterers and kashrut supervisors, the butchers, restaurateurs, bakers and so on who sell kasher food, various stationers and bookshops that supply prayer-books, Bibles and Talmuds, as well as many Habad publications. Moreover, given the importance of the Lubavitch scholastic system in France, many followers (both men and women) work as religious instructors at every level, schoolteachers, school heads and so on. Despite the range of professional activities worldwide, the existence of many professions with a religious connection therefore characterizes Lubavitch in France, like many other Hasidic communities worldwide.[29]

NATIONAL AND 'COMMUNITY' POLITICS

It is in relation to schools, in particular the Chaya Mushka development in the Rue Petit, that Lubavitch has become deeply involved in political matters. The construction of the development proved to be extremely expensive, with an overall cost of more than FF 100,000,000 (€15,000,000). Lubavitch asked the regional council of Île-de-France for a subsidy and an underwritten loan but despite the support of the two centre-right parties, the RPR and the UDF,[iii] this project was rejected on four occasions in 1994. A left-wing majority on the Council – the Greens, the Communist party and the Socialist party – as well as the extreme right-wing Front National, rejected these requests in the name of secularism. Nevertheless, the City of Paris, under the leadership of the mayor Jean Tibéri, granted a subsidy to the school development and state guarantees for a loan of FF 10,000,000. In October 2000, the City of Paris had also allocated a subsidy for facilities of FF 3,500,000 and a maintenance grant of FF 875,260 for the crèche established in Rue Petit.[30] Furthermore, Jean Tibéri attended the school's inauguration in November 2000 and the commemorative plaque affixed in the building states in large letters that 'the scholastic and socio-cultural development of Beth Chaya Mushka was built with the support of the City of Paris'.

The Lubavitcher seem to have learnt some lessons from the support of the RPR. Hillel Pevzner, a leading Lubavitch rabbi, called on people to vote for Chirac at the presidential election of 1995, although this appeal caused some friction within the movement.[31] Certainly, for the Lubavitch spokesman, the rabbi Haim Nissenbaum, followers' political choices are an individual matter, but he adds: '… even if, for Lubavitch, Jacques Chirac had a strong margin of sympathy because of the support that he contributed in community matters'.[32]

It is therefore clear that Lubavitch is involved in French politics, undoubtedly to protect its own direct interests, both at local and at national level. More recently, the vicissitudes of the Israeli-Palestinian conflict, resulting in many

---

iii RPR: 'Rassemblement pour la République', the main political party of the Gaullist right; UDF: 'Union pour la démocratie française', the centre-right party (*Translator's note*).

anti-Semitic incidents of varying severity, have affected the movement, as well as other Jewish circles, particularly in districts where Jews and Muslims have coexisted for a very long time, hitherto without major incidents. On 10 April 2002, stones were thrown at a bus taking pupils and teachers to a Lubavitch school, and the pupils were sworn at by some 'young North Africans'.[33] On 15 January 2003, a gang attacked another Lubavitch school and for a very long time its pupils had been the object of jostling, verbal abuse, kicking and so on. At the end of July 2003, a Lubavitch oratory in Saint-Denis was vandalized. With their high visibility due to the beards and black hats worn by the men, the children's skull-caps and so on, the Hasidim are very easy to identify and they are particularly targeted by the troublemakers. Often, attacks are also directed at isolated individuals; families are threatened and abused; graffiti is scrawled over the doors of apartments in which Jews are living, and so on. It seems that the movement, which has certainly taken various precautionary measures – with women and children no longer going out after nine o'clock in the evening in certain areas – trusts the forces of law and order to protect its property and its followers.

Lubavitch has also succeeded, over the years, in becoming a significant partner in the Central Consistory, the officially recognized institution of orthodox Judaism in France, in spite of the persisting conflicts, particularly in relation to kasher meat. From 1991, two Lubavitch rabbis decided to create their own form of ritual slaughter, particularly in order to finance their institutions, including the Sinai school.[34] To this end, Lubavitch conducted a subtle but multi-faceted campaign to obtain institutional recognition for this slaughter in order to gain access to the slaughterhouses. Since a decree in 1981, the slaughterer's permit that provides this access has been issued exclusively by the Chief Rabbi of France on the specific recommendation of the rabbinical court of the Paris consistory, which supervises the validity of the kashrut.[35] Lubavitch applied pressure to this rabbinical court, liaised with butchers and wholesale butchers and held a meeting with Jean-Louis Debré, the minister for the interior and for religion. Neither the Consistory nor Lubavitch wanted the conflict to lead to a trial with an uncertain outcome; four years later an agreement was finally reached. Lubavitch obtained official slaughterers' permits from the Paris Consistory and the rights concerning slaughter passed partly to the 'Association consistoriale israélite de Paris' (ACIP, the Jewish consistorial association of Paris) and partly to Lubavitch.

Moreover, the movement was given authorization to affix its own labels certifying the kashrut at the butchers' sponsored by the movement – six in Paris and the surrounding region – and around twenty restaurants (including several pizzerias and a Chinese restaurant), but it promised not to challenge the validity of the consistorial kashrut.[36] None of this prevented Lubavitch from creating its own *Vaad Rabbanéi Loubavitch*, a council of Lubavitch rabbis, which is almost equivalent to a rabbinical court, since like the consistorial *bet din*,* it guarantees the kashrut of many products, accords its guarantee to restaurants, butchers', bakeries, caterers and so on. Since the year 2000, this council has also issued a list of institutions under its supervision. In other words, it is almost a second Consistory!

Relations between Lubavitch and the Consistory are therefore not easy. Nevertheless, for a very long time, Lubavitch *shohetim** have been working for the Consistory, particularly the rabbi Belinov, who is in charge of poultry slaughter, and also one of the instigators of the contentious Lubavitch slaughter method. Now Belinov, in accordance with the agreement concluded in 1995, has become a *dayan*,* a judge in the *bet din*, the consistorial rabbinical court of Paris, where he has specific responsibility for all the slaughter activities.[37] Both the 1995 agreement and the role of this rabbi demonstrate the influence of Lubavitch in a field in which – as we saw in relation to Williamsburg – economics and religion are especially closely interrelated, particularly owing to the financial contributions that the slaughter brings to those who, like the Lubavitch and the Consistory, govern the various professionals involved.[38]

Furthermore, the Lubavitch rabbi Haim Nissenbaum is today one of the eight vice-presidents of the Paris Consistory. The institutionalization of Lubavitch has also continued in a secular context, with the movement joining the CRIF in 2001, a coalition uniting most Jewish organizations – both secular and religious – whose major objective is to exert political influence on the State authorities, the media and so on. Apart from the struggle against anti-Semitism, this organization has a long-standing major objective: to support, against all odds, the State of Israel.[39] The Lubavitcher in France are certainly rather reticent about their support for Israel, particularly concerning the movement's annexationist stance (see pp. 73–4), but the reconciliation with the CRIF is certainly connected with some ideological convergences on this issue.[40]

It therefore seems that Lubavitch has managed to integrate itself into the Jewish Establishment in France, at both the religious and the political level. It is interesting that the messianic fervour (see pp. 76–9) of the 1990s, with the belief that the last rebbe, Menahem Mendel Schneerson, will come back to life and reveal himself as the Messiah, does not seem to shock either the Consistory or the CRIF. It appears that the vast majority of Lubavitch rabbis and other Lubavitch leaders in France do not share this belief, or at least, if they do, they remain silent on the subject; neither do the movement's pamphlets or other recent publications make any reference to it. In fact, for the vast majority of Jews in France who have had contact with Lubavitch or have been confronted with their missionary activities, it is essentially a respectable and efficacious religious organization of a more or less fundamentalist nature.

CONCLUSION

As a country strongly imbued with secular values, in which many of the 'French of Jewish origin' were very much assimilated before 1939, France was not a fertile ground for Hasidism until the 1970s; even during the 1919–1939 period, with the substantial immigration from Eastern Europe, the number of Hasidim in the country remained extremely small. As we know, Lubavitch did not have a community there at this time. After 1945, as we saw in relation to reb Ytsekl

(p. 21), Lubavitch could not establish a community in Paris and, although it is not unknown to encounter a Satmarer, a Gerer or a Belzer in the Marais on a rare occasion, he will be passing through and attending an orthodox synagogue such as the one on the Rue Pavée in the 4th arrondissement. While a small community has recently been created by followers of the Bratzlav movement, which has an oratory on Rue Manin in the 19th arrondissement, this has few more than thirty followers.

'French-style' Hasidism certainly has a specific character, with its quasi-monolithic Lubavitch movement. This is the only one that has managed to establish a significant Hasidic presence in the country. At the outset, the two successive rebbes who led the movement from Crown Heights in the post-war period persuaded some of their followers, particularly from the Soviet Union, to safeguard the movement's presence in France: the yeshive in Brunoy, created back in 1946, strongly attests to this desire for a presence. The extraordinary expansion of Lubavitch in France – from a few dozen people after the war to over 10,000 today – is undoubtedly, as for many other Hasidic communities, partly due to the followers' observance of the commandment to 'be fruitful, and multiply', which has created many large families. However, it owes more to the adherence of North African Sephardim, predominantly from the second and third generations, who are susceptible to the proselytism and the 'love of Israel' practised by the movement.

However, unlike the situation in Crown Heights, the expansion is not only due to the support of the *baalei tshuve*, non-religious penitents, who have often travelled a great distance ideologically and socially; in fact, many Sephardic adherents were already at least traditionalist Jews. In fact, these new followers undergo a form of reintegration that involves a two-fold rejection: both of the Judaeo-Arabic past and of a less than benevolent and 'cold' 'consistorial' Jewish culture.[41]

The large-scale 'Sephardization' of Lubavitch in France is a new sociological phenomenon within the movement. Certainly, the principal rabbis in control are still followers of Russian origin, some now French-born, but in spite of everything most officials in the various Habad centres are now Sephardim.[42] This strong Sephardic presence conditions the experience of this Hasidism, which is more tolerant, flexible and open here than elsewhere, particularly with its schools that warmly welcome a wide public.

If we also consider that Lubavitch in France, with around 10,000 to 15,000 followers and close sympathizers, represents a significant part of the movement worldwide, it becomes clear that the Sephardic contribution, with its particular characteristics, may have an influence in the long term on the international direction of this form of Hasidism, which as we should recall no longer relies on an omnipotent rebbe who prescribes the stances to be taken by the various branches of the movement.

9
Overview

AN UNEXPECTED REBIRTH

It has not of course been possible to give a detailed account of all the Hasidic movements and groups in Antwerp, the United States and Israel, or all the Lubavitch communities in various towns in France or the groups of communities in other countries, for example in Montreal, where there are more than 5,000 followers,[1] and in London, where there are said to be 18,000 ultra-orthodox residents in the Stamford Hill district alone, the vast majority of whom are Hasidim.[2]

The fact remains that, in Montreal as in London and in all the places that we have visited in the course of the preceding chapters, Hasidism has undergone, between 1945 and the present day, a rebirth and a development that have been remarkable and unexpected in equal measure. For the first four decades of the 20th century, the Hasidic movement, albeit certainly still in existence – principally in Poland, had in fact waned considerably. Zionism and the various socialist movements had won over a substantial part of the Jewish populations of Eastern Europe to their ideas and the emigration of millions of Jews to the United States from the end of the 19th century had not resulted in a significant transplantation of Hasidism in this country. Furthermore, the majority of Jewish emigrants were not Hasidim; the rebbes discouraged their followers from leaving for this country. Some Hasidim, albeit in small numbers, had settled in Palestine, particularly in Jerusalem.

Nevertheless, the strong hostility of most rebbes to Zionist activities restricted any departure of followers to the Holy Land, even at a period following Hitler's rise to power when there was a great increase in Jewish immigration there.[3] It is certainly necessary to note the lack of foresight of most rebbes concerning the disaster that was about to befall their flock in the country where this occurred on the largest scale, which almost delivered the death blow to the Hasidic movement. Certainly, some rebbes visited Palestine before the Second World War but no major Hasidic leader settled there. In the last few years before the Second World War, the Agudath* party and the Gerer rebbe acquiesced at least tacitly in the creation of a Jewish state in Palestine,[4] but this was already very late in the day. From 1933 and particularly after 1935, the Palestinians opposed Jewish immigration, including by violent means, and Great Britain, the mandatory power in the country, considerably restricted the opportunities for immigration there; in the final analysis, the influx of Hasidim remained very small. At the time of the great tragedy of the Shoah, Hasidism therefore did not have much of a presence either in Palestine or in the United States but, by a quirk of fate, it is precisely in North America and in Israel that Hasidism has experienced its main expansion since 1945.

ORIGIN OF THE SURVIVORS: IDENTIFICATIONS PAST AND PRESENT

It was therefore survivors of the Shoah who set about rebuilding Hasidic communities. From the end of the war, in some of the displaced persons camps in Germany, some Hasidim, followers of various rebbes, were already joining together to form prayer groups and to reconstruct a Hasidic Jewish way of life. As we know, some rebbes had also managed to escape or survive the Nazis in various circumstances, such as the Klausenburger, Satmarer, Bobover, Lubavitcher and Belzer rebbes and various others besides. In the displaced persons camps in Germany, these leaders were the catalysts for this rebirth; but support also came from major Jewish organizations that were helping all the Jewish survivors of the Shoah, and finally there was the support of followers or ex-followers who remained 'sympathizers', particularly those who had settled in the United States and England mainly before 1940.

The Polish Hasidim who survived the massacres carried out by the Germans were mainly young survivors of the death camps and followers who had spent the war in remote Siberian and Eastern regions of the Soviet Union. The Hungarian Hasidim experienced deportations mainly from 1944; the late unfolding of the Nazi atrocities there resulted in a relatively higher survival rate among Hungarian Hasidim and other ultra-orthodox. Moreover, in certain regions that had been under Rumanian sovereignty, notwithstanding the anti-Semitism and the bloody pogroms perpetrated by the Rumanian fascists, the arrival of the Soviet troops meant that deportations were only carried out in part.

These relative discrepancies in misfortune have somewhat modified the native composition of the Hasidism that re-emerged after the Second World War. The Hungarian, Rumanian and Slovakian Hasidim – the grouping that George Kranzler (see Chapter 3) calls 'Hungarian' – became as numerous as those of Polish origin, if not more so. Today, in fact, Satmar and Vishnitz are principally communities of Hungarian and Rumanian origin, whereas the Bobov and Ger Hasidism mainly have followers of Polish origin, while Lubavitch was initially established by Jews from the former Soviet Union, including in France.

Are these differences still apparent at the beginning of the 21st century? The answer to this question proves to be a complex one. After the Second World War, there were Hasidim of both Hungarian and Polish origin in the Belz community in Antwerp, and there were undoubtedly differences in their behaviour. For instance, the Hungarians wore slightly different clothes from the Galicians and had more children. They also prayed in a more concentrated way, although, by contrast, not always with a very full knowledge of the details of the liturgical customs belonging to the Belz tradition in Galicia, using the liturgy less frequently at the major festivals and so on. In time, for followers born after 1945, these differences faded as they received the same kind of education in Antwerp and the movement's main *yeshive** in Jerusalem.

In many groups that formed after the Second World War, some of the followers were 'orphans' of rebbes who had perished and they therefore had to adapt to the customs practised by their new community, for example, by the Bobov community, whose leader was one of the few Polish rebbes to have survived the Shoah. As we saw, the Bobover have their own scholastic system, which teaches forms of prayer, variants of liturgical texts, specific Bobov melodies and, of course, loyalty and veneration towards the Bobover rebbe. Moreover, the Lubavitch scholastic system, particularly in France, with its teaching of the *Hessides*,* the legacy of the Habad tradition, inculcates its own perspective in its pupils. Thus, where the major dynasties have been able to establish their own school system, the new Hasidic generations who attend these schools, irrespective of their parents' pre-war affiliation or origin, tend to identify with the common model, whether this belongs to Belz, Bobov, Lubavitch, or another dynasty.

Furthermore, as we know, the Hasidic movement underwent a relatively wide geographical dispersal in Eastern Europe, with two main centres, Poland and Hungary – broadly speaking the pre-1914 Austro-Hungarian Empire. Today, often side by side in the same towns or districts (and sometimes within a single community, such as Belz in Antwerp), there are nevertheless 'Hungarian' and 'Polish' forms of Hasidism. There is also the Russian model, with Lubavitch, which had a relatively small following before the war – the situation in the Soviet Union acted as a strong curb on its activities – but which, as we have seen, has gained a great deal of influence today.

With its 40,000 Hasidim, Williamsburg is the almost uniform prototype of the 'Hungarian' Hasidic district, characterized by a fierce loyalty to a Jewish fundamentalism brought from their regions of origin. By contrast, 'Polish' Hasidism, the Belz, Bobov and Ger dynasties, with a strong but far from homogeneous presence in Borough Park, Antwerp, Jerusalem, Bene Beraq and elsewhere, certainly has ultra-observant followers but there is a less absolute rigidity there. Crown Heights is an even more uniform district than Williamsburg, in which the 'Russian-style' Habad model rules, deriving from an ancient tradition that synthesizes rationalism and mysticism, combined with an intense missionary activity at present. This type of Hasidism has a different spirit, which combines rigorous observance, modernity and openness to (Jewish) otherness. These relatively diverse mentalities endure in the young generations who have grown up in their respective communities.

Some differences between *minugem*,* customs of the various dynasties, sometimes local customs, certainly secondary to the common observance of Jewish rules, persist in all the movements. The distinctions relate to the details of the liturgy, the melodies and songs, *nigunim*,* used in religious celebrations and various festivities, clothing and the way in which it is worn and the sidelocks, which are of varying length and visibility and may even be absent and so on. Furthermore, as marriages among the Hasidim are arranged by the families or friends of the future spouses, they tend to be concluded mainly between couples of similar or close Hasidic affiliation, which like the customs, contributes to preserving differences of origin. Finally, as we know, there are also political divergences between various movements, above all concerning Zionism and Israel, or concerning membership of or support for one or other religious party in this country.

Since the end of the communist regimes in Eastern Europe, tour operators active in Hasidic circles, and sometimes leaders from one or other community, have begun to organize pilgrimages to Eastern Europe to the founding sites of the movement and particularly to the tombs of various rebbes. Generally, these tours include the synagogues of the past and cemeteries in various places. The Hasidim visit the new tombstone and mausoleum of Baal Shem Tov and other Hasidic leaders who lived in Miedzyboz in Ukraine. As Shifra Epstein notes, as an ethnologist who recently took part in two Hasidic pilgrimages in Poland, one from the United States and the other from Israel, the travellers belonged to various communities but mainly to two in particular, both of 'Hungarian' origin, Satmar for those coming from the United States, Vishnitz for those from Israel.[5] Most of the sites that are visited are situated in Poland (Krakow, Sanz, Gorlice, Lyzhansk, Ger etc.). By visiting these places and praying there, usually together, 'the participants often rediscover during their journey their sense of belonging to the wider Hasidic community, beyond the different sectarian identities'.[6]

These pilgrimages also contribute to establishing Hasidism within its remote Eastern European past. The Hasidim and their rebbes appear to be increasingly attached to these roots. Most of the rebbes, often from the smaller movements, who have emerged since the war, have called themselves after a particular town or village in Eastern Europe; a good example is the dynasty founded by the reb Ytsekl in Antwerp, which is already on its third rebbe; they call themselves Przeworsker rebbes; Przeworsk is a small town in Galicia where the founder, reb Ytsekl, was never the rebbe.[7]

THE COMMUNITY COCOON: A SOURCE OF PSYCHOLOGICAL SUPPORT

It is well known that Hasidism subscribes to a philosophy of joy, or *simhe*.* 'It is a great *mitsve* (obligation) to be constantly in joy. Sadness is the exile of the divine presence', as the rebbe Nahman of Bratzlav said.[8] Dancing, as an expression of this joy, forms part of the Hasidic liturgical practices at many festivals. Nevertheless, I had been struck during my field research among the Belz Hasidim in Antwerp, which lasted over five years, from 1960 to 1965, that this joy, particularly at rather happy festivals such as Purim* and Simhat Torah, remained very restrained, especially among the adults. This was easy to understand; after the Shoah, the survivors had to overcome the traumas of the tragedies experienced during the persecutions. Having experienced the loss of their parents, brothers and sisters, and in some cases their spouses and their children, they then had to endure physical and material hardship and adapt to the new environment in Antwerp, the United States, Israel or elsewhere. The reunions between companions in belief within a *shtiebl** or a shared oratory, in which after years of persecution it was finally possible again to practise, pray and study the sacred texts several times daily and talk to like-minded people, especially about shared concerns, which were many and various, certainly formed a favourable setting for a much needed psychic recuperation.

Moreover, the Hasidim from a single group, who studied and prayed every morning and evening in their oratory, and who also wanted to avoid long journeys on foot on the Sabbath and festival days, settled near to each other, which led to the formation of districts with Hasidic populations of varying sizes in Antwerp, Brooklyn, Jerusalem and elsewhere. Sometimes, as in Antwerp but also in New York, the Hasidim would also meet on a daily basis in a professional context, particularly in the diamond industry and trade – in Antwerp on Pelikanstraat and in New York on 47th Street between 5th Avenue and 6th Avenue.

This intense community life mainly concerned the men, but to a lesser degree and in a different way it also operated among the women. They certainly did not have as many religious obligations as the men – only going to pray at the *shtiebl* on Saturday mornings and certain festival days – but they lived in close proximity to each other and all kinds of intense informal exchanges rapidly ensued. Hasidic wives also have a shared subject of concern: exchanging information about the material questions of daily life, particularly concerning the purchase of food; knowing if a particular new preserve – sauce, vegetable, cheese spread etc. – conforms to the strict criteria of the *kashrut*,* or if a particular baker, fishmonger, grocer or butcher is trustworthy. At the beginning, the Hasidim did not have their own networks of traders and they therefore had to turn to other suppliers, often including non-Jewish ones. Then when, following marriages, the children grew up, and with schools for young boys and girls having been created, usually near the places of prayer, these schools became another important meeting place for the mothers of the young children. Moreover, many mothers played an active part in support organizations for the schools or, on another level, mutual assistance organizations for families or individuals in difficulty. Finally, there were, as there still are, all the informal meetings in the shops and in the street. People chat, gossip and exchange information there.

My own field research among the Belz Hasidim in Antwerp in the early 1960s, at a period when the adults in the community were almost all survivors of the Shoah, enabled me to observe, especially among the men, completely ordinary behaviour with no visible signs of psychological distress. Of course, it is very difficult in an environment that was particularly reticent on such matters at the time to discover deep psychological difficulties among the followers, but participant observation would certainly have enabled me to detect any slightly strange behaviour. Accordingly, the Hasidic community, with its timeless religious practices associated with an intense sociability, which in no way precludes the possibility of conflicts and disputes, certainly appeared to constitute a haven for psychological rehabilitation.[9]

MARRIAGE AND DEMOGRAPHY

A major element in the restoration of Hasidism was the rapid formation of new families. The survivors, widowers or widows and single people, married as soon as possible. The marriages, especially in the immediate post-war period, were concluded without any requirement for homogamy, that is to say, without the spouses adhering to the same rebbe or originating from the same region of Europe. Beyond considerations such as the age, financial resources and possibly the physical appearance of the future spouses,[10] the principal concern of the marriage-brokers was that the man should be devout, if possible instructed in Talmudic subjects, and that the woman should observe the laws of female purity, *taharas mishpohe*,*[11] and that she should be willing and able to run a household that observes the strict rules of the kashrut and so on.

To this day, community endogamy, for example among the ultra-traditionalist Satmar Hasidim, is a trend rather than an obligation.[12] Moreover, in the case of unions between a man and woman who have hitherto been living in two different towns or countries, the couple usually settles where the husband lives. Thus, in the 1960s, the Belz Hasidim in Antwerp often married women who were living in Israel, all of whom came to settle with their spouse: furthermore, the economic position of the Antwerp Hasidim was much better at that time than the situation in Hasidic circles in Israel. Among the Lubavitcher, the presence of many *baalei tshuve*,* recent converts, is accompanied by a homogamy between the latter; marriages between 'original' Hasidim and these 'penitents' are thus avoided, if not prohibited, which amounts to a persistence within the movement of a specifically Habad hierarchy, with an 'aristocracy of elders' as guardians of the tradition.[13]

Whatever the subtle differences in the matrimonial system between the Hasidim of the various dynasties and communities, there is a general increase in large families; as we have seen, five, six or more children are a common occurrence, which for over fifty-five years has produced a major expansion of the number of followers in the various groups. This growth is in evidence in almost all the Hasidic movements, the most traditionalist such as the Satmar being among the most fertile, whereas the Lubavitcher have a lower fertility rate, particularly because of the adherence of *baalei tshuve*, who are often single and relatively old, but their expansion is ensured by the constant influx of the 'penitents'.

Despite the lack of precise data available, we can estimate that there are around 400,000 Hasidim (men, women and children) worldwide, of whom the majority, around 200,000, are in Israel, with a further 150,000 in the United States, and another 50,000 to 60,000 in the rest of the world, such as Antwerp, Canada, Great Britain and France. Even if these figures are only approximate, this indicates a substantial expansion of Hasidism. At the end of the Second World War, the Hasidim, including the survivors from Eastern Europe and some communities in Israel and the United States comprised 20,000 to 30,000 people at the very most.

It is true that not all the Hasidic centres have experienced similar levels of growth. In Crown Heights, for instance, there may even have been a decline, for three main reasons: there have been racial tensions and incidents in the district; since the Lubavitcher rebbe's death in 1994, the district has had less appeal; and, finally, because many young followers settle more or less everywhere in the world to spread 'the good word', as 'emissaries' of the movement. Moreover, there has only been limited growth in Williamsburg because a large 'migratory' current has left this 'old' Hasidic bastion for Kiryas Joel, Monroe, Monsey and so on. The Hasidim in Borough Park have also spread into the neighbouring areas. By contrast, in Jerusalem and Bene Beraq but also elsewhere in Israel, the Hasidic population is increasing.

This demographic dynamism stands in stark contrast to the situation in other parts of the Jewish population. After the Nazi genocide and the massacre of six million people, there were eleven million Jews left worldwide in 1945.[14] Whereas Germany, Italy and Japan, as defeated nations that had experienced large-scale human losses during the Second World War, increased in population by 25% to 33% between 1940 and 1960, the Jewish demographic expansion remained well below this level. In 1960, the Jewish population reached 12,800,000, an increase of only just over 16% since the end of the war. In 1997, the Jewish population worldwide was estimated to be 13,092,000;[15] this clearly represents a very limited growth over nearly fifty years: negligible against a worldwide population increase of 36% between 1948 and 1968. The relative stagnation among the Jews is not due to a higher mortality rate but predominantly to a lower birth rate, whereas among Hasidim the number of children was growing almost exponentially. Admittedly, if we accept, for example, the estimate of 400,000 Hasidim worldwide, they nevertheless represent only a small proportion, 3.05%, of the Jewish population worldwide in 1997. Nevertheless, Hasidic demography contrasts sharply with the Jewish population as a whole. Everywhere in the world, the overall fertility rate among the Jewish population is substantially lower than it is among the Hasidim. In Israel, although the birth rate is higher than in other developed countries, the number of children per adult female, estimated at 2.6% in 1991 for the Jewish population as a whole, is nevertheless well below the figure in Hasidic circles.[16]

Furthermore, intermarriage between Jews and 'gentiles' is increasingly common; for example, in the United States, in first marriages, the phenomenon is increasing; in 1990 it reached more than 50%.[17] In France, a recent survey gives a lower percentage, 30%, but this figure, representing an increase on the findings of a survey in 1986, excludes spouses who have converted to Judaism; furthermore, among young people, from 20 to 29 years old, the exogamy rate is over 40%.[18] Many of the children from these marriages have few if any ties with Judaism. In Israel, the arrival of hundreds of thousands of immigrants from the former Soviet Union has brought many mixed couples and families, whose children, at least according to the strictest interpretation of the Halohe,* the Jewish law, are not Jews.[19] Clearly, this intermixing and its consequences are unthinkable among the Hasidim;[20] in any case, demographically the Hasidim still constitute a hard core of the Jewish identity.

The remarkable demographic expansion of Hasidism is certainly not solely due to the observance of the Biblical prescription 'be fruitful, and multiply' or to homogamous marriage. It is clear that infant mortality among the Hasidim, as in the populations of most of the countries in which they have a particularly strong presence, has decreased considerably in relation to the past both in Eastern Europe and elsewhere. Finally, whether in Belgium or the

United States, in Israel or France, large families receive assistance from the State and charitable organizations, which certainly facilitates the adherence to the Biblical prescriptions.

TRADITIONALISM AND MODERNITY

Despite its traditionalism, Hasidism in no way rejects modernity, at least insofar as its benefits do not pose any threat to its beliefs and way of life. The Hasidim are particularly frequent airline travellers, whether this is for visiting their rebbes in Jerusalem, Bene Beraq and Brooklyn or their relatives, or for business trips and so on. Anyone who travels between Tel-Aviv, New York, Montreal or Brussels often encounters Hasidim in the international airports that serve these cities. Hasidim generally have modern appliances in their homes: refrigerators (sometimes two in order to separate the meat-based from the milk-based foods according to the kashrut rules), electric ovens, telephones and so on.

However, the highly rigorous defence of Hasidic customs imposes some strict rules concerning use of the media. Reading religious and 'serious' (as opposed to sensationalist newspapers with their images with sexual overtones) secular newspapers and weeklies is more or less permitted – although with reservations among many followers of the strictest movements, such as the Satmarer. By contrast, going to the cinema is forbidden, and radio, television and, especially more recently, the internet pose a problem. Radio is tolerated, mainly for listening to the news, but television with its pervasive sexuality and profane music is generally condemned. This certainly does not prevent young Hasidim from looking at a particular programme being broadcast on the screen just as they are going past an audio-visual shop, or visiting a non-Hasidic neighbour to watch a particular important event.

Once again, the Lubavitcher differ in all these respects in having embraced modernity; they make extensive use of audio-visual equipment to disseminate the movement's messages, particularly the rebbe's addresses. As we know, Lubavitch in Crown Heights has also developed a sophisticated interactive website, 'Chabad Lubavitch in Cyberspace', and many Habad communities from various countries, including France, have their own websites as well. There is therefore no prohibition at all on the ownership and use of televisions, video recorders and computers with internet access. However, the Lubavitch attitude is not remotely shared by the Hasidic movements in general. It is the proliferation of pornographic websites that is the main cause of concern to the ultra-orthodox. In 1998, some Hasidic and orthodox authorities in the United States had warned against the danger of internet use.[21] In January 2000, twenty-nine *gdoilim*,* religious leaders in Israel, including several rebbes, published a declaration warning against the dangers of private use of the internet; viewing CD-Roms and playing games and films on the computer was also condemned.[22] Among the twenty-nine signatories of the declaration, which was published in newspapers and posted in the orthodox districts in Israel, were the Vishnitzer and Belzer rebbes and some other less influential *admorim*.*[23] The Gerer rebbe, however, such a powerful figure in the Agudath* party in Israel, did not sign this declaration. Admittedly all the Hasidic persuasions – including Lubavitch – share the concerns about the 'detestable' uses of the internet, but the use by many Hasidim of e-mail and the web for practical and professional purposes prevents many rebbes from adopting excessively trenchant positions on this matter. The Belzer rebbe, who had even condemned the very presence of computers in followers' homes, has since allowed them to use these in a professional capacity.

THE POSITION OF WOMEN: SOME MINOR ADVANCES

Some significant changes apart, the situation of women in the Hasidic environment is essentially the same as in the past in Eastern Europe. Everywhere, it is still men who run the affairs of each community, who carry out the religious activities in the oratories on a daily basis, who control the power structures and are heads of families.[24] Furthermore, the circumcision and the *bar mitsve*,* the attainment of masculine majority at the age of 13 years, are essential rites of passage that are lacking for girls; among the Hasidim there would be no question of a *bat mitsve*, a feminine majority, which is the more egalitarian practice followed in conservative and reform religious circles.

Furthermore, as in the past, women retain responsibility for their religious purity, *taharas mishpohe** (see p. 139 above and note 11), the care and education of young children (for boys this generally passes when they are three or four years old to the *melamed** in the *haider*,* the children's school) and running the household, in particular with the meticulous supervision of the kashrut* in the food that they provide to the family. They also mostly take charge of the material preparations for the religious celebrations and festival meals.

They also prepare the collations and meals that are carried away by their close male relatives when they attend certain *sides*,* festive meals in the oratory, particularly the weekly *shaleshides** at the end of the Sabbath. As we know, only the men attend these gatherings, just as with the *tish halten** of the rebbes, a ceremony that is so highly esteemed by the followers. Many women, because of recurrent pregnancies and the presence of small children, rarely go to the oratory, not even for the weekly service on Saturday morning or those on festival days.

Despite everything, there are some developments taking place. Admittedly, from the immediate post-war period, in accordance with the ultra-orthodox rule that states that only men truly have access to Talmudic knowledge, most of the Hasidic schools for girls were offering religious curricula that were considerably more limited than those provided for the boys. Furthermore, these same schools had more extensive 'profane' teachings than the boys' schools. At the outset, it was a case, as for example with the Belzer in Antwerp, of providing useful instruction for the home, with the learning of household tasks but also an indispensable minimal familiarization with the languages of the countries of residence. Thus, in Israel, in most of the ultra-religious schools, the girls were taught modern Hebrew[25] – whereas many Hasidic leaders condemn the use of the 'sacred language' in daily life. Increasingly, in these schools, in Israel and elsewhere, undoubtedly for economic reasons but also because many young women are developing an awareness of the outside world, the teaching includes specialized classes in subjects that have previously been unknown in these circles, such as information technology but also interior décor. In France, as we have seen, certain subjects from the baccalaureate and some taught at the first university level are even included.

The great difficulties in making ends meet that affect many Hasidic families, bearing in mind their many children and the modest earnings of the husbands, who do not practise very lucrative professions, also increasingly force the women, at least before having had their first child, and as soon as possible thereafter, to work outside the house, if only part-time. They often work as secretaries, schoolteachers, employees or sales staff, and sometimes they run highly profitable shops (children's clothing, crystal-ware, jewellery), particularly in Williamsburg and Borough Park. Furthermore, many married Satmar women seek a salaried job in order to get out of the house and to do work that is more interesting than the domestic tasks.[26]

Among the Lubavitcher, this process is even more in evidence, because of the presence of numerous 'penitents', with a university education and sometimes qualified occupations and posts. The Lubavitch campaigning, particularly during the struggle against the hippy movement and other alternative groups on the campuses, has also left its mark on the situation of women in this movement. In 1972, some women's study groups for the 'penitents' emerged in Crown Heights and in 1974 the rebbe authorized the creation of *Machon Chana*, an institute for the study of Judaism that was specially designed for women:[27] in addition to Hebrew and Yiddish, they study Biblical and Talmudic texts and Jewish history. Since 1958, the Lubavitch women have had their own quarterly, *Di Yddishe Heim*, 'the Jewish household', which is nevertheless run and written by the men, rabbis within the movement.

Moreover, since 1956, and more successfully every year, hundreds of Lubavitch women from all over the world meet for several days for annual conventions in Crown Heights. On the Sunday afternoon, the rebbe Menahem Mendel Schneerson would address this female audience, who had been granted exceptional permission to sit in the male section of the large synagogue on 770 Eastern Parkway (in the absence of the men, who listened to the rebbe's addresses from outside via loudspeakers).

Paradoxically, this increase in visible militant female activities among the Lubavitcher is due to the desire to counteract the influences of the feminist movement more effectively, particularly in the United States, where this is especially strong. Although the traditional situations and the role-division between men and women among the Lubavitcher remain, the 'ladies and young women are no longer the useful and docile members of a community that will allow them some latitude in exchange for good and loyal services'.[28] What form does family life take among the Lubavitcher? There is usually reciprocal cooperation, as well as discussions and debates on religious matters.[29] Even among the Satmarer, who are a long way removed from the modern-style practices of Lubavitch, the men now participate in household tasks;

furthermore, cooperation and joint decision-making are very much on the increase among them.[30]

The above processes also apply to Hasidic women in Israel. Those from the ultra-traditionalist district of Mea Shearim, much more than the men, read newspapers, including secular dailies; many of them also listen to the radio, particularly musical programmes and stories.[31] Furthermore, increasing numbers of ultra-religious women are working outside the home.[32] Most of them speak Hebrew – despite the above-mentioned disapproval – as well as Yiddish. Moreover, even in Mea Shearim the men more often carry out household tasks.[33]

Over the last fifty years, the position of women in Hasidic circles has therefore unquestionably advanced to some extent: economic necessities have played a major part in this, but so has the indirect influence of prevailing feminism. Furthermore, from Satmar to Lubavitch, it is proclaimed that women are highly respected and praised, particularly for their essential role in the home. However, this progress remains limited; in the main, prevailing norms maintain the subordinate status of women. This applies both within the family, where at least in principle the husband is in charge, and within the social structure of the Hasidic communities, in which the men almost without exception (we have seen the case of the rebbetsen* Feiga Teitelbaum among the Satmarer) have an exclusive claim to all the positions of leadership. Access to religious learning and Talmudic studies – the only forms of knowledge that are truly valued in this environment[34] – remains a male prerogative.

Furthermore, the women continue to be sequestered in a separate section of the oratories, where they have to be invisible and their prayers must be inaudible to the men. In Israel, the Hasidim have some means of exerting pressure to introduce sexual segregation in certain situations through their political parties. Whereas in the United States the Hasidim in Kiryas Joel have to charter buses from private companies to drive them to New York while ensuring the separation of men and women within them, in Israel by contrast, Egged, a state-subsidized organization, has provided a bus service since 2001 between Bene Beraq and Jerusalem, with a separate entrance and section for women at the back.[35] There is also sexual segregation at wedding celebrations and in many other situations. It would be possible to give many further examples of this segregation, which is still being widely observed.

How do Hasidic women avoid 'contamination' from the secular world – particularly in Israel, where young women wear many kinds of shorts and mini-skirts and lead highly emancipated lives – when by the very nature of their more extensive secular education than men they are on a closer wavelength to this world? Let us mention just a few reasons. First, the set of values, norms and rules imposed by the parents and the traditionalist school system teach the girls from the earliest age that their task in life is to create an ultra-religious family and to help their future husband to devote himself, outside his paid employment, to the study of the sacred texts. Furthermore, it is more or less explicitly stated that the *haredim** have a much higher social and cultural status than other Jews, even more so than goyim,* non-Jews.[36] Does this prevent women from deviating or leaving the fold? Although this is a rare occurrence, it is not unheard of, as certain testimonies reveal, particularly from women writers who have left the 'inner circle' and a very few studies relating to this subject.[37]

A SPIRITUAL OR INTELLECTUAL REVIVAL?

In the Hasidic movement today, are there any new spiritual or intellectual leaders like Baal Shem Tov, Dov Baer, the Maggid of Mezhirech and others in the past who spearheaded the first expansion of Hasidism? According to certain authorities in the field, the response seems to be in the negative on a strict definition of spirituality: 'Not only are new ideas apparently absent, but the old spiritual teachings are giving way to a new emphasis on the external features of Jewish life', writes Joseph Dan, a contemporary specialist in Hasidic spirituality. Marc-Alain Ouaknin, another expert, writes: 'From the outside this Hasidism is still alive, it has many followers, but it lacks what created the Hasidic revolution: the strength to try out something new and to be inventive.'[38]

However, does the rebirth of the movement through some dynamic survivors not testify to an intense faith and spirit, and therefore to a spirituality that inspires their actions? Furthermore, then as now, the rebbes, especially the most famous ones, are among many other things the authors of *toyres*,* teachings, addresses, speeches and writings (often recorded by their followers) that enrich the lives of their followers and are intended to have exemplary value for others. It is true that these teachings remain private, being known and appreciated predominantly by the authors' closest followers.

Furthermore, the *devekuss*,* the mystical communion with God, one of the foundations of the Hasidic doctrine, remains very much alive among the 'rank and file' disciples and it manifests itself mainly in the spontaneous fervour of their religiosity. Certainly for many of them, this is also in part a practice acquired in early childhood; this is a result of culture in the ethnological sense. We might paraphrase Max Weber here and refer to a 'routinization of fervour', which is not in fact purely a contemporary phenomenon. Despite everything, fervour was and remains one of the specific fundamental contributions of Hasidism to the Jewish religion.

Specific contributions have nevertheless been made by particular important leaders, with repercussions beyond the innermost circle of followers. Joel Teitelbaum, the Satmarer rebbe, produced many texts and addresses in order to criticize Zionism and to warn his followers against the deviations represented by the State of Israel. Certainly, his thought, despite its religious foundations, seems at least in terms of its conclusions, to be more ideological than truly spiritual; however, it remains faithful to the Hasidic anti-Zionism of the past and it demonstrates that criticism of the Hebrew State can come from Jews ... intensely Jewish ones.

A further contribution to Hasidic thought seems to me to be the concept of Ahavat Israel,* love of Israel, in fact love of all Jews, developed by the Lubavitch rebbe, Menahem Mendel Schneerson, a concept that underpins all the intense campaigns implemented by his followers in order to awaken the

Jewish faith in large numbers of *baalei tshuve*. To put this doctrine into practice, much of the Lubavitch activity consists in creating organizations, particularly the Habad houses, but also in publishing texts for reflection and edification in all languages. Although Hasidism achieved its initial success as a movement among the Jewish populations of Eastern Europe, this dynamic – spontaneous rather than truly organized – is very different from the systematic campaigns of the Lubavitcher. Furthermore, the Lubavitch attitude contrasts with that of the other major Hasidic persuasions which, at least until recently, tended rather to be inward-looking, to despise non-orthodox Jews and to feel little concern for their fate. However, the doctrine of 'Ahavat Israel' has recently spread into other communities. As we know, from 1997 (see p. 99 above) some rebbes, mainly from the Ger movement, set up a series of schools for thousands of non-religious children.

Despite their isolationism, even the Satmarer had established some centres called Rav Tov ('in abundance') in several European cities from 1973, particularly in Vienna, to help Iranian, Russian and other Jews fleeing their countries: as well as material aid, they were given instruction in special yeshives to help them rediscover their Jewish heritage. However, it is mainly since the 1980s that Satmar, turning its back on its customary inward-looking attitude, has increased its efforts by establishing *keruv** centres for approaching new converts, particularly among the children of refugees.[39]

A missionary dynamic that extends beyond the Lubavitch movement seems to have become a doctrinal component of the Hasidic revival.

The Hasidic world today is also making a substantial intellectual contribution, although it is not often highly developed or innovative. This clearly concerns the daily practice of Talmudic study by male followers – from school to the everyday life in the oratories.[40] There are certainly some non-Hasidic orthodox, such as those from the Ponevez yeshive* in Bene Beraq, who pursue Talmudic studies that have evolved differently from those of most Hasidim and today there are known to be Talmudic circles that hold sometimes very thorough discussions in certain Jewish university circles, especially in the United States.

However, within the range of groups or sub-groups interested in this activity, the Hasidim are at present the only ones who practise it both extensively and highly consistently. Especially among the adults, attending the *shtiebl* daily and for long periods, the study of the sacred texts is not only an intellectual exercise but also an intense form of social activity; the accompanying *lernen** and discussions take place in a singing tone and in a Yiddish with particular stresses, usually in small groups that meet on a permanent basis. The study is sometimes interrupted for conversation, chatting, gossip and so on. The *lernen*, the Talmudic study, is therefore also an important social event that helps to strengthen the bonds between followers. Certainly the Hasidim, in their very great majority, do not aspire to be Talmudic scholars and Satmar is known to place particular emphasis on the study of texts that deal with religious obligations and their practical application. But in any case, although it may not provide an intellectual revival for its practitioners, Hasidic Talmudic study nonetheless constitutes a significant form of intellectual activity.

It should be emphasized, incidentally, that the Kabbala does not form part of the customary studies, although it is an essential foundation of the development of Hasidism; only a few eminent figures, rebbes or scholars – there are some – devote themselves to this to some extent.

It is a rather paradoxical fact that a movement that began with an explicit rejection of the elitist and scholarly nature of Talmudic study in the mediaeval Jewish world is today the most assiduous upholder of this major Jewish tradition, which has provided a distinct cultural and social identity over the centuries and in many places.[41]

In the final analysis, it is mainly figures from outside the movement, particularly Martin Buber before 1945 or Gershom Scholem, despite the critical side of his reflections, or writers such as Elie Wiesel, Chaim Potok and Isaac Bashevis Singer, who have popularized and, particularly in the cases of Martin Buber and Elie Wiesel, idealized Hasidism. However, the spiritual and intellectual record of the movement today is in no way negligible. It consists in a dynamic missionary approach that undoubtedly helps to reinforce or revive the Jewish identity in its religious form, the fervent support for Talmudic study as the essential historical foundation of a specifically Jewish culture; and, last but not least, the daily use of Yiddish, a linguistic treasure from Ashkenazi Judaism that would now be a relic on the verge of disappearing completely had it not been practised by many Hasidim.

A FAVOURABLE CONTEXT

The Lubavitcher missionary campaigns, which date from the beginning of the 1960s, have certainly brought some Jews to Hasidism – in Israel, as we have seen, half of the 4,500 families who belong to the movement are people who have 'returned' to the religion and in France, as we know, most followers are newcomers of Sephardic origin. More recently, other movements have instigated such missionary activities but the remarkable and unexpected expansion of Hasidism since 1945 clearly derives largely from its demographic expansion and the commitment among Hasidim to the prescription to 'be fruitful, and multiply'. Whereas since the end of the 19th century there have been innumerable defections in Hasidim among the young people who leave Talmudei Torah* and yeshives and who become involved in secular political movements – socialist, communist, Zionist etc.– today, however, although desertions certainly take place they remain a marginal occurrence.[42]

Defections in the past were mainly due to the deplorable economic, social and political conditions in which the Jews were living, in particular the Hasidim in the small towns, which resulted in the most dynamic young people migrating to the cities and abroad, with everything that this uprooting then entailed in terms of social reintegration and unfamiliar ways of life, new forms of political awareness, adherence to less all-embracing forms of religiosity or, in more extreme cases, a total rejection of the traditional world.

Why is this no longer the case at a time when, even today, some followers are having difficulty making ends meet? Let us examine the question by returning to the starting-point of the contemporary expansion.

In the post-war years, the political, social and economic context in Belgium, the United States and Israel, or in Canada or England, was somewhat favourable to the rebirth of Hasidism. The Hasidim from Eastern Europe found refuge there in conditions that were at the very least acceptable. In Antwerp, the restoration sought by the city authorities of a Jewish community that was strongly associated with the revival of a flourishing diamond industry ensured a relative tolerance towards the settlement of many Hasidim from Eastern Europe. Moreover, the local Jewish philanthropic associations helped the Hasidim to obtain residence permits, suitable accommodation and so on. In the United States, the traditional immigration policy facilitated the settlement of many orthodox Jews. In Israel, the so-called 'law of return' has clearly enabled Hasidim to immigrate without restrictions, supported on their arrival by institutions that help the new emigrants, in addition to the support provided to the ultra-religious communities and their followers as a result of the presence, since the country's accession to independence, of ministers and representatives from the Agudath* party.

All the countries in which there has been a substantial settlement and development of Hasidic communities – Belgium, the United States, Israel, France, Canada and England – are democratic states, in principle non-discriminatory towards Jews. This was clearly far from the case before the Second World War in most of their countries of origin but also after 1945 in the 'popular democracies', in which ultra-religious groups, particularly Jewish ones, were certainly not welcome. By contrast, Hasidic institutions were thenceforth able to develop almost entirely as they pleased. Moreover, the attitudes of Jewish organizations in general, despite the reservations of some of their leaders who abhor the extreme religious model of the Hasidim, have generally been favourable to them. This was self-evidently the case in Antwerp, where following the inter-war period and from 1945 the influence of figures from the orthodox tradition who were close to Hasidism was substantial. As for the United States, from the immediate post-war period there was substantial aid from charitable organizations to the survivors of the Shoah, which also benefited the Hasidim. Subsequently, Hasidim such as the Lubavitcher obtained subsidies from these organizations for their educational activities, particularly from the counter-culture period of the 1960s and 1970s, because they clearly contributed to maintaining the Jewish identity, which accorded with the underlying ideology of these organizations. Through groups of 'friends of Lubavitch', Habad has also managed to mobilize a public that appreciates their missionary activities and provides them with financial assistance.

In Israel, the state was certainly strongly influenced at the outset by left-wing secular Zionist parties such as the socialist Mapai party, to which David Ben Gurion belonged, and the extreme-left Mapam (United Workers) party, as well as the conservative parties, Zionists in general and Cherut. However, the founders of Zionism ultimately based their doctrine concerning the return to Zion on all kinds of Biblical references and these religiously based ideas have influenced these secular parties and national life from its beginnings. Time in Israel has a rhythm that is structured by the Sabbath as a day of rest and the major festivals of the Jewish calendar, and schools constantly commemorate the major events of Jewish history in Biblical times. From before the founding of Israel on 19 June 1947, a 'status quo' letter, signed by Ben Gurion, then the main leader of the Jewish Agency, co-signed by a rabbi from the orthodox Zionist party, was sent to the leaders of Agudath Israel. This document was intended to establish the relations between religion and the future State. 'The Zionist leaders stated their intention: to guarantee the exclusivity of the rabbinical courts in matters of individual statute for Jews; to make the Sabbath and Jewish festivals officially recognized as days of rest that could thus be observed without hindrance; to guarantee the observance of the dietary laws [the kashrut] in all the public institutions that are part of the State; and to preserve the autonomy of the ultra-orthodox education system.'[43]

In essence, this agreement has been maintained to this day and we know that the ultra-orthodox, including Hasidim, have obtained many other advantages; accordingly, in this country that has remained in a state of alert since its foundation, most Hasidim are exempted from military service by their Talmudic studies, as are also young women from ultra-orthodox circles, including Hasidim. Moreover, since the country gained independence, the ultra-religious parties, very often including Agudath Israel and still to this day 'United Torah Judaism', have almost constantly formed part of successive governments, whether of a left-wing or a right-wing complexion.[44] This situation has clearly enabled the ultra-orthodox to obtain many advantages in terms of subsidies, civil service posts, housing, social services and so on. All this is certainly subject to disagreements and conflict on occasion, for example concerning a particular benefit given to large families, or recently on the scale of the exemptions from military service, with some advances for the orthodox but also some setbacks. However, in general, the Hasidim and the ultra-orthodox live in a State that accords them what can unquestionably be termed privileged status.

Thus, in all the countries in which they have settled since the Second World War, the Hasidim have experienced much more favourable material conditions than before the war, although many of them have low incomes, often below the poverty threshold. Nevertheless, Hasidim in difficulty, particularly the many large families, generally receive various forms of aid and subsidy in the states in which they live. Finally, mainly in the United States and Israel, the Hasidim have established a highly effective system of mutual social assistance that also helps to alleviate the difficulties of disadvantaged followers. This aid certainly has material but also psychological effects, which reduce the sense of abandonment that might be experienced by followers in difficulty. The active solidarity seems to me to be a significant factor in explaining why followers so seldom leave the movement.

We should mention once again the contemporary intellectual climate surrounding Hasidism. Before 1940, it was often extremely negative; we need only think of Dubnow and his history of Hasidism, which was at best highly critical of the way in which the charismatic cult of the rebbe had developed and other aspects of the movement – particularly, its 'fanaticism'. The historian Raphael Mahler, who certainly emphasizes the positive role of Hasidism in its beginnings, particularly through its rebellion against 'fossilized orthodoxy', nevertheless states that it went on to become an obstacle to the development of Jewish culture.[45] In Israel today, the expansion of Hasidism and its political and religious role still arouse highly unfavourable reactions in broad secular circles that have launched a full-scale cultural war on both Hasidism and other ultra-religious movements.[46]

By contrast, in Europe and the United States Hasidism is rather in vogue; as I stated previously, outstanding intellectual figures present subtle and positive albeit often idealized images of Hasidism and Hasidim in high-quality works that are read by Jews and non-Jews alike. In particular, the praises of Martin Buber, as a philosopher who is very fond of Hasidic tales – he is extremely reticent, however, about the contemporary experience of Hasidism[47] – and Elie Wiesel as a writer are not necessarily inaccurate but I am bound to point out that their writings generally overlook the less attractive aspects of the movement. First, there is its dogmatism concerning the immutability of Jewish laws, along with its total refusal to allow more open religious organizations (reform and liberal Judaism) to participate in the conduct of religious affairs – this is an attitude shared by non-Hasidic ultra-orthodox in Israel and accepted by the State and most of the political parties as prisoners of the 'status quo' in religious matters as mentioned above. There is also the monopoly exercised by the Hasidim, again in conjunction with the same ultra-orthodox, over essential proceedings of everyday life such as marriage, divorce and the validity of conversions.[48] Furthermore, their misogynistic viewpoints make women, whatever the rebbes may say, into second-class citizens. Other less positive aspects are the almost universal rejection, principally for men but also for women, of a modern education and the acquisition of 'profane' knowledge for anything other than practical purposes; the highly restrictive and parochial nature of their type of Jewish culture; and, finally, the fundamentally conservative nature of their value system.

A GENETIC NUCLEUS?

With several hundred thousand followers, Hasidism can certainly pride itself today on an incontestable success, which, particularly through the two political parties, Agudath and Degel Hatorah, extends to participation in government in Israel. Hasidism cannot therefore be described as a 'sect' that is set apart from the Jewish world. In fact, the movement is more like a 'genetic nucleus' or a structure that contains the essential characteristics of a distinct Jewish identity. In practice, its followers' intense religious life, their assiduous Talmudic studies, their predominant use of Jewish languages – Yiddish and Hebrew – their social withdrawal combined with a strong endogamy, their highly distinctive appearance, in many cases their work as religious officials – as teachers, kashrut supervisors etc. – and as small artisans and shopkeepers, also in the service of the Jewish and Hasidic prescriptions concerning food, clothing, objects of worship and so on, and their strong community life, make them exemplars of an enduring *Yiddishkait*,* of Ashkenazi* Judaism from both a historical and a contemporary perspective. The Hasidim of today seem to me to be the most direct upholders of the highly distinctive traditional Jewish way of life within the Jewish communities in Eastern Europe, in the *shtetleh** of the past.

Of course, contradictions and internal conflicts always existed within the *kahalim** of the Middle Ages and then in the *shtetleh*; furthermore, forces of dissolution, the Haskalah,* the Zionist and socialist movements, sometimes assimilationist, had contributed at least since the 18th century to reducing the importance of traditional community life. In fact, however, if we adopt a structural perspective, the emergence of Hasidic communities in the 18th century, with their development and success in Poland and the surrounding areas, appears to have been a compensatory phenomenon, like a counterweight, in confrontation with these forces of dissolution. Certainly, the extreme cult of the rebbe, which persists strongly today, in particular among the Lubavitcher, who are nevertheless relatively modern-style Hasidim, may cast doubt on the witness-bearing role of Hasidism. However, this cult is only an exaggerated version of the ancient Jewish traditions of the intellectual and spiritual master, the *rebbe*, in the original sense of the word. As for miracles and hagiography,[49] also so typical of the movement, they have been part of Jewish life for a very long time and Hasidism has only adopted and amplified them.

Finally, from a contemporary perspective, the various Hasidic movements introduce, as I have said, wherever they have a presence, a maximal form of Jewish identity that is simultaneously religious, cultural and social. By contrast, in most other forms of Jewishness, while there is not always an assimilation to the non-Jewish world (usually through intermarriage), this identification is to say the least considerably blurred.

However, a 'genetic nucleus' is intimately associated with the cell that contains it. Without wishing to take the biological metaphor too far, is this not also the case with the Hasidim? In Antwerp, the Belzer, Vishnitzer, Gerer, Bobover and other groups, with their extreme form of observance, have certainly had the effect of making the individuals, families and communities with other religious approaches more rigorous themselves, when confronted with these paradigmatic maximalist attitudes. Furthermore, the Hasidim belong in fact to the orthodox religious establishment of the town, to which they provide male and female teachers, ritual slaughterers and so on, and kasher shops and restaurants. We know that the situation is more or less the same in France. In the United States, the most traditionalist and isolationist Hasidim, especially the Satmarer, have exerted their influence on the food industry, particularly through the introduction of *glatt kasher** meat, which has imposed much greater rigour on the non-Hasidic firms in this sector. The revivalist fervour of the Lubavitch Hasidim is certainly also a component of the activities of the most influential Jewish organizations in the country in their efforts to reinforce the Jewish identity.

As I have demonstrated in detail, Hasidism forms part of the national political landscape in Israel, with all the religious but also economic and social interdependencies that this entails. These interactions in Israel are certainly often conflict-ridden but they undoubtedly contribute to an active participation of Hasidism in national life, on which it confers a strong Jewish hue, particularly in the holy city and in Bene Beraq, but also beyond. Furthermore, although the Hasidim have not formally converted to Zionism, many of them, with the notable exception of Satmar and some groups in Mea Shearim, accept at least tacitly and sometimes much more explicitly, the nationalist and colonizing policy in the occupied territories implemented by recent Israeli governments. Some Hasidim, including the Lubavitcher, even militantly support the annexation of these territories – ostensibly for the sake of national security and not Zionism – finally, others have even settled in villages and towns created in the occupied Palestinian territories since 1967. The links with the government action in this domain have therefore intensified.

The Hasidic movement, despite the vague impulses towards withdrawal by a minority, particularly in Mea Shearim, is therefore not set apart from international society; the interactions with other wider circles, albeit conflictual or difficult to detect, are nonetheless real. The Hasidic 'nucleus' is undoubtedly connected with its 'cell', Judaism in general, which it imbues perforce with a strong form of identity and ethnicity that is maintained to a far lesser degree in other spheres.

Appendix

THE RESEARCH

Various methods were deployed in the research that has led to this book. The first, absolutely essential, is my familiarity with Hasidic circles, through the 'fieldwork' investigations that I have conducted on several occasions over the years. This direct observation also enabled me to make use of information from printed material of specifically ultra-religious origin, such as the weekly *Hamodia*, the publication of the Agudath Israel party, which has been strongly influenced by the Hasidim and is well-informed about the movement both in Israel and elsewhere.

It was not possible for me to conduct extensive and deep observation personally in all the major Hasidic centres, but I was nevertheless able to refer to the work of excellent colleagues, mainly ethnologists and sociologists, who have skilfully described the Hasidic movement in various locations. I am thinking primarily of Jerome R. Mintz,[1] sadly deceased in 1997, but also of many others, particularly Israel Rubin and George Kranzler, who have both studied Williamsburg and Satmar Hasidism in their beginnings in the United States, but also more recently.

For the Hasidim in Israel, researchers such as Daniel Meijers and Tamar El-Or have certainly described the life of some communities but unfortunately we have almost no other monographic research available on the rich Hasidic tapestry in this country. Nevertheless, there is detailed information on the recent history of the movement and the various Hasidic leaders in the books of Tzvi (Harry) Rabinowicz: furthermore, certain books by experts, such as Samuel Heilman and David Landau, are a valuable source of information. Moreover, there is a vast literature on the Lubavitch (also called Habad) Hasidic movement. This certainly verges on panegyric, particularly in relation to its last rebbe, Menahem Mendel Schneerson, but there is a wealth of interesting detail in these accounts of the movement.

There are also many magazines and newspapers, in the United States and in Israel, that provide news and high-quality reports on Hasidism. It is here that the internet, as a recent and highly effective research tool, makes a valuable contribution. The websites of newspapers such as the *New York Times* or *Haaretz* and the *Jerusalem Post*, are sources of various types of news on the Hasidim. Moreover, it is possible to access their archives and therefore, without having to resort to microfilm or microfiche that are often very difficult to consult, to find the relevant articles using well-chosen key words and to print them out immediately. Finally, there are the main search engines – in particular Google – that make it possible to expand the range of sites being searched and to find information scattered here and there, particularly including some specialized sites with information about the Hasidic world. The internet has been an incomparably useful research tool in compiling this book.

Of course, I am solely responsible for my expositions, analyses and reflections, but I thought it would be useful to explain at least in outline the process by which it has been possible to produce this book.

Notes

INTRODUCTION

1. Participant observation is an essential technique in ethnology. It consists in a more or less extensive and intense period of immersion in the environment that is being studied.
2. Jacques Gutwirth, *Vie juive traditionelle. Ethnologie d'une communauté hassidique* [Traditional Jewish life. Ethnology of a Hasidic community]. Paris, Éditions de Minuit, 1970.
3. From the outset, it should be stated that the figures for Hasidic demography are provisional, even in Israel, where there is no separate count for their communities. There are only some more or less precise data from localized surveys in restricted groups.
4. On these figures, see 'Population' in *Encyclopaedia Judaica*, CD-Rom edition, Judaica Multimedia, Israel, 1997; Sergio Dellapergola, 'World Jewish Population 1997', *American Jewish Yearbook*, ed. D. Singer & R. Seldin, New York, American Jewish Committee, 1999: 548.
5. I encountered an example of this in Frankfurt, Germany, where an 'emissary', *shlieh*,* a *Habad* Hasidic rabbi, until recently almost the sole Hasidic follower in this city, has run a summer day camp for the last twelve years, with the support of the local Jewish community and various sponsors. This is attended by around eighty children who play, make things and sing, but of course are also given Jewish and Hasidic instruction. More recently, the same emissary established a small international Talmudic academy, with headquarters based in an oratory that forms part of the premises of the city's main synagogue. As we will see, in France this reinforcement of religiosity is powerfully exercised through a group that comprises Jewish schools of various kinds.
6. Unless it has been conducted abroad, because the government authorities require the civil state authorities to register these unions. Of course, these rules do not apply to Christians or Muslims, but it will be clear that marriages between spouses from different religious faiths are not conducted by the relevant Jewish authorities, except where the non-Jewish partner has converted, in which case the conversion has to conform to their very strict criteria.

1. FROM THE BIRTH TO THE REBIRTH

1. Concerning the reception of Shabbetai Tzevi's message in Poland and Eastern Europe, see Gershom Scholem's magnum opus, *Sabbatai Zvi, the Mystical Messiah. 1626–1676*, Princeton, Princeton University Press, 1973: 591–602. See also Stephen Sharot, *Messianism, Mysticism and Magic. A Sociological Analysis of Jewish Religious Movements*, Chapel Hill (NC), University of North Carolina Press, 1982, Chapters 7–8: 86–129; Bernard D. Weinryb, *The Jews of Poland. A Social and Economic History of the Jewish Community in Poland from 1100–1800*, Philadelphia, Jewish Publication Society of America, 1973: 206–236.
2. On Frank, see Weinryb, 1973, Chapter 11: 236–263; also see 'Frankists' in *The New Encyclopaedia of Judaism*. Coedited by Fred Skolnik & Shmuel Himelstein. New York, New York University Press, 2002 (1st ed. 1989).
3. According to Scholem 1973: 798; the latter discusses only Tzevi but his analysis seems to me to be equally applicable to Frank.
4. On the tense situations that prevailed in these communities, see Benzion Dinur, 'The origins of Hasidism and its social and messianic foundations' in *Essential Papers on Hasidism*, ed. Gershon David Hundert, New York, London, New York University Press, 1991: 86–208 (translated from Hebrew).
5. See Lloyd P. Gartner, *History of the Jews in Modern Times*, Oxford, Oxford University Press, 2001: 77.

6. See Simon Dubnow, *Geschichte des Chassidismus* [History of Hasidism], Berlin, 1931, 2 vols (reprinted 1969): I, 90. Some factual details concerning the life of Baal Shem Tov are missing.
7. See Moishe J. Rosman, 'Social conflicts in Miedzyboz in the generation of the Besht', in *Hasidism Reappraised*, ed. A. Rapaport-Albert, London, Portland (OR), Littman Library of Jewish Civilization, 1997: 51–62. Jews were able to practise commercial activities and crafts in favourable conditions.
8. It was not until 1814, forty-four years after the death of the Besht, that a collection of writings appeared concerning his life and his miracles. See these accounts in *In Praise of the Baal Shêm Tov [Shivhei ha-Besht]. The Earliest Collection of Legends about the Founder of Hasidism*, translated and edited by Dan Ben-Amos and Jerome R. Mintz, Bloomington, London, Indiana University Press, 1970.
9. Like *Besht*, the *maggid* did not leave any writings, but his ideas were transmitted by his followers.
10. Compiled by Joseph Caro (1488–1575) in a code that remains authoritative.
11. Gershom Scholem, *Major Trends in Jewish Mysticism*, New York, Schocken, 1961: 344.
12. See Gartner, 2001: 83.
13. On Hasidic ritual slaughter, see Dubnow 1931, I: 249–250 and also Julien Bauer, *Les Juifs hassidiques* [The Hasidic Jews], Paris, PUF, 'Que sais-je?', 1994: 25–26.
14. See Shmuel Ettinger, 'Hassidism and the *Kahal* in Eastern Europe', in *Hasidism Reappraised*, ed. A. Rapaport-Albert, London, Portland (OR), Littman Library of Jewish Civilization, 1997: 63–75.
15. Gartner, 2001: 82.
16. See Stephen Sharot, 1982: 149 and Ettinger, 1997: 65, 70.
17. On this decentralization, see 'Hasidism after 1772: structural continuity and change' in Rapoport-Albert, 1997: 76.
18. On the dynastic spirit among rebbes, see Rapoport-Albert 1997: 76–140, particularly pp. 91–92, 102, 109–110.
19. See David Assaf, 'Un petit État dans un grand État: la cour "royale" hassidique au XIXe siècle' [A small state within a large state: the Hasidic 'royal' court in the 19th century], *Les Cahiers du judaïsme*, 2000, 8 ('Hassidismes'): 37–53. On the Belz rebbe's rather modest court before 1940, J. Gutwirth, *Vie juive traditionnelle. Ethnologie d'une communauté hassidique* [Traditional Jewish life. Ethnology of a Hasidic community], Paris, Éditions de Minuit, 1970: 31–32.
20. Followed, ten days later, by the festival of Yom Kippur,* the great atonement; the cycle of festivals closes with Simhat Torah,* the joyous festival of the Torah.
21. Furthermore, particularly from the Middle Ages, non-Jewish authorities, especially in Eastern Europe, had themselves decreed that Jews should wear distinctive hats and signs (see Alfred Rubens, *A History of Jewish Costume*, London, Valentine Mitchell, 1967: 125). On the Hasidic appearance, see also Tamar Somogy, *Die Schejnen und die Proste, Untersuchungen zum Schönheitsideal der Ostjuden in Bezug auf Körper und Kleidung unter besonderer Berücksichtigung des Chassidismus* [The beautiful and the plain: a study of the ideal of beauty among Eastern European Jews in relation to the body and clothing, with particular reference to Hasidism], Berlin, Dieter Reimer, 1982: 125.
22. On the distinctions between elements of the Hasidic male appearance in a specific community, see Gutwirth 1970: 133–170, Chapter VII, 'L'aspect traditional masculin'.
23. See Wolf Zeev Rabinowitsch, *Lithuanian Hasidism*, New York, Schocken, 1971: 2–3.
24. See Raphael Mahler, *Hasidism and the Jewish Enlightenment. Their Confrontation in Galicia and Poland in the First Half of the Nineteenth Century*, Philadelphia, Jewish Publication Society of America, 1985, (1st edition 1961): 32.
25. This was accompanied by a degree of intolerance, as well as some attempts to persuade the non-Jewish authorities to ban Hasidic writings, to prohibit their distinctive appearance and so on. See Mahler, 1985: 123.
26. See Dubnow, 1931, I: 70.
27. See Dubnow, 1931, II: 234.

28. A Yiddish abbreviation for *Alguemayner Bund Fun Yiddishe Arbeter in Russland, Poylen un Lite*, that is, 'General union of Jewish workers in Russia, Poland and Lithuania'.
29. See Celia S. Heller, *On the Edge of Destruction. Jews of Poland between the Two World Wars*, New York, Columbia University Press, 1977: 174.
30. Dubnow, 1931, I: 69–70.
31. To use the judicious term coined by the sociologist and writer, Albert Memmi.
32. During the war, they were able to leave Siberia for more temperate regions of the Soviet Union. Most of the Jews, including Hasidim, who remained in Soviet-occupied Poland, were caught out by the Germans' lightning invasion and met with the dire fate of the overwhelming majority of Polish Jews. On this episode, see in particular, 'Holocaust survivors in the USSR', *Encyclopaedia Judaica*, 1992 (CD-Rom edition), Jerusalem, Judaica Multimedia, 1997.
33. See Jerome R. Mintz, *Hasidic People. A Place in the New World*, Cambridge (MA), London, Harvard University Press, 1992: 27. See also Gutwirth, 1970: 38–39.
34. See Wolfgang Jacobsmeyer, 'Der Lager der jüdischen Displaced Persons in der Deutsche Westzonen 1946/47 als Ort jüdischer Selbstvergewisserung' [The Jewish displaced persons camp in the West German zones 1946/1947 as a place of Jewish self-reassurance], in *Jüdisches Leben in Deutschland seit 1945* [Jewish life in Germany since 1945], ed. M. Brumlik et al., Frankfurt, Jüdische Verlag (Jewish Press), Athenäum, 1986: 37.
35. See Tzvi [Harry] Rabinowicz, *Hasidism in Israel. A History of the Hasidic Movement and its Masters in the Holy Land*, Northvale (NJ), Jerusalem, Jason Aronson Inc., 2000: 59–60.
36. See Peter Honigman, 'Talmuddrucke in Nachkriegsdeutschland' [Editions of the Talmud in post-war Germany], in *Überlebt und Unterwegs. Jüdische Displaced Persons in Nachkriegsdeutschland* [Survivors on the move. Jewish displaced persons in post-war Germany], ed. Fritz Bauer Institute, Frankfurt, New York, Campus Verlag, 1997: 250.

2. A EUROPEAN STAGING-POST: ANTWERP

1. See Ludo Abicht, *De Joden van Belgien* [The Jews of Belgium], Amsterdam, Antwerp, Atlas, 1994: 58–59. 55,000 Jews represented approximately 10% of the city's population. Concerning the often rather unpleasant way in which the Jews were perceived and treated by part of the population, the press and the Flemish political parties, see a remarkably well-documented book: Lieven Saerens, *Vreemdelingen in een wereldstaad. Een geschiedenis van Antwerpen en zijn joodse bevolking* [Foreigners in an international city. A history of Antwerp and its Jewish population], Antwerp, Lannoo, 2000.
2. See Jacques Gutwirth, 'Le judaïsme anversois aujourd'hui' [Judaism in Antwerp today], *Revue des études juives*, 1966, CXXV, 4: 366–367.
3. See Ephraim Schmidt, *Geschiedenis van de Joden in Antwerpen* [History of the Jews in Antwerp], Antwerp, Uitgeverij Ontwikkeling, 1963: 262. Hasidic communities feature in a list of Jewish institutions (nos. 5–11 and 22).
4. See Schmidt, 1963: 269–271.
5. See Roger van Ransbeek, *1920–1970. 50 jaar centraal beheer van joodse weldadigheid en maatschapelijk hulpbetoon* [1920–1970. Fifty years of the Central administration for Jewish charity and mutual assistance], Antwerp, 1970: 79–80.
6. During the 1960s, I examined the records from the immediate post-war period for the thousands of refugees who had come to seek help from the Jewish philanthropic institution at the time, the HISO, the initials of its Dutch name meaning 'Aid for the Jewish war victims'. Today this is known as the Centraal Beheer van Joodse Weldadigheid en Maatschapelijk Hulpbetoon [Central administration for Jewish charity and mutual assistance], abbreviated to 'Centraal'.
7. The Belgian government initially granted permanent residence permits to 2,000 Jewish refugees, a figure that rose to 5,000 in 1947 (van Ransbeek, 1970: 80).
8. Today the use of laser equipment removes the need to account for crystallization planes in the diamonds, which makes the craft of cleaving obsolete in many cases.

9. On Hasidism and the diamond industry in Antwerp, see Gutwirth, 1966: 371–375 and J. Gutwirth, *Vie juive traditionnelle. Ethnologie d'une communauté hassidique* [Traditional Jewish life. Ethnology of a Hasidic community], Paris, Éditions de Minuit, 1970: 71–113.
10. On the various communities in Antwerp in this period see Jacques Gutwirth, 'Hassidisme de notre temps' [Contemporary Hasidism], *Les Nouveaux Cahiers*, 1966, 7: 56–62.
11. On Belz, see Gutwirth 1970.
12. In Montreal, the Belz community formed after the Second World War was constituted of followers of Hungarian origin. In Israel and elsewhere, the Belz communities are somewhat mixed, as in Antwerp.
13. Given the way of life and the specific culture of the Hasidim, to describe them as Polish or Hungarian does not mean a great deal unless the term 'Jew' is implicit.
14. See in particular the illustrated works of George Kranzler (with photographs by Irving I. Herzberg), *The Face of Faith, an American Hassidic Community*, Baltimore, Baltimore Hebrew College Press, 1972 and Maud B. Weiss/Michel Neumeister, *Die Fromme in New York. Die Welt der Satmar-Chassidim* [The orthodox in New York. The world of the Satmar Hasidim], Munich, Gina Keyahoff Verlag, 1995.
15. In particular in the morning worship on the Sabbath – the only form of worship apart from certain festivals that women regularly attend, although they are also present at circumcisions, weddings etc.
16. See H. Rosenberg, 'Joodse verenigingen in Antwerpen' [Jewish organizations in Antwerp], *Virtueel Israelitisch Weekblad*, 1999, <www.goedkosjer.org/JoodsAntwerpen.htm>.
17. The veneration of a particular rebbe by followers cannot always be taken for granted. In this particular case, it should be remembered that the current Belz rebbe was chosen by the community elders when he was under twenty years old and there was already opposition from a minority of enthusiasts for the previous rebbe at that time. Schisms of this kind occur within other communities. The divisions do not relate only to the rebbe's personality but also to matters such as a greater or lesser degree of traditionalism and in this case to school education.
18. There are no precise demographic data available for the Jews of Antwerp, for either before the war or the present day. The Belgian censuses ignore religious affiliation and, to my knowledge, no university or other institution has ever conducted a demographic survey of this kind. The usual estimates vary between 15,000 and 20,000, and 18,000 seems to me to be the best working figure.
19. On the beginnings of this dynasty, see Jacques Gutwirth, 'Anvers: naissance d'une dynastie' [Antwerp: the birth of a dynasty], *L'Arche*, 1968, 139: 54–59.
20. The tradition of the *kvitel* has Kabbalistic origins; the note contains a particular statement; for example, 'With the grace of God. Isaac [the supplicant], son of Sarah – may he recover from his illness'. See Jacob S. Minkin, *The Romance of Hassidism*, Hollywood, CA, Wilshire Books (first edition 1935), 1971: 332–333.
21. This use of a diminutive form, which is in no way disrespectful, is not current practice among the Hungarian Hasidim.
22. A scan of the news-in-brief columns and the photographs of social events in the ultra-orthodox weekly *Hamodia* (in the English language) gives some idea of the proliferation of these small dynasties, of which the one instigated by reb Ytsekl provides a successful example.
23. See Ingrid Carlander, 'Anvers la cosmopolite, Anvers la brune' [Cosmopolitan Antwerp, dark Antwerp], *Le Monde diplomatique*, May 1995: 7–8.
24. Of course, non-religious or not highly religious Jews buy food from non-Jewish suppliers today.
25. For an account of these Hasidic influences, see Henri Rosenberg, 'Those were the days: about past and present', *Virtueel Israelitisch Weekblad*, 1991, <www.goedkosjer.org/JoodsAntwerpen.htm>.
26. Only the Lubavitch Hasidim, who proselytize among other Jews (see Chapter 5), have a presence in the Belgian capital.

3. WILLIAMSBURG, A SATMAR BASTION

1. See Marshall Sklare, *America's Jews*, New York, Random House, 1972: 20.
2. Reform Judaism rejects the idea that the *Halohe*,* the Jewish laws, are immutable and adapts Jewish thought and practice to the spirit of the age. Originating in Germany in the 19th century, the movement has undergone a strong expansion in the United States, first among the Jews of German origin and then, more widely, in the Western USA (California) among third-generation and fourth-generation Jews. Conservative Judaism also rejects the rigidity of the Jewish laws but it seeks to preserve their essence while adopting behaviour that is adapted to the needs of the current time. This pragmatism (for example, going to the synagogue by car on the Sabbath, when it is too far away to walk there) proved to suit many of the Jews who immigrated from Eastern Europe who, having arrived in the United States, had abandoned orthodoxy but took exception to the Reform movement, finding it too solemn and insufficiently warm. Conservative Judaism has become broadly the majority movement and has experienced a very strong advance in suburban areas, particularly on the West coast of the USA.
3. See Nathan Glazer, *American Judaism*, Chicago, London, University of Chicago Press (1st edition 1957), 1972: 105.
4. See William B. Helmreich, *The World of the Yeshiva. An Intimate Portrait of Orthodox Jewry*, New York, Free Press, 1982: 12; Ilan Greilsammer, *Israël. Les hommes en noir. Essai sur les partis ultra-orthodoxes* [Israel. The men in black. A study of the ultra-orthodox parties], Paris, Presses de la Fondation des sciences politiques, 1991: 129.
5. See Jerome R. Mintz, *Hasidic People. A Place in the New World*, Cambridge (MA), London, Harvard University Press, 1992: 71.
6. There are several key works on the Williamsburg Hasidim. First there are those by George Kranzler, *Williamsburg. A Jewish Community in Transition*, New York, Feldheim, 1961, and thirty-four years later a new updated and very thorough but also somewhat romantic study of the district and its Hasidim: *Hasidic Williamsburg. A Contemporary Hasidic Community*, Northvale (NJ), London, 1995(a). Israel Rubin has published *Satmar. Two Generations of an Urban Island*, New York, Peter Lang, 1997. This is a revised and updated edition of a work published by the same author in 1972 under the title *Satmar, An Island in the City* (Chicago, Quadrangle Books). Satmar is the principal Hasidic movement in Williamsburg. See also Solomon Poll, *The Hasidic Community of Williamsburg*, Glencoe, Free Press of Glencoe, 1962. Finally, the book by Jerome Mintz (1992), cited above, is also an essential source on Hasidic Williamsburg.
7. See Kranzler (1961: 15 and 1995[a]: 287–288).
8. A rough translation of an expression that is difficult to translate.
9. There were many border changes during the 20th century, particularly during and after the two world wars and following the disintegration of the former Soviet Union. Today, the sites of the rebbes' former 'Austro-Hungarian' residences are mainly in Hungary and Rumania but also in Moldavia, Slovakia and Ukraine.
10. As Kranzler (1995[a]: 11) rightly observes.
11. On these figures, all of which are approximate, see Poll 1962: 30; Mintz, 1992: 190; Kranzler, 1995(a): 11 and George Kranzler 'The economic revitalization of the Hasidic community of Williamsburg', in *Ethnographic Studies of Hasidic Jews in America*, ed. Janet S. Belcove-Shalin, Albany, State University of New York Press, 1995(b): 191.
12. Accordingly, these tailors sell gentlemen's clothing with buttoning from right to left instead of the more usual buttoning from left to right. Moreover, as good orthodox Jews they observe the Biblical prescriptions (Leviticus 19: 19, Deuteronomy 22: 9–11) of the *Shatnes*,* which prohibit combining animal fibres such as wool and fur with plant fibres such as linen and cotton.
13. The non-Hasidic orthodox Jews generally wear them more discreetly under their clothing.
14. Kranzler, 1995(a): 170.
15. Kranzler, 1995(a): 39–41.
16. On the diamond traders in New York, see the book by Renée Rose Shield, *Diamond Stories. Enduring Changes on 47th Street*, Ithaca and London, Cornell University Press, 2002.

17. Married women, who are supposed to have shaven heads, cover their heads with a scarf or wig that is often itself then covered with a scarf or a hat.
18. See Kranzler, 1995(a): 37.
19. For a great deal of information on this subject, see Kranzler, 1995(a) and 1995(b).
20. See Mark Zborowsky and Elisabeth Herzog, *Life is with People. The Culture of the Shtetl*, New York, Schocken Books, (1st edition 1952), 1962: 191–213.
21. See Kranzler, 1995(a): 243–244.
22. The kashrut,* 'properness', a set of prescriptions governing food authorized for consumption. These are complex laws that ordain the purity or impurity of food as well as incompatibilities. The main characteristics of the system can be outlined as follows. The consumption of game and certain animals, such as pigs and equidae, fish without scales, crustaceans and molluscs, is completely forbidden. Authorized foods are divided into three categories: 1) meat-based, *flaishig*,* foods, that is all meats, animal fats, and all the by-products (soups, sauces etc.); 2) milk-based, *milchig*,* foods, milk, cheese and by-products; 3) neutral, *parve*,* foods, including vegetables, fruit, fish, eggs, cereals, vegetable fats (margarine, oil), coffee, tea etc. The meat-based and milk-based categories have to be kept strictly separate, whereas the 'neutral' foods can accompany both meat-based and milk-based foods.
23. These are foods that are called 'neutral'.
24. There are complex and very detailed rules for the slaughter of authorized animals, which requires the use of a very finely sharpened knife, with no roughness. The Torah (Deuteronomy XII: 23–24; Leviticus VII: 26–27; XVII: 10–14) prohibits the consumption of blood; the ritual slaughterer, *shoihet*, an orthodox Jew, must therefore drain the maximum possible amount of blood from the animal. Later, during preparation, the meat has to be meticulously soaked and salted and then rinsed to remove any trace of blood. On the kashrut, see in particular Julien Bauer, *La nourriture cachère* [Kasher food], Paris, PUF, 'Que sais-je?', 1996.
25. This does not prevent conflicts, almost a permanent feature of the history of the kashrut in France (and elsewhere); see Chapter 8 and Sophie Nizard, 'La cacherout en France. Organization matérielle d'une consummation symbolique' [The kashrut in France. Material organization of a symbolic consumption]. *Les Cahiers du judaïsme*, 1998, 3: 64.
26. See Bauer, 1996: 50.
27. On the mysteries of the kashrut 'industry', an important economic activity, especially in areas where the traditionalist Jewish communities are highly developed, see Bauer, 1996, Chapters 3 and 4; Nizard, 1998, 3: 64–73.
28. See Kranzler, 1995(a): 140.
29. To use Kranzler's term (1995[a]: XV, 108). This 'Hungarian' hard-line style prevailed particularly in Transylvania, a region that is now part of Rumania, but which formed part of Hungary from 1867 to 1940. This rigour derives from a historical situation in which communities were sharply divided with respect to the Jewish laws. In fact, under the Habsburg Empire, Hungary had three types of religious community from 1871: the ultra-strict orthodox, the 'neologists', who belonged to the modern-style reform movement, and finally some traditionalists situated between these two forms. With a few minor variations, this is the situation that still prevails in the United States, with its three large currents – orthodox, conservative and reform (see note 2 of this chapter).
30. See Kranzler, 1995(a): 270. In the 1960s, during my research on the Belz Hasidim in Antwerp (Gutwirth, 1970), I had already been struck by the religious rigour and extreme gravity that characterized the religiosity of the Hungarian followers in this community, composed of Hungarian and Polish Hasidim.
31. This did not relate only to food products. The Hasidim, and the Satmarer in particular, set about producing and selling many articles connected with worship, such as phylacteries, prayer-shawls, candles and religious books (see Poll, 1962: 153–175). *Der Yid* (the Jew), a weekly Satmar publication, provides a good illustration of the advertising for these products.
32. See Poll, 1962: 76–77; Rubin, 1997: 78–79; 206–207.
33. *Glatt kasher*: ultra-kasher. The word *glatt* in German means 'smooth', which refers to the slaughter knives and the condition of the animal, especially the lungs, but 'glatt' also means 'absolutely', which by extension refers to the kashrut in general. In fact, the 'glatt kasher'

concept has been applied to many other products that have no connection with slaughter. For instance, there is 'glatt kasher' smoked salmon today for which the supplier's packaging is guaranteed to have no forbidden additive. From the beginnings of Hasidism, the ultra-smooth knives adopted by the movement were at the heart of the disputes with the *misnaggedim*,* the adversaries of Hasidism (see 'Shehita' in *Encyclopaedia Judaica*, CD-Rom edition, Jerusalem, Judaica Multimedia, 1997; Bauer, 1996: 46). However, today the Hasidic technique is the 'exemplar' of the most advanced slaughter method.

34. See 'Hungary' in *Encyclopaedia Judaica*, CD-Rom edition, Jerusalem, Judaica Multimedia, 1997.
35. The convoy in which the rebbe was travelling reached Switzerland on 7 December 1944 (21 Kislev in the Jewish calendar); this arrival is commemorated every year by the Satmarer. Eichmann had suggested to Kasztner that the Hungarian Jews' lives could be saved in exchange for the delivery of 10,000 trucks (destined for the Eastern front against the Soviet Union) and other goods. He was hoping for a reversal of alliances, which would have united Germany and the Western forces against Stalin. On this convoy, see Harry Rabinowicz, *A World Apart. The Story of the Chassidim in Britain*, London and Portland (OR), Valentine Mitchell, 1997: 163–164; see also Simon Epstein, *Histoire du peuple juif au XXe siècle. De 1914 à nos jours* [History of the Jewish people in the 20th century: 1914 to the present day], Paris, Hachette, 1998: 184–186.
36. See Rubin, 1997: 47. By way of comparison, we know that at the same time the Belz community in Antwerp comprised no more than 74 families.
37. See Rubin, 1997: 11.
38. Thus, the rabbi Lipa Friedman, who had been a banker before the war, was made president of the community from the outset, and remained so until his death (see Mintz, 1992: 31).
39. See Rubin, 1997: 178.
40. See note 29.
41. See Kranzler, 1995(a): 277–278.
42. See Rubin, 1997: 182.
43. On this subject, see Rubin, 1997: 171–172.
44. The city of New York has nevertheless made disused municipal school buildings available to the Satmarer for minimal sums of money.
45. Teitelbaum has addressed this subject in his book in Yiddish, *Va-yo'el Mosheh* [And Joel Moshe] (New York, Sefer Detsch, 1959); there have been later editions in both Hebrew and Yiddish. See Rubin, 1997: 60–61 and Aviezer Ravitsky, *Messianism, Zionism, and Jewish Religious Radicalism*, Chicago, London, University of Chicago Press, 1996 (translated from Hebrew): 63–66. In fact, there are two other oaths connected with the first: 'Israel will not overcome the wall of Exile' and 'the Jews will not rebel against the nations of the world'.
46. Statement in the *New York Times*, 11 February 2001 (source: <www.jewsnotzionists.org>).
47. See Mintz, 1992: 189–190.
48. See Rubin, 1997: 208.
49. See Kranzler, 1995(a): 95–96, 261.
50. Kranzler, 1995(a): 64.
51. Kranzler, 1995(a): 65.
52. See Rubin, 1997: 124.
53. On the development of Kiryas Joel, see Mintz 1992: 206–215.
54. See note 20.
55. See 'Waldman v. Village of Kiryas Joel', *United States Court of Appeals for the second circuit*, decision of 21 March 2000, Docket, n° 99–7830, p. 3.
56. On this matter, see Eric J. Greenberg, 'New York state investigates fraud among Satmar', *Jewish Bulletin of Northern California* (now *The Jewish News Weekly of Northern California*), 4 October 1996; Robert Hennely, 'One man – how many votes?', *Village Voice*, 22 October 1996: 15–16; Christopher Mele and Paula McMahon, 'Voter fraud in KJ continued, investigation shows', *Times Herald Record*, 17 October 1997.
57. This was help that they had received for some time, but in 1984 the US Supreme Court had forbidden state school teachers from working for religious private schools (Mintz, 1992: 310).

58. Tamar Lewin, 'Controversy over, enclave joins school board group', *New York Times*, 20 April 2002 (Metropolitan Desk): B.4.
59. See Mintz (1992: 84), who gives a good description of this 'third meal' and demonstrates Joel Teitelbaum's role among his followers.
60. On Joel Teitelbaum, see Kranzler, 1995(a): 267–283.
61. On this subject, see Mintz, 1992, Chapter 12, 'The succession in Satmar', 126–138.
62. See Joseph Berger, 'Hasid rebels sue main sect for religious persecution', *New York Times*, 5 March 1997: B.8; Joseph Berger, 'Dissident gain with Kiryas Joel pact', *New York Times*, 12 March 1997 (Metropolitan Desk).
63. See Daniel J. Wakin, 'The heir unapparent', *New York Times*, 24 January 2002 (Metropolitan Desk).
64. See Susan Edelman, 'Satmar sibling rivalry hurting them all', *New York Post*, 10 March 2002.

4. BOROUGH PARK: A 'BOURGEOIS' DISTRICT

1. I should remind readers that there are no reliable statistical data concerning the Hasidim in the various districts of Brooklyn.
2. Figures from Egon Mayer, *From Suburb to Shtetl. The Jews of Boro Park*, Philadelphia, Temple University Press, 1979: 31. Mayer uses a spelling of the district's name that is a current phonetic abbreviation of its official name, Borough Park. In particular, his book provides information on the history and the sociology of the district before the mass arrival of the Hasidim. On Hasidic Borough Park, see especially Janet S. Belcove-Shalin, 'Home in exile: Hasidim in the New World', in *Ethnographic Studies of Hasidic Jews in America*, ed. Janet S. Belcove-Shalin, Albany, State University of New York Press, 1995: 206–236; Janet S. Belcove-Shalin, 'Becoming more of an Eskimo: fieldwork among the Hasidim of Boro Park', in *Between Two Worlds. Ethnographic Essays on American Jewry*, ed. J. Kugelmass, Ithaca and London, Cornell University Press, 1988: 77–102; J. R. Mintz, *Hasidic People. A Place in the New World*, Cambridge (MA), London, Harvard University Press, 1992: 100–111.
3. See Michael Taub, 'My mother's Borough Park', in *Jews of Brooklyn*, ed. Ilana Abramovitch and Sean Galvin, Hanover (New Hampshire), London, University Press of New England, 2002: 137–138.
4. Twenty-five electoral districts. See the socio-demographic study conducted by Egon Mayer, *The Borough Park Community Survey, 1992–1993*, New York, Council of Jewish Organizations of Borough Park, 1993; a similar study had been conducted ten years earlier, also by Egon Mayer.
5. Figures according to Belcove-Shalin, 1995: 232, note 18.
6. See Mayer, 1993: 47.
7. See Taub, 2002: 137.
8. See Deborah Sontag, 'Orthodox neighbourhood reshapes itself', *New York Times*, 7 January 1997, A:1 (Metropolitan Desk).
9. See Taub, 2002: 138.
10. On the COJO, Council of Jewish Organizations of Borough Park, see Belcove-Shalin 1995: 216; Mintz 1992: 101–102. With reference to the corruption matter, see James Dao and Alan Finder, 'Jewish Council under scrutiny is known for political clout', *New York Times*, 2 December 1996 (Metropolitan Desk); Joseph P. Fried, 'Brooklyn rabbi is accused of stealing grant money', *New York Times*, 28 March 1997 (Metropolitan Desk); Joseph P. Fried, 'Jury acquits assemblyman Hikind of corruption charges', *New York Times*, 14 July 1998 (Metropolitan Desk).
11. 2,000 families, which in the Hasidic environment, with its large families, represents approximately 10,000 to 12,000 people; see Mintz, 1992: 122. More recently, official Bobov representatives have put forward similar figures.
12. In Mintz, 1992: 122.
13. On the Bobov dynasty see Robert Kamen, *Growing up Hasidic: Education and Socialization in the Bobover Hasidic Community*, Ann Arbor (MI), University Microfilm, 1975; Mintz, 1992:

120–125. Belcove-Shalin, 1995: 218–230; Shifra Epstein, 'The Bobover Hasidim Piremshpiyl: from folk drama for Purim to a ritual of transcending the Holocaust', in Belcove-Shalin (ed.) 1995: 227–255; Harry Rabinowicz, *A World Apart. The Story of the Chassidim in Britain*, London and Portland (OR), Valentine Mitchell, 1997: 182–186; Tzvi [Harry] Rabinowicz, *Hasidism in Israel. A History of the Hasidic Movement and its Masters in the Holy Land*, Northvale (NJ), Jerusalem, Jason Aronson, 2000: 244–247.

14. Zanz was a famous dynasty of the region, but it has disappeared as such; it survives today mainly through the Bobov and Klausenburg dynasties, for which the rebbe founded a district called Kiryat Zanz in Natanya, Israel (see Chapter 7).
15. Harry Rabinowicz, *Hasidism and the State of Israel*, Rutherford, Madison, Teaneck, Farleigh Dickinson University Press, 1982: 246.
16. See Rabinowicz, 1997: 183–184.
17. On this period, see Belcove-Shalin, 1995: 219–220.
18. Belcove-Shalin, 1995: 220.
19. See Avrohom Birnbaum, 'Rebbe and father: the *avoda* of rebuilding in America after the Holocaust'. *Hamodia* (magazine section), 20 July 2001: 12–13.
20. The festival of Passover commemorates the liberation of the Jews from Egypt and the exodus into the desert. It takes place from the 14th to the 20th of the Jewish month Nisan, in March or April according to the year. During these eight days, no leavened food can be eaten or kept, including bread, which is replaced by unleavened breads.
21. Purim also commemorates a deliverance – that of the Jews of the Persian Empire under Ahasuerus, whose chief minister, Haman, wanted to massacre all the Jews.
22. See Shifra Epstein, 'Drama on a table: the Bobover Hasidim Piremshpiyl', in *Judaism Viewed from Within and Without. Anthropological Studies*, ed. Harvey E. Goldberg, Albany, State University of New York Press, 1987: 200.
23. See Renata Singer, 'A Hasidic woman in Borough Park' in *Jews of Brooklyn*, ed. Ilana Abramovitch & Sean Galvin, Hanover (New Hampshire), London, University Press of New England, 2002: 140. Touro College incorporates three types of institute: in human sciences, law and medical sciences.
24. Mintz, 1992: 123–124.
25. The community's financial needs, as well as greed on the part of some of its members, can give rise to severe financial irregularities. In 1997, a rabbi who was a high-level administrator at the Bobov yeshive, and some other Hasidim from the community, were accused – and were then found guilty and sentenced – of laundering millions of dollars from traffickers in Colombian drugs through bank accounts of the yeshive, the community and a mutual assistance society based at the Bobov headquarters. Between 15% and 18% of the value of the transactions was received by the community or by some of the intermediaries who were implicated. See Joseph Berger, 'Drug arrests give a jolt to a sect of Hasidim', *New York Times*, 18 June 1997 (Metropolitan Desk); Eric J. Greenberg; 'Chassidic rabbis implicated in Columbian drug trade', *Jewish Bulletin of Northern California* (now *Jewish News Weekly of Northern California*), 20 June 1997; Jessica Steinberg, 'Bad day in Boro Park', *Jerusalem Post*, 13 September 1997: 8 (magazine); Joseph Fried; 'Guilty plea to money charge', *New York Times*, 17 December 1997 (Metropolitan Desk): 5.
26. See Mintz, 1992: 123–124.
27. Mintz, 1992: 125.
28. See Shari Troy, 'The Mother of all Purimspielen', *Jerusalem Report*, 12 March 2001: 40–41.
29. See Epstein, 1995: 237–255.
30. This was particularly the case in Antwerp between the two world wars.

5. CROWN HEIGHTS, SEAT OF THE LUBAVITCH MOVEMENT

1. Again I should repeat that the figures for the Hasidic population are usually uncertain.
2. See Mark Naison, 'Crown Heights in the 1950s', in *Jews of Brooklyn*, ed. Ilana Abramovitch & Sean Galvin, Hanover (New Hampshire), London, University Press of New England, 2002: 144.

3. On this type of property dealing, called 'blockbusting', in Crown Heights, see J. R. Mintz, *Hasidic People. A Place in the New World*, Cambridge (MA), London, Harvard University Press, 1992: 139f.
4. Mintz, 1992: 141. On Crown Heights, and the Lubavitch movement in particular, there are various valuable works and articles available. In his 1992 book, Mintz devotes several chapters to Crown Heights and Lubavitch. See also Edward Hoffman, *Despite of All Odds. The Story of Lubavitch*, New York, Simon & Schuster, 1991; Sydelle Brooks Levy, 'Shifting patterns of ethnic identification among the Hasidim', in *The New Ethnicity: Perspectives from Ethnology*, ed. John W. Bennet, St. Paul, New York, etc., West Publishing, 1973; Sydelle Brooks Levy, *Ethnic Boundaries and the Institutionalization of Charisma*, Ann Arbor, University Microfilms (Ph.D. 1973) and also Schlomoh Brodowicz, *L'âme d'Israel. Les origines, la vie et l'oeuvre de Menahem Mendel Schneerson, Rabbi de Loubavitch* [The soul of Israel. The origins, life and works of Menahem Mendel Schneerson, Lubavitcher rebbe], Paris, Éditions du Rocher/ Bibliophane, 1998. Despite its hagiographic quality and its somewhat uneven structure, this is a useful work. Other contributions concerning specific points will be indicated below.
5. As we have seen in relation to blockbusting (note 3), property is often a source of criminal activities. The property company created by Lubavitch had used some illegal manoeuvres to recover housing occupied by blacks and Hispanics, which had in fact given rise to a letter of reprimand from the New York mayor (see Mintz, 1992: 148–150, 329). Moreover, in 1994, a Lubavitch rabbi who was directing the Council's housing programme to encourage Hasidim to remain in the area carried out some excellent work but he also took out mortgages on the properties for redistribution and used the proceeds to buy some buildings for himself for around $20,000,000, even extorting some state loans for this purpose. As with COJO in Borough Park, these transactions were facilitated by donations to political parties and figures (on this subject see Jeffrey Goldberg, 'Tsuris in Crown Heights', *New York*, 12 December 1994: 24, 26).
6. See Ari L. Goldman, 'Hasidic group expands amid debate on future', *New York Times*, 5 September 1988.
7. See Mintz, 1992: 241.
8. On these matters, see Mintz, 1992: 328–347; see also Michael Kamber, 'Faded rage', *Village Voice*, 16 January 2002.
9. According to Brodowicz, 1998: 250.
10. See Eve Jochnowitz, 'Holy rolling, making sense of baking matzo', in Abramovitch & Galvin (eds), 2002: 72–77. On the highly specific way in which this is made, see Jacques Gutwirth, 'Les pains azymes de la Pâque chez les *hassidim*' [Unleavened bread at the Passover among the Hasidim], *Objets et Mondes*, 1976, 16, 4: 137–148.
11. On the appearance of the Lubavitch in Crown Heights, see Henri Goldschmidt, 'Suits and souls. Trying to tell a Jew when you see one in Crown Heights', in Abramovitch & Galvin (eds.), 2002: 214–221.
12. On this subject, see Rhonda Berger-Sofer, 'Political kinship alliances of a Hasidic dynasty', *Ethnology*, 1984, 23, 1: 49–62; Avrum M. Ehrlich, *Leadership in the HaBad Movement*, Northvale (NJ), Jerusalem, Jason Aronson, 2000: 253. See also the Schneersohn family tree in *Encyclopaedia Judaica*, CD-Rom Ed., Jerusalem Judaica Multimedia, 1997.
13. On the circumstances of the marriage, see Ehrlich, 2000: 314–315. According to Ehrlich, the rebbe Joseph Schneerson wanted to put his future son-in-law to the test, living as he was in the secular city of Berlin.
14. Brodowicz, 1998, p. 207. See this author's description of the ceremony (pp. 205–208).
15. On this subject, see Avirama Golan, 'Missing brother-in-law found in Paris', *Haaretz*, 21 April 1998. The information contained in this article was provided by Menahem Friedman, an Israeli sociologist, who conducted a survey in Paris on this subject.
16. Brodowicz, 1998: 211.
17. Hoffman, 1991: 38.
18. Ehrlich, 2000: 356.
19. See a text by the rebbe from the 1950s entitled 'Science and technology' (pp. 188–197) in his book *Toward a Meaningful Life: The Wisdom of the Rebbe Menachem Mendel Schneerson*, ed. Simon Jacobson, London, Piatkus, 1995.

20. See Ehrlich, 2000: 298 and Jan Feldman, *Lubavitcher as Citizens. A Paradox of Liberal Democracy*, Ithaca, London, Cornell University Press, 2003: XIII.
21. Ehrlich, 2000: 367–368.
22. Brodowicz, 1998: 234.
23. See J. Immanuel Shochet, 'The philosophy of Lubavitch activism', *Tradition*, 1972, 13, 1: 18–35 and William Shaffir, *Life in a Religious Community: The Lubavitcher in Montreal*, Toronto and Montreal, Holt, Rinehart & Winston of Canada, 1974: 181.
24. On the Bostoner rebbe, see Jacques Gutwirth, 'Field methods and the sociology of Jews: case studies of Hassidic communities', *Jewish Journal of Sociology*, 1978, XX, 1: 53–56 and *Les judéo-chrétiens d'aujourd'hui* [Judaeo-Christians today], Paris, Cerf, 1987: 250–255.
25. As every male adult Jew is supposed to do every morning except on the Sabbath and festival days.
26. See *Chabad Lubavitch Chasidism Today*, California, Chabad-Lubavitch Editions, 1972: 119–120.
27. See Beverly Beyette, 'A telethon with tradition', *Los Angeles Times*, 29 August 2000: E-2.
28. See Neil Sandberg, *Jewish Life in Los Angeles*, Lanham (MD), London, University Press of America, 1986: 41.
29. See Rabinowicz, 1997: 175.
30. This concerns an article in a journal of the Bnei Brith organization in California, reproduced in *Chabad Lubavitch Chasidism Today*, 1972: 38–39.
31. See Bonnie J. Morris, *Lubavitcher Women in America. Identity and Activism in the Postwar Era*, Albany, State University of New York Press, 1998: 58–59. These meetings took place at the annual conventions for Lubavitch women. Like the conventions themselves, these meetings stem from the indirect influence of the feminist movement in this period. The Lubavitch women established some major institutions, including a journal, *Di Yiddishe Heim* (the Jewish home); they are nevertheless all supervised by men in authority in the movement.
32. See Morris, 1998: 48–50.
33. See the European Lubavitch office, 'Les institutions Chabad Lubavitch en France et Afrique du Nord' [Habad Lubavitch institutions in France and North Africa], <www.Chabad-fr.org>, 2002.
34. He states: 'So the current technological revolution is in fact the hand of God at work' (in Jacobson, 2000: 191).
35. See Laurence Podselver, 'Le mouvement Lubavitch: déracinement et insertion des Sépharades' [The Lubavitch movement: the uprooting and integration of the Sephardim], *Pardès*, 1986, 3: 54–68; Ilan Greilsammer, *Israël. Les hommes en noir…* [Israel. The men in black …], Paris, Presses de la Fondation nationale des sciences politiques, 1991: 215.
36. Hoffman, 1991: 89–90.
37. See Ellen Koskoff, 'The language of the heart: music in Lubavitcher life', in Belcove Shalin, 1995: 105, note 1; the *baalei tshuve* from then on outnumbered those who were followers by birth!
38. Usually new utensils have to be bought or, at least, the oven and the equipment have to be 'purified' with fire before they can be used again. See Mintz, 1992: 47, 376.
39. Five Satmarer cut the beard of a Habad rabbi who had made the 'mistake' of teaching the Tanya, the movement's founding work, to a young Satmarer: see Mintz, 1992: 160–162.
40. On this establishment of the Lubavitch business within a non-Jewish agricultural environment, see the somewhat anecdotal book by Stephen G. Bloom, *Postville. A Clash of Cultures in Heartland America*, New York, San Diego, London, Harcourt, 2000.
41. See Bauer, 1996: 58–59; on the kashrut in Paris, see S. Nizard, 'La cacherout en France. Organisation matérielle d'une consommation symbolique' [The kashrut in France. The material organization of a symbolic consumption], *Les Cahiers du judaïsme*, 1998, 3: 64–73.
42. On local politics in Crown Heights, see many details in Mintz, 1992, Chapter 13, 'Politics and race in Crown Heights': 139–153.
43. The 'anti-Semitism' imputed to Hillary Clinton was largely due to the fact that she had publicly expressed support for the creation of a Palestinian state a year previously. On this, see Peter

Noel, 'Hillary "banned" in Crown Heights', *Village Voice*, 25 August 1999. The Democrat party selected not Dinkins but another candidate for the New York mayoralty.
44. On Habad in Washington, see Feldman, 2003: 51–52.
45. See Aviezer Ravitzky, *Messianism, Zionism and Jewish Religious Radicalism*, Chicago and London, University of Chicago Press, 1996 (1st edition in Hebrew, 1993): 14–15.
46. Extract from a statement by the rebbe in New York during the celebration of the Passover in April 1943, quoted in Allan Nadler, 'Last exit to Brooklyn', *New Republic*, 4 May 1992: 32.
47. A rabbinical term that is applied to the essential duty to save a human life in a situation of danger. This obligation is based on part of a line from Leviticus (19: 16) and is supported by some references in the Talmud (Yoma tractate, 85a).
48. 'With regard to the liberated areas', the Rebbe has observed, 'military experts, Jewish and non-Jewish, agree that in the present situation, giving up any part of them would create serious security dangers' (Hoffman, 1991: 163).
49. See Greilsammer, 1991: 233. In May 1976, I myself heard Schneerson refer very explicitly to 'our territories' at the annual parade of the Lag be Omer festival on Eastern Parkway in Crown Heights. His speech, delivered in Yiddish, was being simultaneously interpreted into English: the rabbi and interpreter simply omitted this passage; there were many non-Jews nearby in the audience massed on the avenue.
50. On the 'Lubavitch hawks', see the enlightening observations in Greilsammer, 1991: 233–235.
51. See Greilsammer, 1991: 233–234; Hoffman, 1991: 163–165.
52. On this subject, see Mintz, 1992: 357–358; Greilsammer, 1993: 115, 210; the incident created acute tensions in Israeli Hasidic circles; the Vishnitzer rebbe (see Chapter 7) threatened the two representatives who had not followed the recommendation of the Agudath party leaders with severe reprisals.
53. This campaign was unsuccessful; the amendment was not adopted.
54. (Associated Press), 'Orthodox Jews protest peace talks', *New York Times*, 4 January 2000.
55. In their publications, the Lubavitcher give ample evidence that the former Israeli president, Zalman Shazar (1889–1974), from the Labor party, had an excellent relationship with the rebbe, whom he often visited on his trips to the United States; Shazar was the son of a Lubavitcher who had lived in Tzarist Russia. Shazar strongly supported the Habad movement in Israel; he is an example of these 'sympathizers' of the movement, who are found particularly in the associations of 'friends', who provide it with all kinds of support.
56. See Shaffir, 1974: 61–62; see also Michael Specter, 'The oracle of Crown Heights', *New York Times Magazine*, 15 March 1992. All the Lubavitch literature – books, brochures, leaflets etc. – bears witness to the veneration and the cult dedicated to the rebbe.
57. According to the rabbi Adin Steinsaltz, a renowned Talmudic scholar and a follower of the rebbe, quoted in Specter, 1992.
58. Jacques Gutwirth, 'Religion télévisée: les télévangélistes et Jean-Paul II' [Televised religion: the televangelists and John-Paul II], *Ethnologie française*, 2000, XXX, 3: 427–437.
59. The rebbe's birthday was the occasion for countless messages of congratulation from non-Jewish authorities, including from the United States president (see Hoffman, 1991: 212). Again recently, President George W. Bush received a Lubavitch delegation on the centenary of the rebbe's birth. He even signed a document declaring that this anniversary was 'the day of education and faith'. See Shlomo Shamir, 'Bush meets Lubavitch rabbis to mark late Rebbe's 100th birthday', *Haaretz*, 28 March 2002 (English internet edition).
60. The main prayer of the daily services, the *Amida*, with its eighteen blessings, contains five blessings that express the messianic expectation.
61. On Lubavitch messianism, see Ravitzky, 1996: 193f.
62. Quoted in Ravitzky, 1996: 196.
63. In Ravitzky, 1996: 195.
64. Quoted in William Shaffir, 'Interpreting adversity: dynamics of commitment in a messianic redemption campaign', *Jewish Journal of Sociology*, 1994, XXXVI, 1: 44. See also Ravitzky, 1996: 197.

65. See William Shaffir, 'Jewish messianism Lubavitch-style: an interim report', *Jewish Journal of Sociology*, 1993, XXXV, 2: 118.
66. Quoted in Ravitzky, 1996: 197.
67. See Ravitzky, 1996: 207.
68. Ravitzky, 1996: 205; see also David Gonzalez, 'A "family in stress" over its stricken rebbe', *New York Times*, 12 March 1994: 23.
69. On the events following the death of the rebbe, see William Shaffir's illuminating article 'When prophecy is not validated: explaining the unexpected in a messianic campaign', *Jewish Journal of Sociology*, 1995, XXXVII, 2: 119–136.
70. Shmuel Butman, 'It's all in what the rebbe said', *Haaretz*, 7 April 1998.
71. David Berger, 'The rebbe, the Jews and the Messiah', *Commentary*, 2001, 112, 2: 23–30; David Berger, *The Rebbe, the Messiah, and the Scandal of Orthodox Indifference*, London, Littman Library of Jewish Civilization, 2001.
72. On the followers' convictions, see Mintz, 1992: 352–354; William Shaffir, 1995. These messianic beliefs are said to feature particularly strongly among the followers in Israel; see Yigal Schleifer & Gershom Gorenberg; 'Chabad's Messiah complex', *Jerusalem Report*, 21 June 1995: 32–33. In 2001, a *shlieh*,* a Lubavitch emissary, told me that the followers certainly believe that messianic times are approaching but he did not pronounce on Schneerson's messianic attributes. Given the movement's missionary activities within a large Jewish public that does not share such a conviction, the *shlihim* are well aware that this is an awkward question.
73. See ITIM, 'Schach says Schneerson is a false Messiah', *Jerusalem Post*, 31 January 1993; Ravitzky, 1996: 280 n. 104; Allan Nadler, 'A historian's polemic against "The madness of false messianism"', *Forward*, 19 October 2001 (internet version).
74. See Deborah Nussbaum Cohen (Jewish Telegraphic Agency), '1000 orthodox rabbis reject claim rebbe was messiah', *Jewish News Bulletin of Northern California* (now *Jewish News Weekly of Northern California*), 21 June 1996. Furthermore, in the same article the rabbi Butman is quoted as stating: 'The belief that the Messiah can die and be resurrected before redemption is an integral part of Judaism... because someone else misuses it does not take anything away from Jewish belief.'
75. Geoffrey Alderman, 'Lubavitch Messianism', *Jewish Journal of Sociology*, 2003, XLV, 1–2: 50.
76. See Feldman, 2003: 43 and Alderman, 2003: 50.
77. Quoted in Ravitzky, 1996: 196.
78. See Shaffir, 1995: 128.
79. For details concerning this, see Feldman, 2003: 35–36; see also Ehrlich, 2000: 117; Aviram Golan, 'Who are you, Rebbe?', *Haaretz*, 20 January 1998 (English internet edition); Liz Leyden, '5 years after death, Messiah question divides Lubavitcher', *Washington Post*, 20 June 1999 (internet edition). As we know, the schism is strongly in evidence in Antwerp, where there are two Lubavitch oratories with opposing views on this subject.
80. A phenomenon that does not seem to be entirely new in Jewish religious history: there were secret followers of Shabbetai Tzevi until well into the 20th century: see Gershom Scholem, 'La secte crypto-juive des Dunmeh de Turquie' [The crypto-Jewish Dunmeh sect in Turkey] in *Le Messianisme juif* [Jewish Messianism], Paris, Calmann-Lévy, 1974: 219–247.
81. See Yossi Klein Halevi, 'Can Chabad outlive the Rebbe?', *Jerusalem Report*, 7 April 1994: 21–22.

6. JERUSALEM

1. A figure recently put forward by Tzvi Rabinowicz, *Hasidism in Israel. A History of the Hasidic Movement and its Masters in the Holy Land*, Northvale (NJ) and Jerusalem, Jason Aronson, 2000: 19.
2. See Jacob Barnai, 'The historiography of the Hasidic immigration to Erets Yisrael', in *Hasidism Reappraised*, ed. Ada Rapaport-Albert, London: Portland (OR), Littman Library of Jewish

Civilization, 1997: 377. This study includes the analyses of many authors, including Dubnow and Scholem, of the emigration of Hasidim to the Holy Land.
3. See J. Bauer, *Les Juifs hassidiques* [The Hasidic Jews], Paris, PUF, 'Que sais-je?', 1994: 72; Barnai, 1997: 384.
4. There is nevertheless an exception – the rebbe Nahman of Bratzlav (1772–1811), who spent several months in Palestine in 1799 and explicitly supported the financial measures in favour of the Jewish colonists in the country (H. Rabinowicz, *Hasidism and the State of Israel*, Rutherford, Madison, Teaneck, Farleigh Dickinson University Press, 1982: 52). Concerning Nahman, see p. 84.
5. See Arnold Mandel, *La Vie quotidienne des juifs hassidiques du XVIIIe siècle jusqu'à nos jours* [The everyday life of Hasidic Jews from the 18th century to the present day]. Paris, Hachette, 1974: 101–102.
6. On this subject, see the illuminating discussion by Ilan Greilsammer (*Israël. Les hommes en noir. Essai sur les parties ultra-orthodoxes* [Israel. The men in black. A study of the ultra-orthodox parties], Paris, Presses de la Fondation des sciences politiques, 1991: 41–46).
7. See Julien Bauer, *Les Partis religieux en Israël* [The religious parties in Israel]. Paris, PUF, 'Que sais-je?', 1998: 32–34.
8. Bauer, 1998: 35. The other half originated from Africa and Asia.
9. See 'Demography of Jerusalem' in <www.jewishpeople.net>, based on the *Statistical Yearbook of Jerusalem*, 1996, and Israel Central Bureau of Statistics, 1996, Data.
10. See Josette Alia, *Étoile bleue, chapeaux noirs. Israël d'aujourd'hui* [Blue star, black hats. Israel today]. Paris, Grasset, 1999: 25–26. See also Tom Sawicki, 'The ultra-orthodox takeover of Jerusalem', *Jerusalem Report*, 29 December 1994: 23.
11. There are no official statistics for the district and the number of inhabitants can only be an estimate.
12. Greilsammer, 1991: 45.
13. On Mea Shearim, see Daniel Meijers, *Ascetic Hasidism in Jerusalem. The Guardian-of-the-Faithful Community of Mea Shearim*, Leiden, New York, etc.; E. J. Brill, 1992; S. Heilman, *Defenders of the Faith. Inside ultra-orthodox Jewry*, New York, Schocken Books, 1992: 145f.; Avigail Baron, 'Meah Shearim', I, II, III, *Hamodia* (magazine section), 12 July, 19 July, 9 August 2002. See also a detailed description of the district in Mandel, 1974, Chapter IV: 98–115.
14. The period spent in a shed or hut commemorates the wandering of the Jews in the desert after the Exodus from Egypt.
15. The Hebrew of the Hasidim is officially intended solely for prayer and the study of religious texts. It is very close to ancient Hebrew and also to Aramaic. Its pronunciation is described as 'Ashkenazi', which, with several variants, was standard in central and Eastern Europe. Modern Israeli Hebrew uses a pronunciation known as 'Sephardic'.
16. On this subject, see Etgar Lefkovits, 'Capital's poverty crisis brewing', *Jerusalem Post*, 20 December 2000 (internet edition). Certainly for the entire territory of Israel, 'The situation is particularly bad in the Arab sector, where poverty affects three times as many people as it does among Jews', writes Ruth Sinai in '20 percent of Israelis live in poverty, says report', *Haaretz*, 20 December 2001 (internet edition). Nevertheless, after them, the haredim are the worst affected. As we will see in the next chapter, in Bene Beraq, an ultra-orthodox town with no Arab population, 28.5% of people subsist below the poverty line. This is defined as 50% of the available income; in 1999, this threshold was set at around $1,000 a month for a family of four; see '25% of Israeli children live in poverty', *Hamodia*, 29 December 2000: 7.
17. See Menachem Friedman, 'Neturei Karta', in *Encyclopaedia Judaica*, Jerusalem, Keter, 1972, 12: 1002–3. By a quirk of fate, in 1965 Amram Blau, this extremist leader, married for a second time, to a Frenchwoman of Catholic origin, called Lucette (Madeleine) Ferraille, who converted to Judaism under the name Ruth Ben-David. This highly active figure within the movement also hit the public eye by helping to abduct a young boy whose ultra-orthodox grandparents wanted to remove him from the influence of his non-believing parents. See Ruth Blau, *Les Gardiens de la cité. Histoire d'une guerre sainte* [The guardians of the city. History of a holy war], Paris, Flammarion, 1978.

18. On the guardians of the city and Satmar, see Norman Lamm, 'The ideology of the Neturei Karta – according to the Satmarer version', *Tradition*, 1971, 13, 1: 31–53.
19. See S. Sharot, *Messianism, Mysticism and Magic. A Sociological Analysis of Jewish Religious Movements*, Chapel Hill (NC), University of North Carolina Press, 1982: 179–181; J. S. Minkin, *The Romance of Hassidism*, Hollywood, (CA), Wilshire Books, 1971 (1st ed. 1935): 261–262.
20. See A. Rapoport-Albert (ed.), *Hasidism Reappraised*, London, Portland (Oregon), Littman Library of Jewish Civilization, 1997: 118.
21. Transported secretly in separate pieces from the former Soviet Union; see Herbert Weiner, *Nine and a Half Mystics. The Kaballa Today*, New York, Macmillan, 1971: 199.
22. See Weiner, 1971: 225.
23. See Russell Miller and Gueorgui Pinkhassov (photographer), 'Shtetl for a week', *New York Times Magazine*, 8 September 1996, section 6.
24. Sharot, 1982: 202.
25. Rabinowicz, 2000: 97.
26. See Meijers, 1992: 63–64.
27. Meijers, 1992: 68.
28. See Heilman, 1992: 147.
29. Even Meijers (1992: 42), the author of a monograph on the community, can only provide an estimate of its number of disciples.
30. There are nevertheless some small groups of reb Arele Hasidim in London and New York, each with around twenty families (Meijers, 1992: 48–49).
31. Figures according to Meijers, 1992: 88.
32. On the girls' school, see Meijers, 1992: 89–90.
33. The *guertel* creates a symbolic divide between the upper part of the body as the site of spirituality from the lower part as the site of animal nature; see T. Somogy, *Die Schejnen und die Proste, Untersuchungen zum Schönheitsideal der Ostjuden in Bezug auf Körper und Kleidung unter besonderer Berücksichtigung des Chassidismus* [The beautiful and the plain: a study of the ideal of beauty among Eastern European Jews in relation to the body and clothing, with particular reference to Hasidism], Berlin, Dieter Reimer, 1982: 173–177.
34. See Meijers, 1992: 54.
35. See Avirama Golan, 'All in the family', *Haaretz*, 18 May 2001.
36. Meijers, 1992: 116.
37. Golan, 2001.
38. See Rabinowicz, 2000: 98–99.
39. See Heilman, 1992: 165–166.
40. See Chris Kutschera, 'Jérusalem: Méa Shearim, la mauvaise conscience d'Israël' [Jerusalem: Mea Shearim, the bad conscience of Israel], *Le Spectacle du monde*, September 1982, 246.S see <www.chris-kutschera.com>.
41. But also other ultra-religious parties, such as Shas,* which has mainly Sephardic supporters.
42. Greilsammer, 1991: 146.
43. Concerning this pilgrimage, see J. Gutwirth, *Vie juive traditionnelle. Ethnologie d'une communauté hassidique* [Traditional Jewish life. Ethnology of a Hasidic community], Paris, Éditions de Minuit, 1970: 280–296.
44. Thirty thousand guests and spectators according to Rabinowicz (1982: 138). On this marriage, see also Herbert Weiner, 'A wedding in B'nai Brak', *Commentary*, July 1965: 39–46.
45. Nini Rubin, 'The heritage and history of Belz', *Hamodia*, 14 December 2001: 16.
46. See Ilan Shahar, 'Religious ministry earmarks huge sums for Hasidic "world centres"', *Haaretz*, 21 September 2000 (English internet edition).
47. Rabinowicz, 2000: 29.
48. On this subject, see D. Landau, *Piety and Power. The World of Jewish Fundamentalism*, New York, Hill & Wang, 1993: 258–259.
49. Concerning these events and the political attitude of the Belz Hasidim, see Greilsammer 1991: 222.

50. Greilsammer, 1991: 203.
51. The election of 120 Knesset representatives is conducted using proportional representation. There is a ballot by list and the candidates' position on this therefore influences their chances of election. The negotiations concerning this ranking between the parties in coalition clearly play an essential role in determining the presence of the representatives from one of the particular groups.
52. See Rabinowicz, 2000: 27.
53. See Haim Shapiro, 'Belzer rebbe blasts PM, Government', *Jerusalem Post*, 7 October 1996.
54. See the text of this agreement in 'Coalition agreement between United Torah Judaism and the Likud', *Hamodia*, 6 April 2001: 8–9.
55. This indifference on the part of Belz accorded with the views of rabbi Schach, who despite being ultra-religious, 'is not really interested in religious coercion, which he considers absurd and futile. He is not interested in secular Israelis being forbidden to eat pork or consume leavened bread at Passover' (Greilsammer, 1991: 106).
56. Rabinowicz, 2000: according to Tamar El-Or (*Educated and Ignorant, Ultra-orthodox Jewish Women and their World*, Boulder & London, Lynne Rienner Publ., 1994), there are estimated to be between 5,000 and 8,000 Ger families, but she reminds us (pp. 15–16) that no one, not even the Ger administrators, knows precisely how many followers the movement has.
57. See Mahler, 1985: 312.
58. See Avraham Ziemba, 'The Chiddushei HaRim's arrest', *Hamodia* (Magazine section), 21 February 2002: 4–5.
59. See R. Mahler, *Hasidism and the Jewish Enlightenment. Their Confrontation in Galicia and Poland in the First Half of the Nineteenth Century*, Philadelphia, Jewish Publication Society of America, 1985: 313.
60. A. Y. Bromberg, *Rebbes of Ger. Sfas Emes and Imre Emes*, New York, Mesorah Publ., 1987: 157.
61. Rabinowicz, 2000: 9.
62. On this subject, see A. Ravitzky, *Messianism, Zionism, and Jewish Religious Radicalism*, Chicago, London, University of Chicago Press, 1996: 157.
63. Rabinowicz, 2000: 15.
64. Landau, 1993: 65.
65. Landau, 1993: 20–21.
66. El-Or, 1994: 84.
67. *Hamodia*, Agudath's English-language periodical, largely controlled by the Gerer, published an article that commemorates the thirtieth anniversary of e-mail and emphasizes that following the attacks of 11 September 2001 in New York it enabled communication to continue when telephone lines were jammed or out of order (Reuters), 'E-mail celebrates its 30th birthday', *Hamodia*, 19 October 2001: 27.
68. El-Or, 1994: 16.
69. See Landau, 1993: 281; El-Or, 1994: 16–19; Rabinowicz, 2000: 14.
70. See El-Or, 1994: 15.
71. Under the auspices of the political coalition 'United Torah Judaism' (see p. 136).
72. See Ilan Shahar, 'The Ashkenazi answer to Shas' education network', *Haaretz*, 7 November 2001 (English internet edition).
73. See Ilan Shahar, 'The growing lure of the Haredi school system', *Haaretz*, 6 November 2001 (English internet edition).
74. 'Agudath Israel to open youth clubs throughout Israel', *Hamodia*, 14 December 2001: 2, and 'Keren Nesivos Moshe: filling a void in Afula', *Hamodia*, 21 December 2001: 16.
75. On this subject, see 'Countering proselytizers', *Haaretz*, 11 November 2001 (English internet edition).
76. Greilsammer, 1991: 213.
77. At each of the last two elections, United Torah Judaism won five of the 120 seats in the Knesset.
78. See Joel Greenberg, 'Orthodox Torah students win Israeli draft exemption', *New York Times*, 24 July 2002.

79. In Yedidya Meir, 'Seventeen synagogues, but no blessing', *Haaretz*, 17 December 2001 (English internet edition). At an attack in December 2001 in Emmanuel that cost the lives of several ultra-orthodox Jews, an article in *Haaretz* recalled the rabbi Schach's opposition to the settlement of the haredim* in this area (Ilan Shahar, 'Focus: an end to the miracle'), *Haaretz*, 13 December 2001 (English internet edition).

7. BENE BERAQ AND OTHER LOCATIONS

1. The population there is growing steadily, with a 3% increase in two years; see A. Cohen, 'Israel's tenth largest city: Bnei Brak', *Deiah Vedibur, Information and Insight*, 19 June 2002 <www.shemayisrael.com>.
2. At the general elections at the beginning of 2003, the 'United Torah Judaism' coalition obtained 32,446 votes in Bene Beraq. Shas had 12,443 electors. There were therefore proportionally nearly three Ashkenazi ultra-orthodox voters for every Sephardic *hared** voter, which gives an indication of the Ashkenazi predominance. The remainder of the parties combined obtained 10,000 votes (see 'UTJ gains in Bnei Brak', *Hamodia*, 7 February 2003: 10).
3. The figure on 31 December 1997: this includes the population of Ramat Gan and Holon (source: Central Bureau of Statistics, Israel).
4. See H. [Tzvi] Rabinowicz, *Hasidism in Israel. A History of the Hasidic Movement and its Masters in the Holy Land*, Northvale (NJ), Jerusalem, Jason Aronson, 2000: 161–162.
5. On the problems in Bene Beraq, see Gilles Paris, 'Bnei Brak, capitale des "barbus" d'Israel' [Bene Beraq, capital of Israel's 'bearded men'], *Le Monde*, 23 July 1996: 10; Larry Derfner, 'Good morning Bnei Brak', *Jerusalem Post*, 9 January 1998: 17; Amira Golan, 'His Honor, the Mayor', *Haaretz*, 16 July 1999 (English internet edition).
6. See Golan, 16 July 1999.
7. See Ari Shavit, 'Elective affinities', *Haaretz*, 27 December 2002 (English internet edition).
8. On the new mayor's role and actions, see Tom Segev, 'All the hungry, where are they?', *Haaretz*, 24 December 1999 (English internet edition).
9. See Dina Shiloh, 'Shopping religiously', *Jerusalem Post*, 30 July 1997: 7.
10. See 'Bnei Brak launches Shabbos water system', *Hamodia*, 3 January 2003: 9.
11. Einat Fishbein, 'Numbers show increase in poverty', *Haaretz*, 21 December 1999 (English internet edition); Segev, 1999; Daniel Zelig, 'Bné Brak poorest city in Israel', *Hamodia*, 16 November 2001: 2.
12. See Chapter 6, note 16.
13. Judith Sudilowsky, 'Bnei Brak's poverty lies in its birthrate', *Jerusalem Post*, 24 January 1997: 9.
14. Cohen, 2002. There are a few discrepancies in the demographic data, which are from various sources, but they all reveal the same trends.
15. See Zelig, 2001: 2. The author refers to figures from the Israel's Central Bureau of Statistics.
16. D. Landau, *Piety and Power. The World of Jewish Fundamentalism*, New York, Hill & Wang, 1993: 261.
17. Landau, 1993: 265.
18. On these activities, see Netty Gross, 'Salvation Army', *Jerusalem Post*, 3 February 2000; Segev, 1999; Landau, 1993, Chapter 30, 'Who helps themselves': 257–266.
19. See Gross, 2000, who refers to the work of Professor Benjamin Gidron.
20. T. El-Or, *Educated and Ignorant. Ultraorthodox Jewish Women and their World*, Boulder (Colorado), London, Lynne Rienner Publishers, 1994: 204, note 35.
21. The Reichmanns were the developers of a huge-scale property renovation project at Canary Wharf on the banks of the River Thames in London.
22. On the Reichmann brothers, see Landau, 1993: 270–271.
23. See Gil Kezwer, 'Brothers can you spare a dime?', *Jerusalem Report*, 1992, 10th anniversary (internet edition).

24. Schach had also become a leader of the ultra-religious Sephardim,* mainly originating from the Near Eastern countries; he had created several yeshives with Sephardic students, directed by some of his disciples. Moreover, in the early 1980s – when Schach was joint president of the Council of Torah Greats of the Agudath Israel party, which until then had done very little to protect the Sephardic religious Jews – he gave his approval, in conjunction with the rabbi Ovadia Yoseph, supreme authority in Israel for the Jews originating from Arab countries, to the creation of Shas, the ultra-orthodox party dedicated to their protection. This party also underwent a remarkable expansion – in 2001, it had seventeen representatives in the Knesset; at the 2003 elections, however, their number was reduced to a much lower level, with just five representatives. As we already know, the rabbi Schach also instigated another major schism within the Agudath Israel party by creating the Degel Hatorah party, an alliance of the Ashkenazi *misnaggedim** and the Belz Hasidim.
25. On this subject, see Rabinowicz, 2000: 178.
26. On the Jews of Lodz, see Rebecca Weiner, 'The virtual Jewish history tour, Lodz', *Jewish Virtual Library*, <www.us-israel.org>; 'Lodz', *Encyclopedia of Jewish Communities in Poland*, ed. Morris Wirth, Jerusalem, Yad Vashem and <www.Jewishgen.org>; on Alexander, see in particular Rabinowicz, 2000: 177–180.
27. The site of the infamous nuclear catastrophe in 1986.
28. On Hasidic marriages see also p. 111.
29. The weekly English version of *Hamodia*, the journal of Agudath Israel, provides two pages of photographs in each issue to illustrate festivities and meetings between the prominent figures, major and minor, in Hasidic and ultra-orthodox circles in Bene Beraq and elsewhere.
30. The name Eliezer of Damascus is mentioned in Genesis, 15: 2. He was the loyal and unselfish servant of Abraham, 'father' of the Jewish people, and he found a wife for his son Isaac (Genesis, 24). He is said to have acquired all his master's virtues and knowledge. The founder of the yeshive of this name has the same forename…
31. My description of Kiryat Vishnitz owes a great deal to Tzvi Rabinowicz's book (2000: 37–39).
32. See the previous chapter, note 15.
33. On this subject, see Rabinowicz, 2000: 40. This author is nevertheless extremely generous towards the rebbes, described in his various books.
34. See a description of the *tish* held by the current rebbe, Moses Joshua Hager, in Landau, 1993: 63–64; Lewis Brenner, in 'Come with me to the Tisch', *Jewish Observer*, April 1972: 7–10, describes this meal being held by Hayyim Meir Hager, the previous rebbe.
35. On this subject, see Haim Shapiro, 'Rebbes hold reconciliation meeting', *Jerusalem Post*, 24 November 1998: 4.
36. See Rabinowicz, 2000: 42–43.
37. Concerning these dances, see J. Gutwirth, *Vie juive traditionnelle. Ethnologie d'une communauté hassidique* [Traditional Jewish life. Ethnology of a Hasidic community], Paris, Éditions de Minuit, 1970: 352–353.
38. On Hasidism in Tel-Aviv, see Ilan Shahar, 'The court is no longer in session', *Haaretz*, 22 October 1997 (English internet edition).
39. Shahar, 22 October, 1997.
40. On Kefar Habad, see Rabinowicz, 2000: 71–74; E. Hoffman, *Despite of all Odds. The Story of Lubavitch*, New York, Simon & Schuster, 1991: 156–159; *Challenge. An Encounter with Lubavitch-Chabad in Israel*, London, Lubavitch Foundation of Great Britain, 1973; see also Morris Freilich, 'Field work: problems and goals', in *Marginal Natives at Work. Anthropologists in the Field*, ed. Morris Freilich, Cambridge (MA), Schenkman, 1977 (1st edition 1970): 283–289. The author, who has confirmed to me himself that this is about Kefar Habad, describes here without identifying it the beginnings of the village, as a moshav, an agricultural cooperative.
41. Freilich, 1977: 285.
42. In particular, JOINT, the American Jewish Joint Distribution Committee, and ORT, the Organization for Rehabilitation through Training (Rabinowicz, 2000: 73).

43. Some of the inhabitants of Kiryat Zanz, particularly the oldest, who have sometimes come to settle there under the rebbe's leadership, are United States citizens, which probably accounts for this subsidy.
44. On 25 February 1994, Dr Baruch Goldstein massacred several dozen Palestinians just by the vault of Patriarchs, a holy site for Jews and Muslims; he was killed there himself. Goldstein belonged to the ultra-nationalist religious movement Gush Emunim. Since the second Intifada, Hebron has also been the scene of countless murderous incidents between Palestinians and Israelis and recently of lengthy occupations by Israeli soldiers with a severe curfew for the Palestinians.
45. Joseph Gutnick, who also gave his name to a Habad kolel in Maaleh Adumim, in the occupied territories, a rich magnate in the Australian mining industry, was appointed a special emissary by the rebbe in the early 1990s. His task was to counteract any concession of territory to the Palestinians, in particular by financing an advertising campaign in the Israeli press.
46. See Georges Marion, 'Tension politique en Israël après le memorandum de Wye River' [Political tension in Israel following the Wye River Memorandum], *Le Monde*, 28 October 1996: 5; 'Hebron sous tension à l'approche de l'accord' [Hebron under pressure from the forthcoming agreement], *Dernières Nouvelles d'Alsace*, 20 November 1996.
47. See 'The 1999 Israeli elections: a view from Judea', *Judea Magazine*, 1999: 7.3: 3, <www.womeningreen.org>.
48. In an article entitled 'Focus: an end to the miracle' (*Haaretz*, 13 December 2001, English internet edition) Ilan Shahar recalls that the rabbi Schach, leader of the non-Hasidic ultra-orthodox, had strongly opposed the creation of this settlement in 1983. He had declared that those who settled there were withdrawing from the protection of God.
49. See Nadav Shragai, 'Settling for less', *Haaretz*, 24 January 2002 (English internet edition); Stephanie Le Bars, 'Le budget maintient les privilèges accordés aux colonies' [Privileges granted to the colonies are retained in the budget], *Le Monde*, 1 November 2002: 2.
50. On this subject, see 'Haredim and politics', *Israel Yearbook and Almanac*, 1996: 88, 90.

8. LUBAVITCH IN FRANCE

1. A recent questionnaire-based survey conducted by Erik H. Cohen (see 'Les résultats de la grande enquête sur les Juifs en France' [Results of the major survey on the Jews in France], *L'Arche*, 200, December 2002, 538: 54f.), estimates there to be 500,000 or 575,000 Jews in France, depending on the criteria used. The first estimate is based on a narrow definition of the Jewish population as it relates only to the interviewees who described themselves as Jewish, including their families; the second indicates all the people living in households of which the head is Jewish, including non-Jewish spouses. For the Hasidim, who as we know are very homogamous, the comparison with the first figure is more pertinent.
2. Since the emancipation of the Jews in 1791.
3. See Chapter 5, p. 65, and note 16.
4. According to the rabbi Shmuel Azimov, the Lubavitch leader, with whom I had a discussion in 1975.
5. See 'Les débuts des institutions "Habad" en France' [The beginnings of the 'Habad' institutions in France] Chapter 2, 'Les premiers pas' [The first steps], *Kountrass*, July 2003, 96: 10.
6. According to the Lubavitch rabbi, Haim Nissenbaum, spokesman of the movement.
7. See 'Les débuts...', 2003: 7.
8. See 'Les débuts...', 2003: 11.
9. We should remember that the Consistory, a community institution under State control, was established under the Empire in 1808; after the separation of Church and State in 1905, it became a voluntary religious organization.
10. For a history and a detailed account, see Dominique Jarrasé, *Guide du patrimoine juif parisien* [Guide to Jewish heritage in Paris], Paris Éditions Parigramme, 2003: 112–113.
11. See 'Les débuts...', 2003: 13.
12. See 'Les débuts...', 2003: 9.
13. See 'Les débuts...', 2003: 16.

14. Because Tunisia and Morocco had protectorate status, Jews also obtained French nationality on request. The decree was named after its instigator, Isaac Adolphe Crémieux (1796–1880), a Jewish French politician.
15. For these observations concerning Lubavitch in the Maghreb, I am greatly indebted to Laurence Podselver's article, 'Le mouvement Lubavitch: déracination et insertion des séfarades' [The Lubavitch movement: the uprooting and integration of the Sephardim], *Pardès*, 1986, 3: 54–68. In fact, Lubavitch maintains two synagogues and some schools in Casablanca to this day.
16. An eating utensil, for a Jew who follows the prescriptions in the code of Jewish laws, the Shulhan Aruh, should first be soaked in 'living' water from a spring, a river or rain.
17. See Podselver, 1986: 61–63.
18. The Mimouna at the close of the Passover included the friendly and welcome presence of Arab neighbours who made a strong contribution to the return of 'normal' food with baklava, couscous etc. This commensalism with Muslims undoubtedly contributed to the rejection decreed by the Hasidim.
19. Podselver, 1986: 64.
20. See Victor Malka (*Les Juifs sépharades* [The Sephardic Jews], Paris, PUF, 'Que sais-je?', 1997: 70–71, 80): historically, in matters of religious prohibition, the Ashkenazim are inclined to be strict, whereas the Sephardim support a more flexible and more liberal interpretation of the Law. Furthermore, spontaneity, hospitality and tolerance are essentially Sephardic values; it is principally the latter two that are particularly practised by Lubavitch.
21. See 'Écoles juives de France' [Jewish schools in France], *Kountrass*, 2000, 70 (internet version).
22. However, once again there are no demographic statistics available.
23. Another orthodox school development, Ozer Hatorah, which was also founded after the war, by North African Jews, is much more exacting.
24. See Laurence Podselver, 'La tradition réinventée: les hassidim de Loubavich en France' [Tradition reinvented: the Lubavitch Hasidim in France], *Revue des études juives*, 1992, CLI: 442, 443.
25. In Michèle Baron; 'De Djerba à Paris XIXe' [From Djerba to the 19th arrondissement in Paris], *L'Arche*, 2000, 508: 69 (68–69).
26. See for example Patrick Simon & Claude Tapia, *Le Belleville des juifs tunisiens* [The Tunisian Jewish quarter in Paris], Paris, Autrement, 1998: 157–158, and Laurence Podselver & Denise Weill, 'La nouvelle orthodoxie et la transmission familiale' [The new orthodoxy and familial transmission], *Pardès*, 1996, 22: 153 (149–159).
27. Concerning these figures, see Podselver; 1992, CLI: 441.
28. Once again, there are no precise data, which makes it impossible to provide a complete socio-professional profile of the movement.
29. Unemployment does not appear to be a major problem among the followers.
30. Florence Hubin, 'La Ville attribue une aide à une crèche Loubavitch' [The City grants aid to a Lubavitch crèche], *Le Parisien*, 28 October 2000 (Internet archives).
31. See Nicolas Weill, 'Essor et désarroi des Loubavitch' [Lubavitch expansion and disarray], *Le Monde*, 21 September 1996: 11. By a decree on 14 July 1997, Hillel Pevzner was made a Chevalier de la Légion d'honneur. President Chirac presented him with this decoration on 4 July 1997 at the Élysée palace and addressed a speech to his 'long-standing friend'.
32. In Weill, 1996: 11.
33. See Sylvia Zappi, 'La banalisation des actes antijuifs, nouvelle cause de tensions urbaines' [The trivialization of anti-Semitic acts, a new source of urban tension], *Le Monde*, 18 February 2002 (internet version).
34. Concerning these matters of kasher meat, see Sophie Nizard, 'L'Économie du croire. Une anthropologie des pratiques alimentaires juives en modernité' [The economy of belief. An anthropology of modern Jewish dietary practices], doctoral thesis, École des hautes études en sciences sociales, Paris, 1995: II: 251–2; S. Nizard, 'La cacherout en France. Organisation matérielle d'une consommation symbolique' [The kashrut in France. The material organization of a symbolic consumption], *Les Cahiers du judaïsme*, 1998, 3: 64–73; J. Bauer, *La Nourriture casher* [Kasher food], Paris, PUF, 'Que sais-je?', 1996: 58–59.

35. See Bauer, 1996: 58, Nizard, 1998: 67.
36. See Bauer, 1996: 59.
37. Nizard, 1996: II: 252.
38. Nizard, 1998: 70.
39. See for example, Roger Cukierman, 'Aujourd'hui, nous parlons tous de la même voix, unis derrière Israël' [Now we are all united in support of Israel], *L'Arche*, June 2001, 520 (internet version) or more recently, on 3 October 2003, the message from the CRIF president at Yom Kippur; <www.col.fr/article-304.html>.
40. On 9 November 2003, the Agence juive pour Israël [Jewish agency for Israel] organized a major exhibition on the subject of 'Alyah', or emigration to Israel, on the premises of the Chaya Mushka school in the Rue Petit. Although Lubavitch was only lending or hiring out its premises, the connection between the movement and the agency was nonetheless obvious to visitors to the exhibition or for anyone who read the relevant public announcements.
41. Podselver, 1986: 57.
42. It is only necessary to scan the list of 'centres and representatives of Beth Loubavitch' – <www.loubavitch.fr> – to see that the overwhelming majority of officials have names that are usual for Jews of North African origin.

9. OVERVIEW

1. See William Shaffir, 'Fieldwork among Hassidic Jews: moral challenges and missed opportunities', *Jewish Journal of Sociology*, 2001: XLIII, 1–2: 56.
2. According to some recent research, this population has doubled over the last twelve years and the average size of families there is 5.9 people, as against the British national average of 2.4 (see 'Stamford Hill Chareidi community to double within ten years', *Hamodia*, 6 December 2002: 44).
3. There were 30,000 immigrants in 1933, 42,000 in 1934 and 62,000 in 1935; the Jewish population doubled in four years and was close to 400,000 at the end of 1935 (see S. Epstein, *Histoire du peuple juif au XXe siècle. De 1914 à nos jours* [The history of the Jewish people in the 20th century: 1914 to the present day], Paris, Hachette, 1998: 116).
4. See C. S. Heller, *On the Edge of Destruction. Jews of Poland between the Two World Wars*, New York, Columbia University Press, 1977: 180–181.
5. On these pilgrimages, see Shifra Epstein, 'Les pèlerinages hassidiques en Pologne' [Hasidic pilgrimages in Poland], *Les Cahiers du judaïsme*, 2000, 8: 100–111.
6. Epstein, 2000: 111.
7. The following are some Eastern European names of dynasties of rebbes that, if not entirely new, are at least relatively unknown, and that relate to this past: Tchakaver, Lutzker, Desher, Bohusher, Makaver, Shidlovtze and there are many others besides. As I have said, the two pages of weekly photographs in *Hamodia*, the publication of Agudath Israel, English version, present illustrious rebbes aplenty, along with these figures who are known mainly to their small groups of followers. I shall nevertheless mention one exception – there are others besides – the Bostoner rebbe, born in Boston in 1921, who thereby proclaims his American origin.
8. In Marc-Alain Ouaknin, *Ouvertures hassidiques* [Introduction to Hasidism], Paris, Jacques Grancher, 1990: 164.
9. These observations do not preclude the possibility of severe psychic problems among some Hasidim who have experienced the tragedies of the Second World War.
10. All this is often decided at the outset by parents or close relatives because, as we know, in Hasidic circles it is common for young people of both sexes never to have seen each other before the engagement is already imminent.
11. Laws mainly governing sexual relations between spouses. These are forbidden during menstruation and the seven days that follow it.
12. See I. Rubin, *Satmar. Two Generations of an Urban Island*, New York, etc., Peter Lang, 1997: 128.

13. See L. Podselver, 'La séparation, la redondance et l'identité: les hassidim de Lubavitch à Paris' [Separation, diffusion and identity: the Lubavitch Hasidim in Paris], *Pardès*, 1988, 7: 173–174.
14. These figures are from 'Population' in *Encyclopaedia Judaica*, CD-Rom edition, Judaica Multimedia, Jerusalem, 1997.
15. See Sergio Dellapergola, 'World Jewish Population 1997' in *American Jewish Yearbook*, ed. D. Singer & R. Seldin, New York, American Jewish Committee, 1999: 548.
16. See Moshe Sicron, 'Growth of the Israeli population, 1983–92', in 'Israel, State of: Population', *Encyclopaedia Judaica*, CD-Rom edition, Judaica Multimedia, Jerusalem, 1997.
17. See Linda J. Waite & Judith S. Friedman, 'The impact of religious upbringing and marriage markets on Jewish intermarriage', *Contemporary Jewry*, 1997, 18: 3.
18. See E. H. Cohen, 'Les résultats de la grande enquête sur les juifs de France' [Results of the major survey on the Jews in France], *L'Arche*, December 2002, 538: 67.
19. 208,000 immigrants from the former Soviet Union between 1990 and 1999 are non-Jews according to this strict interpretation, which under the aegis of the ultra-orthodox rabbinical authorities that govern the religious life of the country is not without consequences for marriages, funerals and so on, which they alone can conduct for the Jewish population – see note 48 below. On the figures, see Natan Sharansky, then Minister of the Interior in Israel, quoted in Bezalel Kahn; 'Non-Jewish mass immigration: a time bomb in Israeli society', *Deyah ve Dibur, Information and Insight*, 15 December 1999, <www.shemayisrael.com>. We should recall that Israel has a large Arab population and also for some time now has had tens of thousands of non-Jewish immigrants, often from the Third World, seeking work there.
20. Although as we saw in Chapter 6, rabbi Blau from the Edah Haredit* community married a non-Jew, she had converted under the orthodox rules.
21. YN, 'What is wrong with the Internet', *Yated Neeman*, 14 January 2001: 20.
22. This declaration and list of signatories can be seen in 'D'as Torah and a stern warning', *Deyah ve Dibur, Information and Insight*, 12 January 2000, <www.shemayisrael.com>.
23. The Satmarer rebbe and the Toldot Ahronot leaders did not sign this appeal but they undoubtedly endorse the rejection issued by their strictest fellow leaders on this matter.
24. See J. Bauer, *Les Juifs hassidiques* [The Hasidic Jews], Paris, PUF, 'Que sais-je?', 1994: 109–111.
25. With the notable exception of the schools sponsored by Neture Karte* and the other anti-Zionist groups in Mea Shearim, where the teaching is conducted in Yiddish.
26. Rubin, 1997: 152.
27. See B. J. Morris, *Lubavitcher Women in America. Identity and Activism in the Postwar Era*, Albany, State University of New York Press, 1998: 48f. The institute, Machon Chana, is named after the rebbe's deceased mother.
28. S. Brodowicz, *L'Âme d'Israël. Les origines, la vie et l'oeuvre de Menahem M. Schneerson, Rabbi de Loubavitch* [The soul of Israel. The origins, life and works of Menahem M. Schneerson, Lubavitcher rebbe], Paris, Éditions du Rocher/Bibliophane, 1998: 254.
29. See Lis Harris, *Holy Days. The World of Hasidic Family*. New York, Touchstone, 1985: 127–128.
30. Rubin, 1997: 124.
31. On this subject, see R. J. Simon, *Continuity and Change. A Study of Two Ethnic Communities in Israel*, Cambridge, London, New York, Melbourne, Cambridge University Press, 1978: 88–90, 93–96, 141–148.
32. See Ilan Shahar, 'For ultra-orthodox women the work is never done', *Haaretz*, 12 May 1998 (English internet edition).
33. See D. Meijers, *Ascetic Hasidism in Jerusalem. The Guardian-of-the-Faithful Community of Mea Shearim*, Leiden, New York, etc., E. J. Brill, 1992: 79–80.
34. Although some male followers privately acknowledge that a great deal of secular knowledge is in fact necessary.
35. I am of course familiar with the religious 'rationale' – particularly concerning the possible female 'impurity' that the men should avoid – that is supposed to justify these forms of behaviour, but it is nevertheless reminiscent of similar segregations between blacks and whites

36. On this subject, see D. Landau, *Piety and Power. The World of Jewish Fundamentalism*, New York, Hill & Wang, 1993: 282–285.
37. In the USA, Pearl Abraham, the author of *The Romance Reader* (London, Quartet Books, 1996) and in Israel, Naomi Ragen, who has published several novels on this subject. On this subject, see also William Shaffir & Robert Rockaway, 'Leaving the ultra-orthodox fold: Haredi Jews who defected', *Jewish Journal of Sociology*, 1987, XXIX, 2: 97–114, and Martine Gozlan, 'Fanatisme ultra-religieux' [Ultra-religious fanaticism], *Marianne*, 17 May 1999: 48–53.
38. See Joseph Dan, 'Hassidism: the third century', in Ada Rapoport-Albert, *Hasidism Reappraised*, London, Portland (OR), Littman Library of Jewish Civilization, 1997: 422; M.-A. Ouaknin, *Ouvertures hassidiques* [Introduction to Hasidism], Paris, Jacques Grancher, 1990: 92.
39. See G. Kranzler, *Hasidic Williamsburg. A Contemporary American Hasidic Community*, North Vale, New Jersey & London, 1995(a): 95–96, 141, 226, 253–254.
40. For a more detailed description of Talmudic study among the Hasidim, refer to my book *Vie juive traditionelle* [Traditional Jewish life] (1970: 186–193).
41. See Mark Zborowski, 'The place of book-learning in traditional Jewish culture', in *Childhood in Contemporary Culture*, ed. M. Mead and M. Wolfenstein, Chicago and London, University of Chicago Press, 1955: 133.
42. See Shaffir & Rockaway, 1987: 97–114.
43. In I. Greilsammer, *Israël. Les hommes en noir. Essai sur les parties ultra-orthodoxes* [Israel. The men in black. A study of the ultra-orthodox parties], Paris, Presses de la Fondation des sciences politiques, 1991: 50.
44. Except from the elections at the beginning of 2003 until January 2005.
45. R. Mahler, *Hasidism and the Jewish Enlightenment. Their Confrontation in Galicia and Poland in the First Half of the Nineteenth Century*, Philadelphia, Jewish Publication Society of America, 1985: XV.
46. See, for example, Israël Shahak & Norton Mezvinsky (*Jewish Fundamentalism in Israel*, London, Pluto Press, 1999: 58–62), who make a particular attack, with supporting quotations, on the Lubavitch rebbe's theories extolling the concept of the Jews as a 'chosen people' whose souls have a holy origin, unlike those of non-Jews.
47. See for example Martin Buber, *Hasidism and Modern Man*, Atlantic Highlands, Humanities Press International, 1988 (1st edition, 1958): 43–44.
48. The rabbinical courts, in which only ultra-orthodox rabbis – Hasidim or *misnaggedim** – preside, have for example total jurisdiction over marriage – conducted only according to the rites prescribed by Jewish law. These courts prevent, for instance, any union between people whom they do not consider to be Jews from a religious viewpoint (particularly people with a Jewish father and a non-Jewish mother); furthermore, they do not recognize the conversions to Judaism conducted by the reform and liberal rabbis. 'The exclusivity of the rabbinical courts in the matter of marriage is the most characteristic feature of the lack of separation between religion and State in Israel', as Ilan Greilsammer writes (1991: 168–169), which confirms once again the major role of the ultra-orthodox in the country in such a sensitive matter. Anyone who is unable or unwilling to submit to the decrees of the rabbinical courts has to get married abroad, generally in Cyprus; these unions are not recognized by the rabbinical courts but the supreme court has ruled that the Minister of the Interior has to register and therefore to legalize these marriages.
49. See in particular 'Miracle' and 'Hagiography' in *Encyclopaedia Judaica*, CD Rom edition, Judaica Multimedia, Jerusalem, 1997.

APPENDIX

1. For the authors quoted here, refer to the Bibliography.

Bibliography

1. BACKGROUND BOOKS AND ARTICLES

ABICHT, L. *De joden van België* [The Jews of Belgium]. Amsterdam, Antwerp Atlas, 1994.
ABRAHAM, P. *The Romance Reader*. London, Quartet Books, 1996.
ALDERMAN, G. Lubavitch Messianism. *Jewish Journal of Sociology*, 2003, XLV, 1–2: 46–50.
ALIA, J. *Étoile bleue, chapeaux noirs. Israël d'aujourd'hui* [Blue star, black hats. Israel today]. Paris, Grasset, 1999: 25–26.
ASSAF, D. Un petit État dans un grand État: la cour 'royale' hassidique au XIXe siècle [A small state within a large state: the Hasidic 'royal' court in the 19th century], *Les Cahiers du judaïsme*, 2000, 8 ('Hassidismes'): 37–53.
BARNAI, J. The historiography of the Hasidic immigration to Erets Yisrael. In Ada RAPOPORT-ALBERT (ed.), *Hasidism Reappraised*. London, Portland (Oregon), Littman Library of Jewish Civilization, 1997: 376–388.
BAUER, J. *Les Juifs hassidiques* [The Hasidic Jews]. Paris, PUF, 'Que sais-je?', 1994.
BAUER, J. *La Nourriture casher* [Kasher food]. Paris, PUF, 'Que sais-je?', 1996.
BAUER, J. *Les Partis religieux en Israël* [The religious parties in Israel]. Paris, PUF, 'Que sais-je?', 1998.
BELCOVE-SHALIN, J. Becoming more of an Eskimo: fieldwork among the Hasidim of Boro Park. In *Between Two Worlds. Ethnographic Essays on American Jewry*, ed. Jack KUGELMASS. Ithaca, London, Cornell University Press, 1988: 77–102.
BELCOVE-SHALIN, J. Home in exile. Hasidim in the New World. In *Ethnographic Studies of Hasidic Jews in America*, ed. Janet S. BELCOVE-SHALIN. Albany, State University of New York Press, 1995: 205–236.
BEN-AMOS, D. & MINTZ, J. R. (translated and edited by), *In Praise of the Baal Shem Tov [Shivhei ha-Besht]. The Earliest Collection of Legends about the Founder of Hasidism*. Bloomington, London, Indiana University Press, 1970.
BERGER, D. The Rebbe, the Jews, and the Messiah, *Commentary*, 2001, 112, 2: 23–30.
BERGER, D. *The Rebbe, the Messiah, and the Scandal of Orthodox Indifference*. London, Portland (Oregon), Littman Library of Jewish Civilization, 2001.
BERGER-SOFER, R. Political kinship alliances of a Hasidic dynasty, *Ethnology*, 1984, 23,1: 49–62.
BLAU, R. *Les Gardiens de la cité. Histoire d'une guerre sainte* [The guardians of the city. History of a holy war]. Paris, Flammarion, 1978.
BLOOM, S. G. *Postville. A Clash of Cultures in Heartland America*. New York, San Diego, London, Harcourt, 2000.
BRENNER, L. Come with me to the Tisch. *Jewish Observer*, April 1972: 7–10.
BRODOWICZ, S. *L'Âme d'Israël. Les origines, la vie et l'oeuvre de Menahem M. Schneerson, Rabbi de Loubavitch* [The soul of Israel. The origins, life and works of Menahem M. Schneerson, Lubavitcher rebbe]. Paris, Éditions du Rocher/Bibliophane, 1998.
BROMBERG, A. Y. *Rebbes of Ger. Sfas Emes and Imre Emes*. New York, Mesorah Publ. 1987.
DAN, J. Hassidism: the third century. In *Hasidism Reappraised*, ed. Ada RAPOPORT-ALBERT. London, Portland (Oregon), Littman Library of Jewish Civilization, 1997: 415–426.
DELLAPERGOLA, S. World Jewish Population 1997. In *American Jewish Yearbook, 1999*, ed. D. SINGER & R. SELDIN. New York, American Jewish Committee, 1999: 543–580.
DINUR, B. The origins of Hasidism and its Social and Messianic Foundations. In *Essential Papers on Hasidism*, ed. Gershon David HUNDERT. New York and London, New York University Press, 1991: 86–208.

DUBNOW, S. *Geschichte des Chassidismus* [History of Hasidism]. Berlin, 1931, reprint: Jewish Publishing House, Tel-Aviv, 1969.
EHRLICH, A. M. *Leadership in the HaBad Movement*. North Vale (NJ), Jerusalem, Jason Aronson, 2000.
EL-OR, T. *Educated and Ignorant. Ultraorthodox Jewish Women and their World*. Boulder (Colorado), London, Lynne Rienner Publishers, 1994 (translated from the Hebrew).
EPSTEIN, S. Drama on a table: the Bobover Hasidim Piremshpiyl. In *Judaism Viewed from Within and from Without*, ed. Harvey E. GOLDBERG. Anthropological Studies, Albany, State University of New York Press, 1987: 195–217.
EPSTEIN, S. The Bobover Hasidim Piremshpiyl: from folk drama for Purim to a ritual of transcending the Holocaust. In *Ethnographic Studies of Hasidic Jews in America*, ed. Janet S. BELCOVE-SHALIN. Albany, State University of New York Press, 1995: 237–255.
EPSTEIN, S. *Histoire du peuple juif au XXe siècle. De 1914 à nos jours* [The history of the Jewish people in the 20th century: 1914 to the present day]. Paris, Hachette, 1998.
EPSTEIN, S. Les pèlerinages hassidiques en Pologne [Hasidic pilgrimages in Poland]. *Les Cahiers du judaïsme*, 2000, 8: 100–111 ('Hassidismes').
ETTINGER, S. Hassidism and the Kahal in Eastern Europe. In *Hasidism Reappraised*, ed. Ada RAPOPORT-ALBERT. London, Portland (Oregon), Littman Library of Jewish Civilization, 1997: 63–75.
FELDMAN, J. *Lubavitcher as Citizens. A Paradox of Liberal Democracy*. Ithaca, London, Cornell University Press, 2003.
FREILICH, M. Field work: problems and goals. In *Marginal Natives at work. Anthropologists in the field*, ed. Morris FREILICH. Cambridge (MA), Schenkman, 1977 (1st ed. 1970): 283–289.
FRIEDMAN, M. Neturei Karta. In *Encyclopaedia Judaica*. Jerusalem, 1973, 12: 1002–3.
GARTNER, L. P. *History of the Jews in Modern Times*. Oxford, Oxford University Press, 2001.
GLAZER, N. *American Judaism*. Chicago, London, University of Chicago Press, 1972 (1st ed. 1957).
GOLDSCHMIDT, H. Suits and souls. Trying to tell a Jew when you see one in Crown Heights. In *Jews of Brooklyn*, ed. Ilana ABRAMOVITCH & Sean GALVIN. Hanover (New Hampshire), London, University Press of New England, 2002: 72–77.
GREILSAMMER, I. *Israël. Les hommes en noir. Essai sur les parties ultra-orthodoxes* [Israel. The men in black. A study of the ultra-orthodox parties]. Paris, Presses de la Fondation des sciences politiques, 1991.
GUTWIRTH, J. Le judaïsme anversois aujourd'hui [Judaism in Antwerp today]. *Revue des études juives*, 1966, CXXV, 4: 365–384.
GUTWIRTH, J. Hassidim de notre temps [Contemporary Hasidism]. *Les Nouveaux Cahiers*, 1966, 7: 56–62.
GUTWIRTH, J. Anvers: naissance d'une dynastie [Antwerp: the birth of a dynasty]. *L'Arche*, 1968, 139: 54–59.
GUTWIRTH, J. *Vie juive traditionnelle. Ethnologie d'une communauté hassidique* [Traditional Jewish life. Ethnology of a Hasidic community]. Paris, Éditions de Minuit, 1970.
GUTWIRTH, J. Les pains azymes de la Pâque chez les hassidim [Unleavened bread at the Passover among the Hasidim]. *Objets et Mondes*, 1976, 16, 4: 137–148.
GUTWIRTH, J. Field methods and the sociology of Jews: case studies of Hassidic communities. *Jewish Journal of Sociology*, 1978, XX, 1: 49–58.
GUTWIRTH, J. *Les Judéo-chrétiens d'aujourd'hui* [Judaeo-Christians today]. Paris, Éditions du Cerf, 1987.
GUTWIRTH, J. Religion télévisée: les télévangélistes et Jean-Paul II [Televised religion: the televangelists and John Paul II]. *Ethnologie française*, 2000, XXX, 3: 427–437.
HARRIS, L. *Holy Days. The World of Hasidic Family*. New York, Touchstone, 1985.
HEILMAN, S. *Defenders of the Faith. Inside ultra-orthodox Jewry*. New York, Schocken Books, 1992.
HELLER, C. S. *On the Edge of Destruction. Jews of Poland between the Two World Wars*. New York, Columbia University Press, 1977.

HELMREICH, W. B. *The World of the Yeshiva. An Intimate Portrait of Orthodox Jewry*. New York, The Free Press, 1982.

HOFFMAN, E. *Despite of all Odds. The Story of Lubavitch*. New York, Simon & Schuster, 1991.

HONIGMAN, P. Talmuddrucke in Nachkriegsdeutschland [Editions of the Talmud in post-war Germany]. In *Überlebt und Unterwegs. Jüdischer Displaced Persons in Nachkriegsdeutschland* [Survivors on the move. Jewish displaced persons in post-war Germany]. Fritz Bauer Institut, Frankfurt, New York, Campus Verlag, 1997: 249–266.

JACOBSMEYER, W. Der Lager der jüdischen Displaced Persons in den Deutsche Westzonen, 1946/47 als Ort jüdische Selbstvergewisserung [The Jewish displaced persons camp in the West German zones 1946/1947 as a place of Jewish self-reassurance]. In *Jüdisches Leben in Deutschland seit 1945* [Jewish life in Germany since 1945], ed. Michael BRUMLIK *et al*. Frankfurt, Jüdische Verlag bei Athenäum, 1986.

JOCHNOWITZ, E. Holy rolling, making sense of baking matzo. In *Jews of Brooklyn*, ed. Ilana ABRAMOVITCH & Sean GALVIN. Hanover (New Hampshire), London, University Press of New England, 2002: 72–77.

KAMEN, R. *Growing up Hasidic: Education and Socialization in the Bobover Hasidic Community*. Ann Arbor, University Microfilms, 1975 (Ph.D. 1975).

KRANZLER, G. *Williamsburg. A Jewish Community in Transition*. New York, Feldheim, 1961.

KRANZLER, G. *Hasidic Williamsburg. A Contemporary American Hasidic Community*. North Vale, New Jersey & London, 1995 (a).

KRANZLER, G. The economic revitalization of the Hasidic community of Williamsburg. In *Ethnographic Studies of Hasidic Jews in America,* ed. Janet S. BELCOVE-SHALIN. Albany, State University of New York Press, 1995 (b): 181–204.

KRANZLER, G. & HERZBERG I. (photos). *The Face of Faith, An American Hassidic Community*. Baltimore, Baltimore Hebrew College Press, 1972.

LAMM, N. The Ideology of the Neturei Karta – According to the Satmarer Version. *Tradition*, 1971, 13,1: 31–53.

LANDAU, D. *Piety and Power. The World of Jewish Fundamentalism*. New York, Hill & Wang, 1993.

LEVINE, S.W. *Mystics, Mavericks and Merrymakers. An Intimate Journey Among Hasidic Girls*. New York, London, New York University Press, 2003.

LEVY, S. B. Shifting patterns of ethnic identification among the Hassidim. In *The New Ethnicity: Perspectives from Ethnology*, ed. John W. BENNET, St. Paul, New York, etc. West Publishing, 1973: 25–50.

LEVY, S. B. *Ethnic Boundness and the Institutionalization of Charisma*. Ann Arbor, University Microfilms, 1973 (Ph.D. 1973).

MAHLER, R. *Hasidism and the Jewish Enlightenment. Their Confrontation in Galicia and Poland in the First Half of the Nineteenth Century*. Philadelphia, Jewish Publication Society of America, 1985 (translated from the Yiddish).

MANDEL, A. *La Vie quotidienne des juifs hassidiques du XVIIIe siècle jusqu'à nos jours* [The everyday life of Hasidic Jews from the 18th century to the present day]. Paris, Hachette, 1974.

MAYER, E. *From Suburb to Shtetl. The Jews of Boro Park*. Philadelphia, Temple University Press, 1979.

MAYER, E. *The Boro Park Community Survey, 1992–93*. New York, Council of Jewish Organizations of Boro Park, 1993.

MEIJERS, D. *Ascetic Hasidism in Jerusalem. The Guardian-of-the-Faithful Community of Mea Shearim, Leiden*. New York, etc. E. J. Brill, 1992.

MINKIN, J. S. *The Romance of Hassidism*. Hollywood, (CA). Wilshire Books, 1971 (1st ed. 1935).

MINTZ, J. R. *Hasidic People. A Place in the New World*. Cambridge (MA), London, Harvard University Press, 1992.

MORRIS, B. J. *Lubavitcher Women in America. Identity and Activism in the Postwar Era*. Albany, State University of New York Press, 1998.

NAISON, M. Crown Heights in the 1950s. In *Jews of Brooklyn*, ed. Ilana ABRAMOVITCH & Sean GALVIN. Hanover (New Hampshire), London, University Press of New England, 2002: 143–152.

OUAKNIN, M.-A. *Ouvertures hassidiques* [Introduction to Hasidism]. Paris, Jacques Grancher, 1990.

PIERKARZ, M. Hasidism as a socio-religious movement on the evidence of devekut. In *Hasidism Reappraised*, ed. Ada RAPOPORT-ALBERT. London, Portland (Oregon), Littman Library of Jewish Civilization, 1997: 225–248.

POLL, S. *The Hasidic Community of Williamsburg*. Glencoe, Free Press of Glencoe, 1962.

RABINOWICZ, H. *Hasidism and the State of Israel*. Rutherford, Madison, Teaneck, Farleigh Dickinson University Press, 1982.

RABINOWICZ, H. *A World Apart. The Story of the Chassidim in Britain*. London, Portland (Oregon), Valentine Mitchell, 1997.

RABINOWICZ, H. [Tzvi] *Hasidism in Israel. A History of the Hasidic Movement and its Masters in the Holy Land*. Northvale (NJ), Jerusalem, Jason Aronson, 2000.

RABINOWITSCH, W. Z. *Lithuanian Hasidism*. New York, Schocken, 1971.

RAPOPORT-ALBERT, A. Hasidism after 1772: Structural Continuity and Change. In *Hasidism Reappraised*, ed. Ada RAPOPORT-ALBERT. London, Portland (Oregon), Littman Library of Jewish Civilization, 1997: 76–140.

RAVITZKY, A. *Messianism, Zionism, and Jewish Religious Radicalism*. Chicago, London, University of Chicago Press, 1996 (translated from the Hebrew).

RITTERBAND, P. The fertility of the Jewish people: a contemporary overview. In *World Jewish Population: Trends and Politics*, ed. S. DELLAPERGOLA & L. COHEN, Jerusalem, Hebrew University of Jerusalem 1992: 93–105.

ROBBERECHTS, E. *Les Hassidim* [The Hasidim]. Maredsous, Éditions Brepols, 1990.

ROSMAN, M. J. Social Conflicts in Miedzyboz in the Generation of the Besht. In *Hasidism Reappraised*, ed. Ada RAPOPORT-ALBERT. London, Portland (Oregon), Littman Library of Jewish Civilization, 1997: 51–62.

RUBIN, I. *An Island in the City*. Chicago, Quadrangle Books, 1972.

RUBIN, I. *Satmar. Two Generations of an Urban Island*. New York, etc. Peter Lang, 1997.

SAERENS, L. *Vreemdelingen in een wereldstad. Een geschiedenis van Antwerpen en zijn joodse bevolking* [Foreigners in an international city. A history of Antwerp and its Jewish population]. Antwerp, Lannoo, 2000.

SANDBERG, N. *Jewish Life in Los Angeles*. Lanham (MD), London, University Press of America, 1986.

SCHMIDT, E. *Geschiedenis van de Joden in Antwerpen* [History of the Jews in Antwerp]. Antwerp, Ontwikkeling, 1963. [French translation: *L'Histoire des juifs à Anvers*. Anvers, Excelsior, 1969].

SCHNEERSON, M. M. Science and technology. In *Toward a Meaningful Life. The Wisdom of the Rebbe Menachem Mendel Schneerson*, ed. Simon JACOBSON. London: Piatkus, 1995.

SCHNELLER, R. Continuity and change in ultra-orthodox education. *Jewish Journal of Sociology*, 1980, XXII, 1: 35–45.

SCHOCHET, J. I. The philosophy of Lubavitch activism. *Tradition*, 1972, 13, 1: 18–35.

SCHOLEM, G. *Major Trends in Jewish Mysticism*. New York, Schocken, 1961.

SCHOLEM, G. *Sabbatai Sevi. The Mystical Messiah, 1626–1676*. Princeton, Princeton University Press, 1973.

SCHOLEM, G. La neutralisation du messianisme dans le hassidisme primitive [The elimination of messianism in early Hasidism]. In *Le Messianisme juif. Essais sur la spiritualité du judaïsme* [Jewish messianism. Essays on Jewish spirituality]. Paris, Calmann-Lévy, 1974: 272–273.

SHAFFIR, W. *Life in a Religious Community: The Lubavitcher in Montreal*. Toronto and Montreal, Holt, Rinehart & Winston of Canada, 1974.

SHAFFIR, W. Jewish Messianism Lubavitch-style: an interim report. *Jewish Journal of Sociology*, 1993, XXXV, 2: 115–128.

SHAFFIR, W. Interpreting adversity: dynamics of commitment in a Messianic redemption campaign. *Jewish Journal of Sociology*, 1994, XXXVI, 1: 43–53.

SHAFFIR, W. When prophecy is not validated: explaining the unexpected in a Messianic campaign. *Jewish Journal of Sociology*, 1995: XXXVII, 2: 119–136.
SHAFFIR, W. Fieldwork among Hassidic Jews: moral challenges and missed opportunities. *Jewish Journal of Sociology*, 2001, XLIII, 1–2: 53–69.
SHAFFIR, W. & ROCKAWAY, R. Leaving the ultra-orthodox fold: Haredi Jews who defected. *Jewish Journal of Sociology*, 1987, XXIX, 2: 97–114.
SHAHAK, I. & MEZVINSKY, N. *Jewish Fundamentalism in Israel*. London, Pluto Press, 1999.
SHAROT, S. *Messianism, Mysticism and Magic. A Sociological Analysis of Jewish Religious Movements*. Chapel Hill (NC), University of North Carolina Press, 1982.
SHIELD, R. R. *Diamond Stories. Enduring Changes on 47th Street*. Ithaca, London, Cornell University Press, 2002.
SICRON, M. Growth of the Israeli Population, 1983–92. In 'Israel, State of Population', *Encyclopaedia Judaica*, CD-Rom Ed. Jerusalem, Judaica Multimedia, 1997.
SIMON, R. J. *Continuity and Change. A Study of Two Ethnic Communities in Israel*. Cambridge, London, New York, Melbourne, Cambridge University Press, 1978.
SINGER, R. A Hasidic woman in Borough Park. In *Jews of Brooklyn*, ed. Ilana ABRAMOVITCH & Sean GALVIN. Hanover (New Hampshire), London, University Press of New England, 2002: 139–142.
SKLARE, M. *America's Jews*. New York, Random House, 1972.
SOMOGY, T. *Die Schejnen und die Proste, Untersuchungen zum Schönheitsideal der Ostjuden in Bezug auf Körper und Kleidung unter besonderer Berücksichtigung des Chassidismus* [The beautiful and the plain: a study of the ideal of beauty among Eastern European Jews in relation to the body and clothing, with particular reference to Hasidism]. Berlin, Dieter Reimer, 1982.
TAUB, M. My Mother's Borough Park. In *Jews of Brooklyn*, ed. Ilana ABRAMOVITCH & Sean GALVIN. Hanover (New Hampshire), London, University Press of New England, 2002: 137–138.
VAN RANSBEEK, R. *1920–1970. 50 jaar centraal beheer van joodse weldadigheid en maatschapelijk hulpbetoon* [1920–1970. Fifty years of the Central administration for Jewish charity and mutual assistance]. Antwerp, 1970.
WAITE L. J. & FRIEDMAN, J. S. The impact of religious upbringing and marriage markets on Jewish intermarriage. *Contemporary Jewry*, 1997, 18: 1–23.
WEINER, H. A Wedding in B'nai Brak. *Commentary*, July 1965: 39–46.
WEINER, H. *Nine and a Half Mystics. The Kaballa Today*. New York, Macmillan, 1971.
WEINRYB, B. D. *The Jews of Poland. A Social and Economic History of the Jewish Community in Poland from 1100–1800*. Philadelphia, Jewish Publication Society of America, 1973.
WEISS, M. B. & NEUMEISTER, M. *Die Fromme in New York. Die Welt der Satmar-Chassidim*. [The orthodox in New York. The world of the Satmar Hasidim]. Munich, Gina Kehayoff Verlag, 1995.
WIGODER, G. (ed.). *The New Encyclopaedia of Judaism*. Coedited by Fred Skolnik & Shmuel Himelstein. New York, New York University Press, 2002 (1st ed. 1989).
WIESEL, E. *Souls on Fire. Portraits and Legends of Hasidic Masters*. Translated by Marion Wiesel. London, Weidenfeld & Nicolson, 1972.
ZBOROWSKI, M. The place of book-learning in traditional Jewish culture. In *Childhood in Contemporary Culture*, ed. Margaret MEAD & Martha WOLFENSTEIN, Chicago and London, University of Chicago Press, 1955: 118–141.
ZBOROWSKI, M. & HERZOG, E. *Life is with People. The Culture of the Shtetl*. New York, Schocken Books, 1962 (1st ed. 1952).

2. INFORMATIVE ARTICLES

BARON, A. Meah Shearim, I, II, III, *Hamodia* (Magazine section) 12 July, 19 July, 9 August 2002.
BERGER, J. Hasid rebels sue main sect for religious persecution. *New York Times*, 5 March 1997: B 8.

BERGER, J. Dissident gain with Kiryas Joel pact. *New York Times*, 12 March 1997 (Metropolitan Desk).
BERGER, J. Drug arrests give a jolt to a sect of Hasidim. *New York Times*, 18 June 1997 (Metropolitan Desk).
BEYETTE, B. A telethon with tradition. *Los Angeles Times*, 29 August 2000: E-2.
BIRNBAUM, A. Rebbe and father: the avoda of rebuilding in America after the Holocaust. *Hamodia* (Magazine section), 20 July 2001: 12–13.
BUTMAN, S. It's all in what the Rebbe said. *Haaretz*, 7 April 1998 (English Internet Edition).
CARLANDER, I. Anvers la cosmopolite, Anvers la brune [Cosmopolitan Antwerp, brown Antwerp]. *Le Monde diplomatique*, May 1995: 7–8.
CHEN, D. W. A Hasidic village gets a lesson in bare-knuckled politicking. *New York Times*, 9 June 2001 (Metropolitan Desk).
COHEN, A. Israël's tenth largest City: Bnei Brak. *Deiah Vedibur, Information and Insight*, 19 June 2002, <www.shemayisrael.com>.
DAO, J. & FINDER, A. Jewish council under scrutiny is known for political clout. *New York Times*, 2 December 1996 (Metropolitan Desk).
DERFNER, L. Good Morning, Bnei Brak. *Jerusalem Post*, 9 January 1998: 17.
EDELMAN, S. Satmar sibling rivalry hurting them all. *New York Post*, 10 March 2002.
FISHBEIN, E. Numbers show increase in poverty. *Haaretz*, 21 December 1999 (English Internet Edition).
FRIED, J. P. Brooklyn rabbi is accused of stealing grant money. *New York Times*, 28 March 1997 (Metropolitan Desk).
FRIED, J. P. Guilty plea to money charge. *New York Times*, 17 December 1997 (Metropolitan desk): 5.
FRIED, J. P. Jury acquits assemblyman Hikind of corruption charges. *New York Times*, 14 July 1998 (Metropolitan Desk).
GOLAN, A. Bnei Brak's War of Independence. *Haaretz*, 2 January 1998 (English Internet Edition).
GOLAN, A. Who are you, Rebbe? *Haaretz*, 20 January 1998 (English Internet Edition).
GOLAN, A. Missing brother-in-law found in Paris. *Haaretz*, 21 April 1998.
GOLAN, A. His Honor, the Mayor. *Haaretz*, 16 July 1999 (English Internet Edition).
GOLAN, A. All in the family. *Haaretz*, 18 May 2001.
GOLDBERG, J. Tsuris in Crown Heights. *New York*, 12 December 1994: 24, 26.
GOLDMAN, A. L. Hasidic group expands amid debate on future. *New York Times*, 5 September 1988.
GONZALEZ, D. 'A Family in stress' over its stricken rebbe. *New York Times*, 12 March 1994: 23.
GOZLAN, M. Fanatisme ultra-religieux [Ultra-religious fanaticism]. *Marianne*, 17 May 1999: 48-53.
GREENBERG, E. J. New York state investigates fraud among Satmar. *Jewish Bulletin of Northern California* [now *Jewish News Weekly of Northern California*], 4 October 1996 (Internet Edition).
GREENBERG, E. J. Chassidic rabbis implicated in Colombian drug trade. *Jewish Bulletin of Northern California* [now *Jewish News Weekly of Northern California*], 20 June 1997 (Internet Edition).
GREENBERG, J. Orthodox Torah students win Israeli draft exemption. *New York Times (International)*, 24 July 2002.
GROSS, N. Salvation Army. *Jerusalem Report*, 3 February 2000.
HELLMAN, P. The Devout raise a city within a city and prosper. *New York Times*, 15 September 1995: C (Weekend Desk).
HENNELY, R. One man – how many votes. *Village Voice*, 22 October 1996: 15–16.
ITIM, Schach says Schneerson is a false Messiah. *Jerusalem Post*, 31 January 1993: 12.
KAHN, B. Non-Jewish mass immigration: a time bomb in Israël society. *Deyah ve Dibur, Information and Insight*, 15 December 1999, <www.shemayisrael.com>.
KAMBER, M. Faded rage. *Village Voice*, 16 January 2002.

KEZWER, G. Brothers can you spare a dime? *Jerusalem Report*, 1992 (10th Anniversary, Internet Edition).
KLEIN HALEVI, Y. Can Chabad outlive the Rebbe? *Jerusalem Report*, 7 April 1994: 18–23.
KUTSCHERA, C. Jérusalem: Méa Shearim, la mauvaise conscience d'Israël [Jerusalem: Mea Shearim, the bad conscience of Israel]. *Le Spectacle du monde*, September 1982: 246 (see <www.chris-kutschera.com>).
LE BARS, S. Le budget maintient les privilèges accordés aux colonies [Privileges granted to the colonies are retained in the budget]. *Le Monde*, 1 November 2002: 2.
LEFKOVITS, E. Capital's poverty crisis brewing. *Jerusalem Post*, 20 December 2000 (Internet Edition).
LEWIN, T. Controversy over, enclave joins school board group. *New York Times*, 20 April 2002 (Metropolitan Desk): B, 4.
LEYDEN, L. 5 Years after death, Messiah question divides Lubavitcher. *Washington Post*, 20 June 1999 (Internet Edition).
MARION, G. Tension politique en Israël après le memorandum de Wye River [Political tension in Israel following the Wye River Memorandum]. *Le Monde*, 28 October 1996: 5.
MEIR, Y. Seventeen synagogues, but no blessing. *Haaretz*, 17 December 2001 (English Internet Edition).
MELE, C. & McMAHON, P. Voter fraud in KJ continued, investigation shows. *Times Herald Record*, 17 October 1997 (Internet Edition).
MILLER, R. & PINKHASSOV, G. (photos). Shtetl for a Week. *New York Times Magazine*, 8 September 1996, section 6.
NADLER, A. Last exit to Brooklyn. *New Republic*, 4 May 1992: 27–30, 32–35.
NOEL, P. Hillary 'banned' in Crown Heights. *Village Voice*, 25–31 August 1999.
NUSSBAUM COHEN, D. (Jewish Telegraphic Agency), 1000 Orthodox rabbis reject claim rebbe was Messiah. *Jewish Bulletin of Northern California* [now *Jewish News Weekly of Northern California*], 21 June 1996 (Internet Edition).
PARIS, G. Bnei Brak, capitale des 'barbus' d'Israël [Bene Beraq, capital of Israel's 'bearded men']. *Le Monde*, 23 July 1996: 10.
ROSENBERG, H. Those were the days: About past and present. *Virtueel Israelitisch Weekblad*, 1991,<www.goedkosjer.org>.
ROSENBERG, H. Joodse verenigingen in Antwerpen [Jewish organizations in Antwerp]. *Virtueel Israelitisch Weekblad*, 1999, <www.goedkosjer.org/JoodsAntwerpen.htm>.
RUBIN, N. The heritage and the history of Belz. *Hamodia*, 14 December 2001: 1.
SAWICKI, T. The ultra-orthodox takeover of Jerusalem. *Jerusalem Report*, 29 December 1994: 20–23.
SCHLEIFER, Y. & GORENBERG, G. Chabad's Messiah complex. *Jerusalem Report*, 21 June 1995: 31–34.
SEGEV, T. All the hungry, where are they? *Haaretz*, 24 December 1999 (English Internet Edition).
SEXTON, J. Welfare reform has Hasidic community on edge. *New York Times* (National/Metro), 21 April 1997.
SHAHAR, I. The court is no longer in session. *Haaretz*, 22 October 1997 (English Internet Edition).
SHAHAR, I. For ultra-orthodox women the work is never done. *Haaretz*, 12 May 1998 (English Internet Edition).
SHAHAR, I. Religious ministry earmarks huge sums for Hasidic world centers. *Haaretz*, 21 September 2000 (English Internet Edition).
SHAHAR, I. The growing lure of the Haredi school system. *Haaretz*, 6 November 2001 (English Internet Edition).
SHAHAR, I. The Ashkenazi answer to Shas' education network. *Haaretz*, 7 November 2001 (English Internet Edition).
SHAHAR, I. Focus: an end to the miracle. *Haaretz*, 13 December 2001 (English Internet Edition).

SHAMIR, S. Bush meets Lubavitch rabbis to mark late Rebbe's 100th birthday. *Haaretz*, 28 March 2002 (English Internet Edition).
SHAPIRO, H. Belzer rebbe blasts PM, Government. *Jerusalem Post*, 7 October 1996 (Internet Edition).
SHAPIRO, H. Rebbes hold reconciliation meeting. *Jerusalem Post*, 24 November 1998: 4.
SHAVIT, A. Elective affinities. *Haaretz*, 27 December 2002 (English Internet Edition).
SHILOH, D. Shopping religiously. *Jerusalem Post*, 30 July 1997: 7.
SHRAGAI, N. Settling for less. *Haaretz*, 24 January 2002 (English Internet Edition).
SINAI, R. 20 percent of Israelis live in poverty, says report. *Haaretz*, 20 December 2001 (Internet Edition).
SONTAG, D. Orthodox neighborhood reshapes itself. *New York Times*, 7 January 1997, A:1 (Metropolitan Desk).
SPECTER, M. The oracle of Crown Heights. *New York Times Magazine*, 15 March 1992 (Magazine Desk).
STEINBERG, J. Bad Day in Borough Park. *Jerusalem Post*, 12 September 1997: 08 (Magazine).
SUDILOWSKY, J. Bnei Brak's poverty lies in its birthrate. *Jerusalem Post*, 24 January 1997: 9 (Internet Edition).
TROY, S. The mother of all Purimspielen. *Jerusalem Report*, 12 March 2001: 40–41.
WAKIN, D. J. The heir unapparent. *New York Times*, 24 January 2002 (Metropolitan Desk).
WEINER, R. The virtual Jewish History Tour, Lodz. *Jewish Virtual Library*, <www.us-israel.org>.
WIRTH, M. (ed.). Lodz. *Encyclopaedia of Jewish Communities in Poland*, Jerusalem, Yad Vashem and <www.Jewishgen.org>.
ZELIG, D. Bné Brak Poorest City in Israël. *Hamodia*, 16 November 2001: 2.
ZIEMBA, A. The Chiddushei HaRim's Arrest. *Hamodia* (Magazine Section), 21 February 2002: 4.

3. ANONYMOUS INFORMATIVE BOOKS AND ARTICLES

Agudath Israel to open youth clubs throughout Israel. *Hamodia*, 14 December 2001: 2.
Bnei Brak launches Shabbos water system. *Hamodia*, 3 January 2003: 9.
D'as Torah and a stern warning. *Deyah ve Dibur, Information and Insight*, 12 January 2000, <www.shemayisrael.com>.
Demography of Jerusalem. In <www.jewishpeople.net> (from Statistical Yearbook of Jerusalem, 1996 and Israel Central Bureau of Statistics, 1996 Data).
Chabad Lubavitch Chasidism Today. California, Chabad-Lubavitch, 1972.
Challenge. An Encounter with Lubavitch-Chabad in Israel. London, Lubavitch Foundation of Great Britain, 1973.
Coalition agreement between United Torah Judaism and the Likud. *Hamodia*, 6 April 2001: 8–9.
Countering proselytizers. *Haaretz*, 11 November 2001 (English Internet Edition).
E-Mail celebrates its 30th birthday. *Hamodia*, 19 October 2001: 27 (Reuters).
EUROPEAN LUBAVITCH OFFICE. Les Institutions Chabad Lubavitch en France et Afrique du Nord [Habad Lubavitch institutions in France and North Africa], <www.Chabad.-fr.org>, 2002.
Focus: an end to the miracle. *Haaretz*, 13 December 2001 (English Internet Edition).
Hagiography, *Encyclopaedia Judaica*. CD-Rom Ed. Jerusalem, Judaica Multimedia, 1997.
Haredim and politics. *Israel Yearbook and Almanac*, 1996: 88, 90.
Hebron sous tension à l'approche de l'accord [Hebron under pressure from the forthcoming agreement]. *Dernières Nouvelles d'Alsace*, 20 November 1996.
Holocaust survivors in the USSR. *Encyclopaedia Judaica*, CD-Rom Ed. Jerusalem, Judaica Multimedia, 1997.
Jerusalem gets first Chareidi mayor. *Hamodia*, 21 February 2003: 1–2, 10.
Keren Nesivos Moshe: Filling a void in Afula. *Hamodia*, 21 December 2001: 16.
Keren Nesivos Moshe schools bring whole families back to Torah. *Hamodia*, 2 February 2002: 29.

Miracle, *Encyclopaedia Judaica*, CD-Rom Ed. Jerusalem, Judaica Multimedia, 1997.
Orthodox Jews Protest Peace Talks. *New York Times*, 4 January 2000 (Associated Press).
Population. In *Encyclopaedia Judaica*, CD-Rom Ed, Jerusalem, Judaica Multimedia, 1997.
'Schneersohn Family'. In *Encyclopaedia Judaica*, CD-Rom Ed, Jerusalem, Judaica Multimedia, 1997.
Stamford Hill Chareidi community to double within ten years. *Hamodia*, 6 December 2002: 44.
The 1999 Israeli Elections: A view from Judea. *Judea Magazine*, 1999, 7.3: 3, <www.womeningreen.org>.
25 % of Israeli Children Live in Poverty. *Hamodia*, 29 December 2002: 7.
UTJ Gains in Bnei Brak. *Hamodia*, 7 February 2003: 10.
Waldman v. Village of Kiryas Joel. United States Court of Appeals for the second circuit, decision 21 March 2000, Docket n° 99–7830.
What is wrong with the Internet. *Yated Neeman*, 14 January 2001: 20.

4. HASIDISM IN FRANCE

BARON, M. De Djerba à Paris XIXe [From Djerba to the 19th arrondissement in Paris]. *L'Arche*, 2000, 508: 68–69.
COHEN, E. H. Écoles juives de France. *Kountrass*, 2000, 70 (internet version).
COHEN, E. H. Les résultats de la grande enquête sur les juifs de France [Results of the major survey on the Jews in France]. *L'Arche*, December 2002, 538: 54–73.
COHEN, E. H. Les débuts des institutions 'Habad' en France, chapitre II: les premiers pas [The beginnings of the 'Habad' institutions in France; Chapter 2, 'The first steps']. *Kountrass*, July 2003, 96: 5–21.
HUBIN, F. La Ville attribue une aide à une crèche Loubavitch [The City grants aid to a Lubavitch crèche]. *Le Parisien*, 28 October 2000 (internet archives).
JARRASÉ, D. *Guide du patrimoine juif parisien* [Guide to Jewish heritage in Paris]. Paris, Éditions Parigramme, 2003.
MALKA, V. *Les Juifs sépharades* [The Sephardic Jews]. Paris, PUF, 'Que sais-je?', 1997.
NIZARD, S. La cacherout en France. Organisation matérielle d'une consommation symbolique [The kashrut in France. The material organization of a symbolic consumption]. *Les Cahiers du judaïsme*, 1998, 3: 64–73.
PODSELVER, L. Le mouvement Lubavitch: déracinement et insertion des séfarades [The Lubavitch movement: the uprooting and integration of the Sephardim]. *Pardès*, 1986, 3: 54–68.
PODSELVER, L. La séparation, la redondance et l'identité: les hassidim de Lubavitch à Paris [Separation, diffusion and identity: the Lubavitch Hasidim in Paris]. *Pardès*, 1988, 7: 167–174.
PODSELVER, L. La tradition réinventée: les hassidim de Loubavitch en France [Tradition reinvented: the Lubavitch Hasidim in France]. *Revue des études juives*, 1992, CLI: 441- 450.
PODSELVER, L. & WEILL, D. La nouvelle orthodoxie et la transmission familiale [The new orthodoxy and familial transmission]. *Pardès*, 1996, 22: 149–159.
SIMON, P. & TAPIA, C. *Le Belleville des juifs tunisiens* [The Tunisian Jewish quarter in Paris]. Paris, Autrement, 1998.
WEILL, N. Essor et désarroi des Loubavitch [Lubavitch expansion and disarray]. *Le Monde*, 21 September 1996: 11.

Glossary

The glossary essentially contains Yiddish (Y) and Hebrew (H) terms, which are indicated in parentheses. The combination of two letters, in particular the most frequent, Y-H, indicates (1) the language of the term and (2) the language of origin. Apart from Y and H, the following are occasionally used: G for German, E for English and P for Polish.

For the transliteration of the Yiddish and Hebrew words such as **H**erem, Mashgia**h** or **H**aredim, which contain a sound that does not exist in English and that corresponds approximately to the 'hota', an aspirated 'h' that comes from the throat, as in Rio**j**a in Spanish or Ba**ch** in German, I have chosen the current usage of the consonant 'h' to transcribe them, which unfortunately does not convey the true phonetic quality of the words in Hebrew and Yiddish. For the Yiddish or Hebrew words with the palato-fricative alveolar 'sh' sound, I have followed the usage of other Hasidic glossaries by using the vowels 'sh'; for example, 'shtiebl' or 'shtreimel'.

Admor, pl. *admorim*, the acronym of *Adoneinu, Moreinu Ve-Rabeinu* (H): 'our lord, teacher and master'; this is a title often given today in Israel to the rebbe*, particularly by the Hasidim themselves.

Agudath Israel (H), *Agudes Isruel* (Y), abbreviated to *Agudath* (H) or *Agudes* (Y): union or association of Israel; an ultra-orthodox political party.

Ahavat Israel (H): love of Israel; in fact, love of all Jews – a key concept in Lubavitch Hasidism.

Ashkenaz, pl. *Ashkenazim* (H): German; this is the term used for Jews of Northern European origin.

Baal, pl. *baalei, shem* (Y-H): 'master of the (divine) name', worker of wonders and miracles.

Baal tshuve, pl. *baalei tshuve*, fem. *baalot tshuve* (Y-H): 'master of repentance'; a person who returns to the Jewish faith.

Bar mitsve, pl. *bar mitsves* (Y), *bar mitzvah* (H): 'son of the commandment'; for a boy, the transition in a religious sense to the stage of adulthood at the age of 13 years; it also refers to the celebrations that take place on this occasion.

Besht: the acronym for Baal Shem Tov, the founder of Hasidism.

bes medresh (Y-H): 'house of study'; room for study and community prayer, a synonym of shtiebl.*

bet din (H): 'house of the law'; the rabbinical court of law.

bikur holim (H): visiting the sick.

dayan (H): a judge in the bet din* or rabbinical court.

Degel Hatorah (H): 'flag of the Torah'; an ultra-orthodox Israeli political party, founded in 1988.

devekuss (Y), *devekut* (H): 'devotion'; mystical and affective communion with God, a major mystical concept in Hasidism.

Edah Haredit (H), abbreviated to *Edah* (H): 'the community of God-fearers'; a politico-religious coalition of Hasidic and ultra-orthodox groups in Israel, mainly active in Mea Shearim.

erlicher Yid (Y-G): 'honest Jew'; faithful to the Jewish prescriptions.

farbrengen (Y-G): in Crown Heights, a large meeting on Saturday afternoons, at which Menahem Mendel Schneerson, a Lubavitch rebbe*, traditionally gave long addresses.

flaishig (Y-G): meat-based; a category of the kashrut,* as opposed to milchig.*

gabbe (Y-H): assistant to the rebbe,* but also a follower in charge of the distribution of honours during the reading of the Torah* in the morning service.

gadol, pl. *gdoilim* (Y-H): 'great'; a prominent ultra-orthodox religious leader.

gemah, pl. *gemahim* (Y-H): abbreviation of 'Gemilut hasadim' (H): 'to give favours'; a charitable organization.

gematria (Y-H): numerology; a form of interpretation that seeks to reveal the deep significance of words by their value in figures; the letters of the Hebrew alphabet all have a numerical value.

glatt kasher (Y-G + Y-H): ultra-kasher. From the German 'glatt', meaning 'smooth', this applies primarily to the slaughter knives used for the meat, the animals' lungs etc., but in a wider sense it also means 'indisputably' (kasher).

goy, pl. *goyim* (Y-H): non-Jew.

guertel (Y-G): ritual belt worn by the Hasidim during prayer, which separates the upper part of the body as the site of spirituality from the lower part as the site of animal nature.

guit shabbes (Y-G + Y-H): 'good Sabbath'; a greeting exchanged with close family, friends and acquaintances.

guit yontef (Y-G + Y-H): a greeting meaning 'happy festival'.

Habad (H): an abbreviation of the Hebrew words 'Hohma, Binah, Daat', meaning 'wisdom, understanding, knowledge'. This term is often used to designate the Lubavitch Hasidic movement.

hahnosses kale (Y-H): 'to lead the bride' (under the canopy of the wedding ceremony); the provision of a trousseau to a fiancée from a poor family.

haider, pl. *haidarim* (Y-H): 'room'; traditional infant school.

Halohe (Y), *Halaha* (H): the set of Jewish religious obligations.

hared, pl. *haredim* (H): 'a person who trembles [before God]' or '[God-] fearing'; Hasidim and other ultra-orthodox in Israel.

Hasid, pl. *Hasidim* (E-H): 'pious one'; a follower of Hasidism.

Haskule (Y), *Haskalah* (H): the Jewish Enlightenment movement.

Hatzoloh (Y-H): rescue; an organization that provides emergency medical care.

herem (Y-H): excommunication.

Hessides (Y-H) or *Hasidut* (H): 'piety'; Hasidism in Hebrew or Yiddish. Among the Lubavitch Hasidim, the set of writings known as the *Tanya*, the work of the founder of Lubavitch, Shneur Zalman of Lyady, as well as the speeches and letters, published in volumes, of various rebbes* of the movement.

hevre, pl. *hevres* (Y-H): circle or group of friends.

hoif (Y-G): court or residence of the rebbe.*

hol-hamoed (H): intermediate semi-holidays during the festival of Tabernacles, the Sukkot,* and during the Passover.

Humesh (Y-H): the Pentateuch and the passages from the prophets that accompany them.

Kabbala (E-H): a set of esoteric Judaic mystical texts collected from the first few centuries of the Christian era.

kahal, pl. *kahalim* (H): Jewish community officially recognized by the authorities, particularly in Eastern Europe, Austria-Hungary and Russia until well into the 19th century.

Kahal Haredim (H): 'gathering' or 'congregation of those who fear (God)'; the name of a dissident Satmar community.

kasher (E-H): 'proper'; conforming to the Jewish dietary prescriptions.

kashrut (E-H): 'properness'; the Jewish dietary laws.

keruv (H): 'approach'; this is a term used by some Hasidim for centres that carry out missionary work (among Jews).

kiddish (Y), *kiddush* (H): 'sanctification'; ritual ceremony sanctifying the Sabbath; more generally, a light meal at a private celebration for reaching the age of religious majority, a forthcoming marriage and so on.

kiryat (H): district.

kloyz (Y-G): synonym for shtiebl;* a Hasidic oratory but also an informal Talmudic school located at the shtiebl.

kolel, pl. *kolelim* (Y-H): a Talmudic academy for married men.

kvitel, pl. *kvitleh* (Y-G): 'receipt'; a note inscribed with the wishes for which the rebbe* is being asked to intercede with God, which is submitted to the rebbe or sometimes placed on a rebbe's tombstone.

landsman (Y-G): a colloquial term for a compatriot.

lernen (Y-G): 'to learn': used as a substantive to refer to Talmudic study.

loshn koidesh (Y-H): 'sacred language'; Biblical and Talmudic Hebrew.

maggid, pl. *maggidim* (Y-H): itinerant preacher.

Marrano, pl. *Marranos* (E-Spanish?): a Jew who has converted to Catholicism while secretly remaining Jewish.

mashgiah, pl. *mashgihim* (Y-H): a supervisor of the application of the kashrut.*

Mashiah (H): the Messiah.

maskil, pl. *maskilim* (H): an 'enlightened' adherent of the Haskule.*

melamed, pl. *melamdim* (Y-H): a religious instructor.

mezuze, pl. *mezuzes* (Y), *mezuzah*, pl. *mezuzot* (H): a small parchment with verses from Deuteronomy, inserted in a case that is fixed to the doorposts of their houses by Jews.

mikve, pl. *mikves* (Y), *mikvah* (H): ritual bath.

milchig (Y-G): milk-based; a category of food in the kashrut,* as opposed to flaishig.*

minek, pl. *minugem* (Y), *minhag*, *minhagim* (H): among Hasidim, a particular custom established by a rebbe* or a dynasty.

misnagged, pl. *misnaggedim* (H): 'the adversary or adversaries'; the orthodox opponents of Hasidism who espouse a Judaism based on the Talmud* and reasoning.

mitzve, pl. *mitzves* (Y-H): a Jewish prescription; also a good deed.

mitzve tank (Y-H + E): 'tank of prescriptions'; trucks used by the Lubavitch movement in missionary work in the street.

mitzve tanz (Y-H + G): at the end of a wedding, a dance between the bride and some of her male family members, or between the latter.

Moetzet Gedolei Hatorah (H): Council of Torah Greats, particularly within the Agudath Israel* and Degel Hatorah* parties.

moshav (H): a co-operative village with an agricultural purpose.

Neture Karte (Y-H): 'guardians of the city'; an ultra-orthodox anti-Zionist organization.

nigun, pl. *nigunim* (Y-H): melody or song, created or adopted by various Hasidic dynasties and communities.

nizozot (H): divine or sacred sparks. A concept in Hasidic thought that originates from the Kabbala.*

Paiseh (Y), *Pesah* (H): the festival of Passover.

parve (Y-H): 'neutral'; a category of food that is neither flaishig* nor milchig* in the kashrut.*

peyes (Y), *peyot* (H): 'sides, edges or ends'; the sidelocks of varying length worn around the temples of Hasidim.

pidyen (Y), *pidyon* (H): 'redemption'; a donation offered to the rebbe* or to his assistants at the submission of a kvitel.*

pikuah nefesh (H): 'respect for the soul or human life': a rabbinical expression applied to the essential duty to save a Jewish life in a situation of danger, even if this means breaking some of the prohibitions in the Jewish laws.

pilpul (Y-H): Talmudic study that takes the form of comparison and debate.

Piremshpil (Y-H + G): the Purim play; a theatrical production that takes place at this festival.

piyyut, pl. *piyyutim* (H-Greek): liturgical poem.

reb (Y-H): before a name, a respectful equivalent of 'Mr' or teacher.

rebbe (Y-H): Hasidic spiritual leader; more literally, 'teacher' who teaches at the Jewish school, Talmud Torah.* Today, a Hasidic spiritual leader is also given the title Admor.*

rebbetsen (Y-H): rebbe's* wife.

Roshe Shoune (Y), *Rosh Hashanah* (H): Jewish festival of the New Year.

rosh yeshivah (H): head of a Talmudic academy.

ruf (Y), *rav* (H): rabbi.

Sabbateanism (E): the religious movement founded by Shabbetai Tsevi (1626–1678).

seder (Y-H): the ceremonial meal on the first and second evenings of the Passover.

Sephardi, pl. *Sephardim* (E-H): originally the Jews of Spain and Portugal, but today used more generally to refer to the Jews of Southern Europe, the Near East and the Middle East.

sefer Torah (H): scroll of the Torah.*

shadhen, pl. *shadhenim* (Y-H): professional or sometimes amateur marriage-broker.

shaleshides (Y), *seuda shelishit* (H): the traditional third meal at the end of the Sabbath.

Shas: the acronym for 'Sephardic guardians of the Torah', the current name for the Sephardic ultra-orthodox party in Israel.

Shatnes (Y): the prohibition on wearing a garment that combines wool and linen fibres.

shikun (H): plot or small district.

Shive (Y), *Shivah* (H): week of mourning immediately following a death.

shlieh, pl. *shlihim* (Y-H): 'delegate' or 'emissary'; among the Lubavitch Hasidim, these are usually rabbis in charge of the activities in Habad* houses.

shmure matses (Y-H): 'guarded' matzot, hand-made with particular care and arranged on a symbolic dish at the seder.* Many Hasidim eat only this type of unleavened bread throughout the Passover.

Shoah (H): 'catastrophe'; Hebrew term to refer to the genocide of the Jews during the Second World War.

shoihet, pl. *shohtim* (Y-H): ritual slaughterer.

shomrim (Y-H): 'supervisors': an organization that patrols and supervises the streets in Hasidic districts.

shrayim (Y-H): the remains of the rebbe's* meal at the tish,* a meal with a mystical significance.

shtetl, pl. *shtetleh* (Y-G): small town in Eastern Europe with a substantial Jewish population; this also refers to a district of a city in which many Jews are living.

shtiebl, pl. *shtiebleh* (Y-G): 'small room'; the Hasidic oratory.

shtreimel (Y-G or P): a wide fur cap.

Shulhan Aruh (H): 'set table'; a code synthesizing the Jewish laws, established in the 16th century by Joseph Caro; this code is still authoritative.

Sidder (Y), *Siddur* (H): prayer-book.

side, pl. *sides* (Y), *seudah*, pl. *seudot* (H): celebration or festival meal.

Simhat Torah (H): joyous festival of the Torah.

simhe (Y-H): joyful celebration.

soiher, pl. *sohrim* (Y-H): businessman, merchant.

spodek (Y-P): a tall fur cap.

Sukkah (H): the shed in which Jews live and take meals during the festival of the Sukkot.*

Sukkot (H): the festival of Tabernacles, at the beginning of the Jewish year.

Taharas Mishpohe (Y-H): 'family purity'; prescriptions concerning women's purity, based on a verse in Leviticus (20: 18); during menstruation and several days afterwards, sexual relations are forbidden. The prohibition has to be lifted by a purification in the mikve,* ritual bath. There is an entire section of the Talmud,* the Niddah, devoted to family purity.

talles (Y), *tallit* (H): prayer-shawl.

talles koten (Y), *tallit katan* (H): a garment with ritual fringes; generally worn under the shirt by Hasidim.

Talmud (E-H): an accumulated set of Biblical commentaries that has been authoritative for many centuries.

Talmud Torah, pl. *Talmudei Torah* (H): a traditional school for pupils from 12 years to around 15 years of age but also, particularly in France, schools that provide Jewish instruction on Sundays.

tfillen (Y), *tefillin* (H): phylacteries; two black leather cubes worn during morning prayer and attached by straps in a prescribed way, one of which is tied around the head, the other rolled around the left hand and arm; each contains a parchment with some verses from the Pentateuch.

Tilem (Y), *Tehilem* (H): the psalms.

tish (Y-G): table; meal of mystical communion with a rebbe,* especially on Friday evening.

tish halten (Y-G): to 'hold table'; the tish* ceremony.

toite (Y-G): Hasidim, literally 'dead Hasidim', the name given to followers of the tzadik* Nahman of Bratzlav, who died two centuries ago.

Torah (H): in the strict sense, the Pentateuch or the written law. More generally, the Biblical texts or the entire Jewish spiritual heritage including the Talmud* and other more recent texts. In an abstract sense, the teaching, the law or the Jewish doctrine.

toyre (Y-H): from the word 'Torah'; the rebbe's* teachings, particularly at a tish* and at shaleshides,* the third meal of the Sabbath.

trefe (Y-H): improper, non-kasher.
trefe medine (Y-H): 'improper country'; used by Hasidim to refer to the United States before 1945.
tzadik, pl. *tzadikim* (Y-H): the holy, the righteous one, a term applied to Hasidic leaders.
tzitses (Y), *tzitzit* (H): the fringes at the four corners of the ritual shawl, the talles koten* or the talles.
tzedoke (Y), *tzeddaka* (H): good works, charity.
waber shil (Y-G): the women's synagogue, part of an oratory reserved for women.
yeshive, pl. *yeshives* (Y), *yeshivah*, pl. *yeshivot* (H): Talmudic academy.
yeshive gdole (Y), *yeshivah gedolah* (H): higher-level Talmudic academy.
Yetev Lev D'Satmar (Y-H): the charitable heart of Satmar; the official name of the Satmar community.
yiddishe tochter (Y-G): 'Jewish daughter'; a girl or young woman who observes the Jewish rules and traditions.
Yiddishkait (Y-G): way of being Jewish; 'Jewishness'.
Yom Kippur (H): the festival of the Day of Atonement, at the beginning of the Jewish year.
yourzeit (Y-G): the anniversary of a death.

Index

Compiled by Sue Carlton

ACIP (Association consistorial israélite de Paris) 131
Agudath Israel 8, 11, 66, 89, 90, 148, 150
  alliance with Degel Hatorah 94, 100, 103, 118, 119
  and Belz Hasidim 93, 94
  and Ger Hasidim 95, 96, 99, 100, 101, 109, 141
  and Lubavitch Hasidim (Habad) 74
  and Vishnitz Hasidim 110, 113
  and Zionism 82, 83, 96, 134, 149
Aharonowitz, Reuben 103
Ahavat Israel 66, 145–6
Akiva, rabbi 103
Alexander dynasty 108
Algerian Jews 70, 120, 123
Alter, Abraham Mordecai (Imre Emes) 82, 95, 96–7
Alter, Isaac Meir Rothenburg 96
Alter, Israel 97, 98, 99
Alter, Jacob Arie 98
Alter, Pinhas Menahem 97–8, 101
Alter, Simhah Bunem 97, 99
Alter, Yehudah Leib (Sfas Emet) 96, 103
anti-semitism 4, 127, 131, 132, 135
Antwerp 15–26, 136
  and Belz Hasidim 17–19, 22, 23, 90–1, 94, 135, 137, 138, 139
  diamond industry 15–16, 22, 23–4, 148
  diverse Hasidic communities 17–19
  Hasidic schools 22–3, 135
  new Hasidic dynasty 19–22
  reb Ytsekl's community 17, 19–22, 137
Arad 81, 96, 97, 98
Ashdod 81, 96, 97, 98, 99, 109, 114
Ashkenazi Jews 4, 8, 100, 118, 122, 125
Ashkenazi Judaism 8, 150–1
Azimov, Shmuel 124

Baal Shem Tov 5–7, 8, 66, 137, 145
  brother-in-law of 37, 81

Barak, Ehud 74
Bat Yam 54, 58, 81, 114
Batei Ungarin 83, 86
Begin, Menachem 94
Beit Hatavshil 106
Belarus 4, 8, 63, 64, 109
Belinov, rabbi 132
Belz Hasidim 10, 17–19, 59, 78, 89–95
  anti-Zionism 90, 93
  in Antwerp 22, 23, 90–1, 94, 135
  in Borough Park 52–3, 90–1, 94
  in Israel 85, 87, 90–2, 108, 115, 118
  and marriage 139
  mutual assistance 92–3
  in occupied territories 118
  and politics 93–4
  schools 91
  success of movement 94–5
  in Tel-Aviv 115
ben Eliezer, Israel (Baal Shem Tov) 5–7, 8, 66, 137, 145
Ben Gurion, David 148, 149
Bene Beraq 19, 52, 54, 81, 94, 102–14, 136, 140, 152
  and Belz Hasidim 95, 108, 115
  and Bratzlav Hasidim 85
  and Ger Hasidim 95–6, 101, 107–8, 109
  mutual assistance 105–7
  rebbes and dynasties 108–9
  religious constituents 107–8
  and Satmar Hasidim 84, 108
  schools 111
  and Vishnitz Hasidim 91, 110–15
Bensonhurst 51
Bergen-Belsen camp 34
Bet Hana school 127
Bet Israel Damasek Eliezer 110
Bet Rivakh school 122, 127
Betar Illit 117–18

192

Biderman, Avraham Shlomo 106
Blau, Amram 84, 86
Bloomberg, Michael 72
Bobov Hasidim 18, 19, 22, 50, 54–9
  in occupied territories 118
  schools 54, 56–7, 136
Bobowa 54
Bohemia 10
Borough Park, Brooklyn 27, 31, 49–59, 140
  and Belz Hasidim 52–3, 90–1, 94
  and Bobov Hasidim 52, 54–9
  Bobov schools 51, 54, 56–7
  and Bratzlav Hasidim 84, 85
  Hasidic diversity 52–4
  Hasidim professions 50, 143
  and kashrut 49, 50
  Sabbath and festival days 52
  and Satmar Hasidim 35, 40, 41, 45, 52
  Satmar schools 37
Bratzlav Hasidim 84–5
Brosovski, Shalom Noah 109
Brunoy yeshive 122, 124, 125, 127, 128, 133
Buber, Martin 147, 150

Central Rabbinical Congress of the United States and Canada 33, 38, 39
Chaya Mushka school 127, 130
Chernobyl dynasty 109
Chirac, Jacques 130
Chné Or school 122, 127
Chortkov Hasidim 17, 18
Cité de l'Éducation Heikhal Menachem 127
Cité de l'Éducation Sinaï 127, 129, 131
Clinton, Hillary 53, 72
COJASOR 121
Consistory of France 121, 124, 131–2
Council of Jewish Organizations of Borough Park, (COJO) 53
Council of Torah Greats 93, 94, 97, 100, 108, 110, 113
CRIF (Conseil Représentatif des Institutions Juives de France) 127, 132

Crown Heights, Brooklyn 27, 56, 60–80, 125, 139, 143
  see also Lubavitch Hasidim
Cuomo, Andrew 53
Cuomo, Mario 43

Dan, Joseph 145
Danziger, Avraham Menachem 108
Danziger, Yitzhak Menachem 108
Debré, Jean-Louis 131
Degel Hatorah 94, 100, 101, 103, 113, 118, 119, 150
Der Yid 39
Di Yddishe Heim 143
diamond industry 15–16, 22, 23–4, 25, 30, 148
Dinkins, David 72
Dov Baer of Mezhirech 6, 8, 63, 103
Dreyfus affair 11
Dubnow, Simon 12, 149

Edah Haredit 38, 83, 93, 97
Edict of Tolerance 10–11
Efrat 118
Egged 144
Eichmann, Adolf 34
Elad 112, 118
Eliezer of Damascus yeshive 111
Elijah ben Solomon Zalman 8
Elimelech of Lyzhansk 7, 103
Emmanuel 81, 100–1, 118
Epstein, Shifra 137
Etz Chaim 54
Ezra Mitzion 105

Flatbush 51
France, and Lubavitch Hasidim (Habad) 120–33
Frank, Jacob 5, 7
French Revolution 1789 11
Friends of Lubavitch 67–8, 148
FSJU (Fonds social juif unifié) 127–8, 129

Galicia 10, 17, 50, 54, 55, 59, 90, 95

Galilee 81, 96, 98
Ger Hasidim 10, 17, 47, 52–3, 85, 87, 95–101, 135
  in Antwerp 17, 18, 19, 23, 151
  in Bene Beraq 107–8, 109
  dynasty 96–8
  missionary work 99–100
  mutual assistance 87, 92
  in occupied territories 118
  and politics 100–1
  professions 98
  relations with Vishnitz Hasidim 113
  schools 99, 146
  in Tel-Aviv 115
  and tradition 98–9
  and Zionism 82, 96, 97, 98
Gerstenkorn, Isaac 102–3
Giuliani, Rudolf 53, 72
Gora Kalwaria 96
Gould, Elliot 67
Grunwald, Levi Y. 33
Gueula 95
Gutnick, Joseph 118

Haaretz 77
Hachoze, Jacob 17
Hager, Barukh (1845–93) 110
Hager, Barukh (1895–1964) 114
Hager, Eliezer 110
Hager, Hayyim Meir 110, 113, 114
Hager, Israel (1860–1936) 110
Hager, Israel (b. 1938) 113
Hager, Menahem Mendel (Vishnitzer rebbe 1830–85) 110
Hager, Menahem Mendel (brother of Moshe) 113
Hager, Moses Joshua 110
Hager, Moshe 113, 114
Haifa 114
Halberstam, Benzion 54–5
Halberstam, Chayim 54
Halberstam, Naftali Tzevi 53, 59
Halberstam, Shlomo 53, 54, 55–6, 58, 59
Halberstam, Shmuel David 117
Halberstam, Yekutiel Judah (Klausenburger rebbe) 13–14, 89–90, 116–17

Hamodia 53, 100
Hasidim
  favourable context for 147–50
  influence of 150–2
  interaction between communities 22–6
  and internet use 30, 69, 98, 141–2
  and modernity 141–2
  mutual assistance 31–2, 41, 87–8, 92–3, 105–7, 149
  and politics 38–9, 53–4, 72–5, 93–4, 100–1, 130–2, 150, 152
  population increase 139–41
  professions 29–31, 40, 50, 70, 98, 130, 143
  and technology 30, 69, 98, 125, 141–2
Hasidism
  after Second World War 12–14
  cult of the rebbe 75–6, 84, 91, 98, 151
  customs 9–10
  defections 147
  differences between movements 135–7
  expansion and decline 8–12
  five stages of 12
  main characteristics 5–7
  rebirth of 134, 145–50
Haskule 10
Hatzolah 32
Hatzor Haguelilit 96, 98
Hebrew language 36, 88, 111–12, 128, 142, 144, 150
Hebron 81
Henich, Chanoch 108
Hikind, Dov 53
Histadrut 103
Holocaust (Shoah) 12, 13, 78, 95, 97, 116, 134
Holocaust survivors 16, 55, 56, 58, 59, 82, 121, 135–7, 138
  and marriage 138–9
  psychological support 137–8
  support from Jewish organizations 148
Hungarian Hasidim 13, 17, 18, 28, 33, 47, 83, 135, 136, 137
Hungary 5, 10, 13, 16, 23, 28, 86, 90
  and Belz Hasidim 17, 90
  and Satmar Hasidim 34, 36, 37
  and Vishnitz Hasidim 110, 111

Israel 14, 15, 54, 81–101, 151–2
  religion and State 148–9
  see also Bene Beraq; Jerusalem; Tel-Aviv

Jerusalem 54, 81–101, 109, 136, 138
  and Belz Hasidim 90–2
  and Bratzlav Hasidim 84–5
  and Ger Hasidim 95–101
  Mea Shearim 82–9
Jesode Hatorah school 23
Jewish People's Council 82
JOINT (American Jewish Distribution Committee) 121
Joseph II 10
Joseph, Ovadia 113

Kahal Haredim 43, 45
Kahan, Avraham Y. 86, 88
Kahan, David 88
Kahan, Jacob Shmuel 87, 88
Kahaneman, Joseph Shlomo 107
Kalish, Joseph Tzvi 102–3
Karelitz, Abraham 107
Karelitz, Avraham (Chazon Ish) 103
Karelitz, Mordecai 103
kashrut 32–4, 39–40, 49, 50, 71, 104, 131–2, 138
Kasztner, Rudolf 34
Kazen, Joseph 69
Kefar Habad 73, 81, 115–16
Kehot 65
Khmelnitsky, Bogdan 4
Kiryas Joel 35, 39, 40, 41–4, 46, 47, 102, 140
  and elections 43
  legislative disputes 43–4
  women 144
Kiryat Belz 92
Kiryat Bobov 114
Kiryat Chassidei Vishnitz 118
Kiryat Ponevez 107
Kiryat Vishnitz 109, 110, 111, 113
Kiryat Zanz 90, 116–17
Koch, Edward 72
Kranzler, George 29, 135

Labor party, Israel 74
Laniado hospital 117
Law of Return 74, 148
Leizer, Yankele (Jacob) 21–2
Levin, Yitzhak Meir 82, 97
Likud 74, 94
Lithuania 4, 8, 10, 63, 107
Lodz 109
London 14, 48, 54, 90
Lubavitch Hasidim (Habad) 9, 19, 23, 47, 60–80, 102, 120–33, 135
  cult of the rebbe 75–6, 151
  expansion in France 123–5, 133
  historical outline 120–3
  in Israel 108, 115–16
  and Israeli politics 73–5, 132, 152
  and kashrut 71, 131–2
  and marriage 139
  messianism 76–80, 84–5, 107
  missionary campaigns 66–9, 92, 95, 146, 147, 148
  and modernity 141–2
  and occupied territories 117–18
  and politics 72–3, 130–2
  professions 70, 130
  and role of women 68, 143–4
  scholastic system 61, 69, 70, 122–3, 126–9, 136
  and Sephardic culture 125–6, 133
  social structure 69–71
  as special case 63–4
  see also Schneerson, Joseph Isaac; Schneerson, Menahem Mendel
Lupolianski, Uri 101
Luria, Isaac 6, 8, 113

Maale Amos 118
Machon Chana institute 143
Mahler, Ralph 149–50
Maleh Adumim 118
Mapai party 148
Mapam (United Workers) party 148
marriage 138–9
Mea Shearim 38, 48, 82–9, 112, 144, 152
  Bratzlav Hasidim 84–5
  Toldot Ahronot 85–9

messianism 4–5, 76–80, 84–5, 107
military service 11, 74, 83, 87, 88–9, 99, 100, 104, 105, 149
Moetzet Gedolei Hatorah 93
Monroe 41–2, 140
Monsey 35, 41, 140
Montreal 14, 48, 54, 71, 90
Moroccan Jews 70, 120, 122, 123
Morocco 123
Muchka, Shmuel 129

Nachalat Har Habad 81, 115, 116
Nagyvarad 110
Nahman of Bratzlav 84–5, 137
Natanya 15, 81, 116–17
Nazi genocide 7, 21, 27, 28, 38, 45, 82, 140
Netanyahu, Benjamin 94, 118
Neture Karte 84, 86, 88, 97
Nissenbaum, Haim 130, 132

Opportunity Development Association (ODA) 31, 41, 47
Oslo Accords 94, 98
Ouaknin, Marc-Alain 145

Palestine 13, 81–2, 90, 102, 134
  occupied territories 74, 81, 94, 100, 112, 117–19, 152
Pardes Katz 102, 103, 108
Paris Consistory 127, 131
Pevzner, Hillel 130
Piremshpil 58
Podolia 84
Poland 4–5, 8, 10, 11, 12, 82, 84, 90, 96, 137
  and Alexander group 109
  and Belz Hasidim 17
  and Bobov Hasidim 55, 57
  and Ger Hasidim 95, 96–7
  Jewish emigration from 15, 55
Polish Hasidim 13, 21, 23, 55, 95, 134, 136, 151
Ponevez yeshive 107, 146
Potok, Chaim 147

Rabin, Yitzhak 98
Rav Tov 146
reb Arele Hasidim 85–9, 98, 101
Rechevot 112, 114
Reichmann brothers 106–7
Rokeah, Aaron 19, 90, 91, 115
Rokeah, Issachar Dov (Berele) 90, 91–2, 93, 94–5
Rokeah, Joshua 19
Rokeah, Shalom 17
Rooney, John 38
Rosenfeld, rabbi 72
Roshe Shoune 85
Roth, Aron (Arele) 86
Rubashkin, Aron 71
Rubin, Israel 36–7
Rumania 13, 16, 25, 28, 34, 110, 135
Russian emigrants 15, 50, 60, 66, 73, 92, 99, 102, 114, 124

Safed 81, 85
Satmar Hasidim 17, 18, 19, 28, 31, 34–48, 52–3, 135, 137, 151
  and American politics 38–9
  in Bene Beraq 108
  economic situation 39–41
  in Jerusalem 82, 84, 101
  Kiryas Joel community 41–4
  and marriage 139
  and occupied territories 118–19
  opposition to Zionism 37–8, 47–8, 73, 82, 84, 118–19, 145, 152
  role of women 30–1, 40–1, 47
  schools 22, 23, 35–7, 40, 43–4, 146
  splits in movement 46–7
  ties with Neture Karte 88
  ultra-orthodoxy 47–8
Satmar Shikun 84
Satu Mare 34
Schach, Eliezer Menachem 78, 94, 101, 102, 103, 107
Schneerson, Dov Baer 64, 73
Schneerson, Joseph Isaac (sixth rebbe) 14, 27, 60, 64, 65, 73, 121

Schneerson, Menahem Mendel (seventh rebbe) 19, 61, 64–6, 69, 73–5, 116, 143, 145–6
  and France 121, 122, 123, 132
  and Israeli politics 73–5
  as Messiah 76–80, 84–5, 132
  personality cult 75–6
  resurrection 80
Schneerson, Mushka Chaya 64
Schneur Zalman of Lyady 63, 122
Scholem, Gershom 7, 147
Sephardic Jews 70, 100, 118, 120, 124, 128–9
  and Lubavitch Hasidim (Habad) 125–6, 129, 133
Seret-Vishnitz 114
Sharon, Ariel 94, 100, 119
Shas party 100, 113, 118, 119
Shefa Mehadrin supermarket 104
Shikun Yoel 108
Shinui party 100
Shoah *see* Holocaust (Shoah)
Shomrim 32
Shulhan Aruh 7, 9, 22
Singer, Isaac Bashevis 147
Six Day War 1967 124
Slonim dynasty 109, 115
Slovakia 10
Slovakian Hasidim 135
solidarity/mutual assistance 31–2, 41, 87–8, 111, 148
Sukkot, festival of 83, 125

Teitelbaum, Aaron 46
Teitelbaum, Chanania 34
Teitelbaum, Feige 40–1, 44–5, 144
Teitelbaum, Hersch 34
Teitelbaum, Joel 34, 37–8, 41, 44–5, 46, 84, 145
Teitelbaum, Moishe 38, 45–6
Teitelbaum, Zalmen 46
Tel-Aviv 97, 102, 103, 110, 114–15
Tibéri, Jean 130
Tiberias 81, 82
Tieberg, Yehuda Moses 108–9
Toldot Ahronot 85–9, 119
Tomchei Tmimim Lubavitch yeshive 122

Transylvania 116
Tunisian Jews 70, 120, 123
Twersky, Menachem Nahum 109
Tzevi, Shabbatai 4–5, 7, 78

Ukraine 8, 10, 84, 85, 109, 110
Uman 85
United Religious Front 90
United States 13
  Jewish emigration to 11, 12, 14–16
  see also Borough Park, Brooklyn, Crown Heights, Brooklyn; Williamsburg, Brooklyn
United Torah Judaism 94, 100, 118, 119

Vishnitz Hasidim 17, 18, 19, 22, 47, 135, 137
  in Bene Beraq 110–15
  conflicts and rivalries 113–14
  and mutual assistance 111
  in occupied territories 118
  relations with Ger Hasidim 113
  role of rebbe 112–13
  schools 111
  in Tel-Aviv 115
  way of life 111–12
Vizhnitsa 110

Weber, Max 145
Weinberg, Avraham 109
Weintraub, Jerry 68
Wiesel, Elie 147, 150
Williamsburg, Brooklyn 13, 18, 27–48, 136, 140
  and Belz Hasidim 90, 94
  Hasidic women 30–1, 40–1, 47
  Hasidic professions 29–31, 40, 143
  and Kashrut 32–4, 39–40
  poverty of Hasidim 31–2
  and Satmar Hasidim 28, 34–48
  Satmar scholastic system 35–7, 40
  see also Kiryas Joel
women/girls 29, 30–2, 40–1, 47, 50–1, 104, 125, 150
  advances 142–5
  education 57, 122, 127–8, 142–3
  feminism 68

women/girls *continued*
  in Israel 86, 89, 105, 106, 144–5
  and military service 38, 89
  separated from men 19, 25, 55, 99, 106, 111, 122, 127

Yad Sarah 101, 105
Yetev Lev D'Satmar 28, 43
Yiddish 25, 36, 57, 88, 111, 128, 144, 146, 150
Yochanan Ben Zakkai 103
Ytsekl, reb (Isaac Gewuerzman) 17, 19–22, 34, 55, 132, 137

Zalman, Dov Baer 64
Zionism 11, 134, 137, 148–9, 152
  opposition to 37–9, 73, 82–3, 84, 89, 134
  see also Satmar Hasidim
Zohar (Book of Splendour) 6